Forty years ago I dreamed of teaching Gurukula students with Śrīla Prabhupāda's *Śrīmad-Bhāgavatam* serving as the central text. Toward realizing that goal, I had compiled the *Bhāgavatam* into its essential stories, for I trusted Śrīla Prabhupāda's words that such study would truly educate and prepare my students on every level for a satisfying and worthwhile life.

But Kṛṣṇa had a more wonderful plan. The opportunity to fulfill Śrīla Prabhupāda's desire – like a fragrant lotus in the form of this *Śrīmad-Bhāgavatam: A Comprehensive Guide for Young Readers* – has been carefully placed into the open hands of Mātājī Aruddhā Devī Dāsī and her team of parents and educators. May the fortunate children who take advantage of their love-laden offering gain a taste for this sweet, potent literature. May those children continue throughout their lives to taste and distribute to others that which they have relished in their childhood and youth. May the *Śrīmad-Bhāgavatam* safeguard their rapid journey to the lotus feet of Śrī Kṛṣṇa. And may Śrīla Prabhupāda bless those who have sought to fulfill his desire by compiling this offering and placing it into his lotus hands.

Gratefully,

– Bhūrijana Dāsa

Śrīmad-Bhāgavatam: A Comprehensive Guide for Young Readers, to our reading and from all reports, is an unsurpassed resource for teachers of *Śrīmad-Bhāgavatam*, both in families and in schools. The variety of materials and amount of work that went into producing the book as a gift to Śrīla Prabhupāda are astonishing.

– Hanumatpreśaka Swami (Prof. H.H. Robinson)

As I travel around United States, I get to personally witness how much devotee families have benefitted from HG Aruddhā Devī Dāsī and her homeschooling methods, which are completely based on Śrīla Prabhupāda's books and his teachings. I am an ardent supporter of her and the models of education which she develops and promotes through her books and various home schooling seminars.

It's very pleasing to note that she and her team has come up with a second project, *Śrīmad-Bhāgavatam: A Comprehensive Guide for Young Readers*. The series' main objective is to provide children with a *Bhāgavatam*-centered education, with lots of activities created by parents and teachers that are geared toward different learning styles, while meeting devotional, cognitive and language objectives of a growing child in Kṛṣṇa consciousness. This innovative and systematic compilation of various activities in book form is a great resource for any homeschooling parents who want their children go deeper in the messages of *Śrīmad-Bhāgavatam*.

– Romapāda Swami

From my reading of Aruddhā Devī Dāsī's book on studying *Śrīmad-Bhāgavatam*, it is evident that she is fulfilling Śrīla Prabhupāda's desire that our children get the best Kṛṣṇa conscious education. As Śrīla Prabhupāda said in a lecture on *SB* 1.5.13 given in New Vrindaban in 1969: "When one can understand *Śrīmad-Bhāgavatam* in true perspective, then he's to be understood that he has finished his all educational advancement. *Avadhi. Avadhi* means 'this is the limit of education.' *Vidyā-bhāgavatāvadhi*."

This book gives the highest knowledge in an interesting way so that children may access the *Bhāgavatam* on many levels, including higher-level thinking and application to their lives, as well as artistic, dramatic, and journalistic approaches. I recommend this book for all parents who want to give their children a higher taste for reading Śrīla Prabhupāda's *Śrīmad-Bhāgavatam*.

– Narāyaṇī Devī Dāsī

Śrīmad Bhāgavatam

– A Comprehensive Guide for Young Readers –

Canto 3, Volume 2

ŚRĪMAD BHĀGAVATAM

– A Comprehensive Guide for Young Readers –

CANTO 3, VOLUME 2

Compiled by

ARUDDHĀ DEVĪ DĀSĪ

Krishna Homeschool

Attention Schools, Temples, Associations, and Professional Organizations:
This book is available at special discounts for bulk purchases for promotions, premiums, fundraising, or educational use. Special books, booklets, or excerpts can be created to suit your specific needs.

Library of Congress Cataloging-in-Publication Data

Śrīmad-Bhāgavatam: A Study Guide for Children / compiled by Aruddhā Devī Dāsī.
Pages: 444
ISBN 978-1-7339272-4-6
1. Puranas. Bhagavatapurana--Textbooks. 2. Hinduism--Textbooks.
I. Aruddha, Devi Dasi.
BL1140.4.B436S745 2014
294.5'925--dc23
2014005526

Cover illustration by Nitiksha Dawar
Cover design by Raivata Dāsa

For more information, contact:

Krishna Homeschool

Contact the author at aruddha108@yahoo.com

RAIVATA DESIGN
Designing with the Soul

Design by Raivata Dāsa
design@raivata.pro
www.raivata.pro

Contents

This book is a tribute to the spiritual master of the entire world, His Divine Grace A. C. Bhaktivedanta Swami Prabhupāda, who gave us the invaluable gift of *Śrīmad-Bhāgavatam.* Śrīla Prabhupāda spent hours each night translating this vast literature from Sanskrit to English and writing his erudite purports. He emphasized that anyone who studies *Śrīmad-Bhāgavatam* will be liberated from misery and directly connected to Kṛṣṇa. It was Śrīla Prabhupāda's great desire that our children be educated in *Śrīmad-Bhāgavatam.*

Acknowledgments

My humble obeisances and gratitude to my spiritual master, His Holiness Gopal Krishna Goswami, a dear and dedicated disciple of Śrīla Prabhupāda, who is untiring in his efforts to preach Kṛṣṇa consciousness throughout the world. He always encourages me to share my experiences of Kṛṣṇa conscious parenting with devotees.

My gratitude to my husband Anantarūpa Prabhu, my sons Rādhikā Ramaṇa and Gopal Hari, and my daughters-in-law Amrita Keli and Devī Mūrti, who greatly supported my efforts in completing these series of books.

My profound thanks to all the contributors for Canto 3, Volume 2, of this book who spent many hours creating resources and other materials. I offer my heartfelt gratitude to the following contributors, who hail from various countries around the world, for their committed efforts in specific areas (in order of country):

Australia

Mādrī Devī Dāsī for word search and crossword puzzles.

Rāṇī Revatī Devī Dāsī for introspective activities.

India

Pūrṇeśvari Rādhā Devī Dāsī for critical thinking and analogy activities.

New Zealand

Bhāva Sandhi Devī Dāsī for creative art activities.

Portugal

Eshani Lasya for her beautiful and professional artwork, which brought the stories to life.

United Kingdom

Vṛndākiśorī Devī Dāsī for her dramatic and engaging chapter summaries.

Kulaśekhara Dāsa for introspective activities.

United States

Anādi Rādhā Devī Dāsī for compiling higher-thinking questions, language activities, and creative, thoughtful activities for younger children.

Amṛta Sundarī Devī Dāsī for action and theatrical activities.

Devī Mūrti Devī Dāsī and Indradevi Vengatesh for small illustrations, created many times at the last minute.

My profuse thanks to Nikuñja Vilāsinī Devī Dāsī (Nirvana Kasopersad) for her excellent editorial work. Her expertise in checking and revising content, correcting grammar, and proofreading, with constant attention to quality and detail, proved to be a great blessing as we put together this voluminous work.

Many thanks to Raivata Dāsa for the design and layout, which made the book polished and attractive to children. Working under tight deadlines, he gave attention to consistency in consecutive volumes.

Special thanks to Amol Bakshi for providing us with a vision, reviewing the content with care and attention, and for his valuable feedback, spotting minute errors with an eye for detail.

This book is the product of many hands, and it would not have existed without the dedication of all these devotees. I am deeply indebted to them for taking time from their busy schedules to create a valuable resource for children everywhere.

Introduction

While conducting seminars on homeschooling and Kṛṣṇa conscious parenting throughout the world during the last seven years, I met many parents who wanted to teach their children *Śrīmad-Bhāgavatam* but who needed more guidance on how to do it. It was then that I started doing workshops, during which we would sit together with their children and I would demonstrate how to guide a discussion in a way that evoked the child's curiosity about the nature of the world, God, the self, and the purpose of life. Together, we would read the translations of a chapter of *Śrīmad-Bhāgavatam* and discuss the stories, main themes, and great personalities. We would talk about the relevance of *Śrīmad-Bhāgavatam* in our own lives – how it provides spiritual solutions to material problems. Both the children and parents were thoroughly enlivened and absorbed in the discussions.

When I explained at my seminars how I taught my boys *Śrīmad-Bhāgavatam* through interactive reading and discussion, hundreds of parents were inspired to follow. However, many parents who wanted to study the *Bhāgavatam* with their children were uncertain about how to do it. They needed a formal curriculum, and I pondered how I could help. I decided to start a collaborative project, involving devotee parents from around the world. I formed an online group in which approximately 15 parents – from Australia, New Zealand, India, South Africa, the United Kingdom, and the United States – worked together to create study resources for each chapter of Canto 1. Every parent would send their creations to others in the group, who would use the material with their own children and offer feedback. I would go through all the materials, offering direction and ideas on content and activities.

All the parents brought special skills – our team included English teachers, musicians, artists, and computer professionals. With children of their own, they were highly motivated to give them a *Bhāgavatam*-centered education. The result? An innovative collection of material on every chapter of Canto 1. The creators used the curriculum with their own children as they designed it, seeing the results firsthand.

However, having all this material in email attachments was beneficial only to a certain extent – it had to be edited, organized, and compiled. So we began the painstaking task of systematically compiling a book for use by parents anywhere, which was published by Torchlight as *Śrīmad Bhāgavatam: A Comprehensive Guide for Young Readers, Canto 1 Part 1*. We then went through a similar process for Canto 1 (Part 2), Canto 2, and now Canto 3, Parts 1 and 2. This second volume is primarily geared for children between the ages of 8 and 16, but much of the material can be adapted for children younger than 8, or older than 16.

WHY STUDY ŚRĪMAD-BHĀGAVATAM?

Śrīla Prabhupāda said that from the very beginning, children "should be taught Sanskrit and English, so in the future they can read our books. That will make them MA, Ph.D. Because the knowledge in these books is so advanced, children would be well-educated, happy, satisfied, and even go back home, back to Godhead." (Letter to Jagadīśa, April 6, 1977)

As is evident in many of his lectures, Śrīla Prabhupāda desired that children in his *gurukula* schools read *Śrīmad-Bhāgavatam*. In 1974, speaking on *Śrīmad-Bhāgavatam* (1.16.22), Śrīla Prabhupāda emphasized that the *Bhāgavatam* would equip one to know any subject: "So in *Śrīmad-Bhāgavatam* you will find everything, whatever is necessity, for the advancement of human civilization, everything is there described. And knowledge also, all departments of knowledge, even astronomy, astrology, politics, sociology, atomic theory, everything is there. *Vidyā-bhāgavatāvadhi*. Therefore, if you study *Śrīmad-Bhāgavatam* very carefully, then you get all knowledge completely. Because *Bhāgavatam* begins from the point of creation: *janmādy asya yataḥ*." (July 12, 1974, Los Angeles)

If we give children this foundation, they become confident of their spiritual identity and also do well academically. Śrīla Prabhupāda's books inspire critical reasoning and creative thinking, which are the main elements of academic education. In addition, *Śrīmad-Bhāgavatam* is pure and perfect and can equip them with the highest knowledge, both material and spiritual.

Parents and teachers who have taught their children *Śrīmad-Bhāgavatam* early in life have experienced how easily they pick up English language skills, especially reading, comprehension, and analytical reasoning. *Śrīmad-Bhāgavatam* is full of analogies, allegories, figurative speech, and metaphors. Even a seven-year-old child can grasp difficult concepts because the subject matter of *Śrīmad-Bhāgavatam* encourages higher-thinking skills.

Śrīmad-Bhāgavatam is a wonderful book to teach from because it gives the philosophy of the *Bhagavad-gītā* through stories, and children love stories. These stories are not fictitious; rather, they are the lives of great saintly personalities and the pastimes of Kṛṣṇa and His *avatāras*. By reading these, children directly associate with the great personalities and their teachings and begin to emulate the character of these personalities. As children grow older, they learn to appreciate the instructions given by Queen Kuntī, Prahlāda Mahārāja, Dhruva Mahārāja, Kapiladeva, and so many others. In fact, many of the devotees described in the *Bhāgavatam*, such as Prahlāda and Dhruva, are children themselves, so our children have perfect examples and heroes to follow.

The scriptures tell us that Śrī Caitanya Mahāprabhu heard the stories of Dhruva Mahārāja and Prahlāda Mahārāja hundreds of times while growing up, and still he was never bored. The example and instructions of these saints are so valuable that no other moral book can compare with them. Children develop good character, saintly qualities, and pure *bhakti* by reading *Śrīmad-Bhāgavatam*. Indeed, *Śrīmad-Bhāgavatam* is the very essence of Lord Caitanya's *saṅkīrtana* movement.

HOW TO USE THE BOOK

(A) *Discussion*

In my book *Homeschooling Kṛṣṇa's Children*, I emphasize the necessity of giving our children a Kṛṣṇa conscious education based on Śrīla Prabhupāda's books. I discuss the methodology of studying *Śrīmad-Bhāgavatam* through interactive reading and discussion – the most important element of the process. We sit in a circle and take turns reading only translations, pausing frequently for discussion. (For children who cannot read, they can listen as their parents read and paraphrase the translations). This method has been followed for thousands of years by the great sages of Vedic India as we see in the *Bhāgavatam* itself.

Discussion is an important part of reading. For children it breaks up the monotony of reading and can add both interest and challenge. By using *Śrīmad-Bhāgavatam* as their basic text, children can learn all aspects of language skills: composition, comprehension, vocabulary, critical thinking, and analytical reasoning. The children often drive the discussion by asking questions, raising doubts, or making observations about what they read. By expressing themselves, children understand the material better, gain self-confidence, and learn communication skills. Parents can pick up on their children's cues and ask questions of their own to encourage deeper understanding. Parents can also present their own realizations, play devil's advocate, and relate the stories to practical life, thus making the *Bhāgavatam* study a dynamic learning experience.

Reading and discussion also lead to good speaking, debate, and logical thinking. The nature of *Śrīmad-Bhāgavatam* is such that it encourages a person to ask questions, think critically, and work creatively because the *Bhāgavatam* is full of analogies, metaphors and figurative speech. For example, the analogy of the car and the driver that Prabhupāda uses to describe the difference between the body and the soul is practical and simple, but it allows a child to appreciate a foundational principle of Kṛṣṇa consciousness. Some analogies may be difficult for a four- or five-year-old, but as he or she grows older, these analogies will become the basis for strong reasoning skills.

Before reading a chapter (translations)

with their children, parents should read the chapter and purports on their own and go through the discussion (higher-thinking questions) provided in this book. These questions give parents ideas of how to inspire discussion as they read with their children. Please remember, however, that the discussion questions are only for the purpose of stimulating ideas, not to create a highly structured "oral exam" atmosphere while reading. The key is to keep the discussion dynamic and student-driven, using the sample questions when needed and adapting/rephrasing them appropriately for the age and personality of the child. During a vibrant discussion, you and your child will, no doubt, come up with questions and topics that were not mentioned in this book, and we encourage you do to so. Here are some suggestions for raising interesting and thought-provoking questions:

- Take turns reading the translations, going in a circle. This keeps the child's attention, because children eagerly await their turn. If your child cannot read, you should read and pause frequently to paraphrase the story at the child's level. Ask your child to tell the story in his or her own words.
- Whenever possible, ask "why" and "how" questions rather than "what" (factual) questions, thus encouraging your child to think and reason.
- Don't be afraid to ask open-ended questions that do not have a clear-cut answer. These questions often lead to beneficial discussions.
- Discuss the many analogies and metaphors in Śrīla Prabhupāda's purports, which are good opportunities to connect the *Śrīmad-Bhāgavatam* to your child's experience and imagination.
- Frequently encourage your child to make comments and raise questions. When your child raises a question for which you don't know the answer, don't be afraid to say so. Discuss his or her question thoroughly, read through purports to find guidance, and you will see many fresh realizations arise.
- Try to relate the story to daily life: "Why did Parīkṣit Mahārāja not retaliate against the boy's curse?" or "What can we learn from Parīkṣit Mahārāja's behavior?" However, don't put your child on the spot by pointing fingers: "How should you have behaved with your friend Johnny the other day?" Such finger-pointing destroys the discussion and intimidates the child.
- Draw connections with other stories from the scriptures that your child may already know: "The boy Śṛṅgi showed anger in an inappropriate way, but when is it okay to feel angry? Can you give an example from other stories in the scriptures?"
- Continue reading until you come to a translation that raises a question or comment. Don't worry if a particular section doesn't raise discussion – some sections will be more interesting to a child than others.
- Have a "realizations session" at the end of a chapter where your child can tell you what they learned from the chapter, and you can tell your child what you learned. Or bring

the family together and ask your child to give a short class on the chapter.

- If you have not read *Śrīmad-Bhāgavatam* before, that is okay. As a parent (or teacher), you have more life experience, and you know your child, which will allow you to lead a discussion and engage your child.
- When you read with an older child (the specific age will vary based on the maturity of the child), take the stance of a fellow reader and learner. This will help your child open up and feel comfortable. Of course, as the teacher, you will still need to correct a mistaken line of reasoning or raise points that are important, but try to do it as a partner rather than as a master.
- Consider these readings/discussions as your time with *Śrīmad-Bhāgavatam*. Stay focused and become absorbed in *Śrīmad-Bhāgavatam*. Just because your study partner is a seven-year old child does not mean that you will gain any less from studying *Śrīmad-Bhāgavatam*.

(B) *Written and Oral Exercises*

Once you have read a chapter of the *Bhāgavatam* translations together, you can use a variety of exercises provided in the book to teach language skills – including writing, comprehension, and vocabulary – which will help in understanding the chapter. This book provides comprehension questions, key themes and messages, language puzzles, arts and crafts, and many other activities. In this volume we have eliminated some language activities and extra resources to not make it too thick and unwieldy for children. However, extra activities are available on request. We also encourage you to use your creativity to compile new interesting activities that would stimulate your child. To decide on which verses children can memorize, please see the related verses from each chapter after the Themes and Key Messages section. Our goal is to provide you with practical tools to make *Śrīmad-Bhāgavatam* a central part of your children's education. Regardless of whether you are homeschooling or sending your children to school, we hope these tools will inspire you to create other innovative ways to help your children.

Here are the different sections you will find in this book:

- Story Summary
- Key Messages and Themes
- Discussion Questions and Higher-Thinking Questions
- Critical-Thinking Activities
- Introspective Activities
- Language and Writing Activities
- Analogy Activities
- Arts, Crafts, Drama, and other Hands-On Activities
- Songs and Poems
- Answers (includes answers to specific questions and puzzles)

The instructions for each activity are addressed directly to the child, but we assume that parents will still need to explain and supervise the activities, especially if the child is younger.

LEARNING OUTCOMES

The book's main objective is to provide children from the ages of 8 to 16 with spiritual knowledge from the *Śrīmad-Bhāgavatam* and the opportunity for personal realization.

The primary process for doing this is by reading chapter translations with the children, discussing the stories and philosophical content of the chapter, and providing the children with the opportunity to make their own inquiries and share their personal experiences.

In addition, the activities in this book develop the key themes and philosophical points presented in each chapter by accommodating different learning styles in a range of learning modes (visual, auditory and kinesthetic).

The activities also meet the following cognitive and language objectives:

- Developing thinking skills (based on Bloom's *Taxonomy of Educational Objectives*):
- Developing comprehension skills
- Acquiring knowledge
- Applying knowledge
- Using knowledge to be creative
- Analyzing information
- Promoting self-evaluation

Language objectives:

- Written language (includes reading and writing)
- Visual language (includes communicating through the visual arts, such as drama and static imagery)
- Oral language (includes communication through speaking)

This book also supplements any existing curriculum that parents or teachers may use to teach language skills. This is not a course designed to teach reading and writing in itself, but it can work together with a formal curriculum to further develop language skills, while providing children with a resource for studying *Śrīmad-Bhāgavatam*.

Śrīmad-Bhāgavatam lies at the heart of Śrī Caitanya Mahāprabhu's philosophy and movement. I pray that this book will help children and their parents develop a lifelong love for this great literature, following in the footsteps of Śrīla Prabhupāda and our previous *ācāryas*. *Śrīmad-Bhāgavatam* is very profound, and this book only skims the surface. Please forgive any faults and shortcomings in our humble endeavors.

Aruddhā Devi Dasi

17

Victory of Hiraṇyākṣa Over All the Directions of the Universe

STORY SUMMARY

The demigods now felt reassured after their meeting with Lord Brahmā. Their gripping fear melted away after hearing of Jaya and Vijaya's curse to be born as demons on Earth and their defeat by the Supreme Lord. They offered gratitude and respects to Lord Brahmā, then boarded their airplanes and returned to their own planets with new-found hope.

However, Diti and Kaśyapa were tortured with worry about the birth of their terrible twins. With all their power, they had managed to keep the twins in Diti's womb for one hundred years, but now the inevitable time had come for the boys to take birth. And, oh, the world would know it.

When they were born, many omens in the form of natural disturbances occurred in the heavenly planets, the earthly planets, and planets in between. You see, when there are natural disturbances in the world, it is to be understood that a demon is being born. When the terrible twins were born, the natural disturbances were eerie and frightening.

The ground shook and trembled; earthquakes shattered the earth and caused fires in all directions. Darkness was everywhere; the sky was covered with dark clouds – horrific lightning with claps of thunder terrified the inhabitants of Earth. Beyond the thunderbolts, they could see comets and meteors flying across the sky and misty halos surrounding the sun and moon during their eclipses. The bad planets shone brightly. A sure omen.

The oceans wailed in sorrow, causing its creatures to weep, while the agitated rivers and lakes caused its lotuses to wither. If you walked to a mountain cave, you would hear eerie rattling sounds like that of chariots getting louder and louder…yet there was nothing there.

She-jackals howled and vomited fire while the he-jackals, along with dogs and owls, wailed. Donkeys stomped the earth, braying loudly, while the birds, frightened by the braying of the donkeys, flew from their nests, shrieking. Terrified cattle passed dung and urine, and instead of milk, only blood came from their udders.

Clouds rained pus instead of water, and images of the demigods in the temples shed tears. Trees fell even without the blast of wind.

Everyone looked on in horror, sure that this marked the end of the world – everyone except the four Kumāras who knew well the cause of these disturbances.

Soon these two demons had bodies hundreds of times stronger than the average person. Their steellike frames grew as big as mountains until their crowns pierced the clouds. Their bodies blocked the view of all directions, and with every step they shook the earth.

Their father Kaśyapa named the eldest

Hiraṇyakaśipu and the younger twin Hiraṇyākṣa. Hiraṇyakaśipu was unafraid of death. He had a benediction from Brahmā that seemingly protected him from death, making him very proud, and so he had all the three worlds under his fingertips.

Hiraṇyākṣa adored his brother Hiraṇyakaśipu and traveled throughout the universe with his club, ready to satisfy his brother in whatever way he desired. With his gigantic mace on his shoulder, he walked with golden anklets that vibrated the sound of impending doom. He also had no fear of death at the hands of anyone.

The demigods in the heavenly planets hid themselves in terror just at the sight of Hiraṇyākṣa.

"Ha! Ha! Ha! I am all powerful!" the demon roared one day, looking around for any sign of life in the heavenly kingdom.

Disappointed, he left that place and dove deep into the ocean that roared terribly. The aquatic creatures swam away in fear.

"Ha! Ha! Ha!" Hiraṇyākṣa laughed again, bubbles emanating from his mouth and nostrils. "Just see my splendor – I didn't even need to deal a blow with my mace!"

He roamed the ocean for many, many years, hitting the mighty wind-tossed waves again and again with his iron mace until he reached Vibhāvarī, the city of Varuṇa. Varuṇa is the demigod of the sea, lord of the aquatic creatures, and guardian of the underworld where the demons reside.

Hiraṇyākṣa fell at Varuṇa's feet. Varuṇa sat on his throne, unsure of Hiraṇyākṣa's motives. Was this a genuine submission? Hiraṇyākṣa lifted his head and gazed at Varuṇa with deep sincerity. Varuṇa sighed with relief. Maybe the demon was reforming.

Bringing his palms together, Hiraṇyākṣa said, "O Supreme Lord, I beg you…"

Varuṇa gave him an encouraging nod. "Yes?" He prodded gently.

"Fight with me!"

Varuṇa was taken aback. Hiraṇyākṣa's eyes narrowed as a sinister smile crept into his face. He chuckled. He chortled. He laughed menacingly and then uncontrollably. Varuṇa was made a fool.

Varuṇa felt a hot anger burning in his chest and rising to his face. He couldn't show this to the demon. He knew he was no match for Hiraṇyākṣa, but he knew who would be. He knew exactly what Hiraṇyākṣa needed.

Varuṇa swallowed his anger, watching the demon as he continued to laugh and howl uncontrollably.

"Oh, dear Hiraṇyākṣa," said Varuṇa gently.

The demon stopped laughing. How was Varuṇa going to reply to his surprise plea?

"Unfortunately, we don't engage in war anymore as we're now too old for combat," Varuṇa said.

Hiraṇyākṣa scoffed at what he considered to be a lame excuse.

"You are such a skilled warrior," Varuṇa continued. "I think you should approach Lord Viṣṇu. He is the only one that can really satisfy your thirst for battle. He is your only match. He'll vanquish your pride as you lie on the battlefield facing death. He assumes various incarnations like Varāha, especially to exterminate wicked demons like you and to show His grace to His devotees."

Themes and Key Messages

The following table summarizes the key messages and themes of this chapter. Use it as a quick reference guide to the verses listed. Can you find the listed verses in your *Śrīmad-Bhāgavatam*? Discuss each theme and message further with your teacher or friends. Can you think of examples in your own life that relate to these key messages?

Theme	Reference	Key Messages
We can overcome fear by hearing from authority.	3.17.1	Everyone in the material world experiences fear. When we are disturbed by something and become afraid, the best solution is to approach a senior devotee who can explain the matter from a spiritual perspective and thereby remove our fear. Just like Arjuna approached Kṛṣṇa on the battlefield, or the demigods approached Lord Brahmā in the previous chapter, we should also hear from authority, take shelter of Lord Kṛṣṇa, and become peaceful.
Natural disturbances in the world and inauspicious omens indicate the birth of impious or demoniac people.	3.17.4–14	Natural disturbances like earthquakes, floods, hurricanes, and many other such disasters is a result of impious and sinful activity in the world. Because nowadays these natural calamities are so common, we can conclude that the demoniac population has increased.
There are two kinds of people in the world. The first is of demoniac mentality (*asuras*).	3.17.16, 17, 19, 20, 25	Demons are concerned simply with physical comforts and material upliftment. They have no interest in Lord Kṛṣṇa. They also try to increase their own power to dominate others, create quarrels, occupy others' property, and are proud of their position. Such people train their family to only pursue sense gratification. They forget that everyone is subject to birth, death, disease, and old age.
The second kind of persons in this world is of demigod mentality (*devas*).	3.17.16, 20	People of demigod mentality are simply concerned with the Supreme Personality of Godhead. They work for the spiritual upliftment of human society. They desire to engage everything and everyone in the service of the Lord. They teach their family members to take shelter of Lord Kṛṣṇa and not spend their life simply for material advancement.

Character Descriptions

Hiraṇyākṣa

- He was born as the son of Kaśyapa Muni and Diti in the Cākṣuṣa millennium.
- He was the first demon in the universe.
- He is called the "great exploiter of the gold rush." (*SB* 2.7.1 purport)
- He is the twin (younger) brother of the demon Hiraṇyakaśipu and the uncle of Prahlāda Mahārāja.
- He dislocated the earth from its orbit and threw it deep into the waters of the Garbhodaka ocean.
- He was killed by Lord Varāha and then pierced by Lord Varāha's tusk.
- In a particular millennium, he was formerly Vijaya, one of the chief doorkeepers of Lord Nārāyaṇa in Vaikuṇṭha.

Varuna

- He is the ninth son of Kaśyapa Muni and Aditi.
- He is the father of the great sages Agastya and Vasiṣṭha.
- He is the controlling deity for all relishable juices and of the tongue, which tastes all different flavors.
- He is the demigod (*adhikāri-devatā*) presiding over the seas and the oceans, the night, and the western sky.
- He is prayed to for forgiveness, since he punishes sin.
- He is the sender of disease.
- His capital, Vibhāvarī, is within his underwater kingdom.
- His daughter Vāruṇī, in the form of liquid honey oozing from the hollows of the trees, captivated Lord Balarāma in the forest of Vṛndāvana.
- He gave the *paśāstra* weapon to Arjuna.

Understanding the Story

Now it's time for you to check how well you understood the story by answering these multiple-choice questions. There can be more than one answer for each question. (Answers can be found at the end of the chapter.)

1. Residents on which planet do not fear death, getting hurt, losing something they love, etc.?
   a) Earth
   b) Moon
   c) Heavenly planets
   d) Vaikuṇṭha planet
2. Where did Jaya and Vijaya appear on the earth after they fell from Vaikuṇṭha?
   a) In Vṛndāvana
   b) In a tree hole
   c) In Diti's womb
   d) In a hospital bed

3. For how long did Diti keep the two boys in her womb?
   a) 9 months
   b) 3 years
   c) 100 years
   d) 1,000 years
4. When inauspicious omens appeared when the demons were born, who knew that they were Jaya and Vijaya from Vaikuṇṭha?
   a) All the animals and trees
   b) The four Kumāras, Brahmā, and the demigods
   c) Inhabitants of the earth
   d) The oceans, lakes, and rivers
5. Why were the four Kumāras not afraid after seeing the terrible omens?
   a) They were totally dependent on Kṛṣṇa and knew that Kṛṣṇa had arranged everything to carry out His pastimes.
   b) They were quite powerful and knew they could protect themselves.
   c) They were little boys, so they did not understand danger.
   d) They were unaffected by happiness and distress.

6. What did Kaśyapa Muni name his twin sons?
   a) Rāma and Lakṣmaṇa
   b) Rāvaṇa and Kumbhakarṇa
   c) Jagāi and Mādhāi
   d) Hiraṇyakaśipu and Hiraṇyākṣa
7. What were the physical bodies of Hiraṇyakaśipu and Hiraṇyākṣa like?
   a) They were like average male human beings.
   b) Their bodies were strong like metal and tall like mountains.
   c) They were delicate and gentle like rose petals.
   d) Their bodies emitted fire constantly.
8. How did Hiraṇyakaśipu and Hiraṇyākṣa behave after receiving benedictions from Brahmā?
   a) They became humble devotees of Lord Brahmā.
   b) They decided to do more austerities to please Lord Viṣṇu.
   c) They were no longer afraid of death, believing they could not be killed by anyone, so they created disturbances everywhere.
   d) They began to trouble other demons.
9. Why were the demigods still afraid of Hiraṇyakaśipu and Hiraṇyākṣa, knowing they were Jaya and Vijaya from Vaikuṇṭha helping the Lord to perform His pastimes on Earth?
   a) The demigods knew the two demons were more powerful than they were, and being attached to their position, they feared being overpowered by the two demons.
   b) Lord Viṣṇu had informed the demigods that He would not protect them from these two demons.
   c) The demigods forgot that they were also very powerful.
   d) Demigods get scared very easily.
10. Why did the demigod Varuṇa not engage in a fight with Hiraṇyākṣa?
    a) Varuṇa and Hiraṇyākṣa were friends from the past.
    b) He was not as powerful as Hiraṇyākṣa and wanted to direct him to Lord Viṣṇu so that Viṣṇu could kill him.
    c) Varuṇa forgot how to use his weapons to fight with Hiraṇyākṣa.
    d) Varuṇa did not want others to watch him get defeated by Hiraṇyākṣa.

Higher-Thinking Questions

Now try to deepen your understanding of this chapter by delving into Śrīla Prabhupāda's purports and reflecting on the following questions:

1. Śrīla Prabhupāda in his purport to verse 1 concludes that by approaching authority one's problems will be solved. Who do you see as authority in your life? Have you experienced any fearful situations that made you take shelter of your authority? Explain.
2. Can people consult scriptures like the *Bhagavad-gītā* and *Śrīmad-Bhāgavatam* for solution to their problems? Do you think those are authorities too? Explain.
3. If someone expresses to you a concern for the increasing natural disturbances in the present age, what will you say in response to him or her?
4. Who are the demigods and demons? What are the differences between them?
5. In the purport to verse 16, Śrīla Prabhupāda explains that the demigods care for the spiritual wellbeing of human society whereas the demons are concerned with only material sense gratification.
   What steps can people take so that instead of constantly thinking about satisfying their senses, they can think about their spiritual wellbeing and the spiritual wellbeing of others?
6. How does the earth react to disturbances created by people who are not God conscious? (see verse 4)
7. Do you believe that there are signs before something happens? Vedic literatures have a branch of science that deals with this called *nimitta śāstra*. Do you think it is a science or superstition? Explain your answer.
8. What was the reason for Hiraṇyakaśipu being so proud and puffed up (see verse 19)? Do you recall any other personalities from the *śāstras* who were similarly proud due to power and position?

ACTIVITIES

In this section you will find many exciting things to do. These activities will get you thinking, moving, drawing, and having loads of fun.

Action Activity . . . to get you moving!

WHAT'S IN A NAME

Description: Prajāpati Kaśyapa named his elder son Hiraṇyakaśipu, which means "one who likes gold and soft cushions." Similarly, Vidura means "one who is wise and intelligent." Kṛṣṇa is also referred to by many names, which describe His qualities or pastimes. Challenge your parents or friends to a game of charades by enacting the meaning of Kṛṣṇa's names.

How to play:

1. Make two teams of two or more players in each team (or you can play with a single opponent).
2. Each player should research at least 20 names of Kṛṣṇa (from *Bhagavad- gītā* or other sources) and memorize their meanings.
3. In front of the opposing team, each player takes turns to enact the quality or pastime that their choice of names represents one by one.
4. Give your opposing team about a minute to guess the name.
5. For each correct answer, they get 2 points, and for every wrong answer, your team gets 1 point.
6. Play till you finish with all your names.

Artistic Activities

. . . to reveal your creativity!

OMENS DRAWING GAME

What you will need:
Paper, scissors, pencils/pens

Description:

1. With your friends go back through the story and make notes of all the terrible omens and natural disasters that occurred when Hiraṇyakaśipu and Hiraṇyākṣa were born.
2. Draw each omen on small pieces of paper.
3. Place them on a flat surface and try to memorize them.
4. One person now starts taking away the omen papers one by one. As each one is taken away, the others have to guess the omen that was just removed, as well as all the missing ones till that point.

For example, after the third omen is removed, you have to remember "trees fell, jackals cried, and lotuses withered." When one more omen is taken away, you would say "trees fell, jackals cried, lotuses withered, and darkness was everywhere."

Use the templates below to create your drawings.

UNDERSEA MURAL

What you will need:
Large paper, paints, brushes, information about sea aquatics, paper, pens, cardboard

Description:

1. Paint a large, blue sea-like background. Undercoat the whole "under water" area with light blue. While your blue undercoat is still wet, blend darker shades of blue and green on top. Wait for it to dry.
2. Research different sea creatures: their size, characteristics, special abilities and strengths.
3. On pieces of cardboard draw or paint your choice of different aquatics and then cut them out.
4. Then draw or paint Hiraṇyākṣa and Varuṇadeva on cardboard and cut out.
5. On your underwater drawing, paint sea details, such as seaweed, sand, stones, etc.
6. Present a "show and tell" about your aquatic creatures and add them onto the sea background to create a mural. Then add Hiraṇyākṣa and Varuṇa and retell the pastime with your undersea mural.

Critical-Thinking Activity
. . . to bring out the spiritual investigator in you!

OMENS AND NATURAL DISASTERS

The dictionary defines "omen" as "an event that foretells good or evil." Vedic literatures mention specific good and bad signs that indicate the nature of future events. For example, in verses 3 to 15 of this chapter, there are many ill omens listed. These omens appeared at the birth of Hiraṇyakaśipu and Hiraṇyākṣa, indicating that these two people would create a lot of trouble in the universe.

With so many omens, superstitions, and blind beliefs being followed around the world today, it is easy to wonder whether Vedic omens really foretell the nature of future events. Complete the following activities to understand the nature of Vedic omens.

Omens or Blind Beliefs?

It is not difficult to test whether omens can indeed exist. For example, there is some evidence that suggests that animals are able to sense the coming of major natural disasters, such as earthquakes, tsunamis, and hurricanes. Many times, animals exhibit warning behaviors and even leave the area before a natural disaster strikes.

Activity 1.1: Animal Behavior Before Natural Disasters

Research the following:

1. Find out some typical animal behavior that is known to have occurred before natural disasters.
2. Find out whether animals tried to flee or escape before the disaster occurred.
3. Can we consider such behavior as omens signaling a natural disaster?
4. From this study, would it be very difficult to believe in the possibility of omens before certain events?

What About Vedic Omens?

Since the animal behavior we studied in the above activity is scientifically verifiable, it is easy to believe that they could indeed be omens predicting a natural disaster. But how do we understand the omens described in Vedic literatures, which are not always directly verifiable?

Vedic literatures, written by the Lord or His pure devotees, are perfect. Therefore, the science of omens they describe are also perfect. Everything, including the science of predicting the nature of certain world events to come, has been perfectly described for the benefit of people. This knowledge is also passed down directly from the Lord Himself through the *paramparā* system, from spiritual master to disciple. We can therefore accept this knowledge to be true.

Activity 1.2: Omens at the Birth of Hiraṇyakaśipu and Hiraṇyākṣa

Purpose of the activity: To learn the Vedic omens that occurred at the time of Hiraṇyakaśipu and Hiraṇyākṣa's birth. To also study some good Vedic omens.
What you will need: Pictures depicting the various ill omens that appeared at the time of Hiraṇyakaśipu and Hiraṇyākṣa's birth; pictures depicting some good omens that are described in the *Bhāgavatam*; chart paper to make a collage
Activity: List and find images for the bad omens that appeared at the time of Hiraṇyākṣa's and Hiraṇyakaśipu's birth. Research the *Bhāgavatam* and find out some good omens that appear when a nice event is going to happen. Then make a collage of omens, with images of good omens filling one half of your sheet and images of bad omens filling the other half.

Are All Omens True?

There are also many wrong beliefs in the name of Vedic religion today. And then there are many non-Vedic blind beliefs, rituals, and superstitions that are current in the world. Learning to distinguish between real and wrong omens and beliefs is very important for us to strengthen our faith in the teachings of the *Śrīmad-Bhāgavatam*.

Every time you come across a practice, omen, or ritual, use the prompts below to help you understand whether it is genuine or not. You should, of course, do this under the guidance of a proper mentor.

1. What is the omen or belief?
2. How did the omen or belief originate? Does it have (or has it been verified by) an authorized Vedic source?
3. In the past, has the omen always correctly foretold the nature of future events?
4. What can you finally conclude? Is the omen authentic or not?

Activity 1.3: Testing Omens

Do a study of some common omens or beliefs in your culture. For each omen or belief, have a set of images that convey your findings. Then present your findings with pictures on a chart. If your friends are also doing this activity with you, share your findings with each other.

Conclusion:
After you have completed the activities in this section, discuss the following:

1. Do you have faith that Vedic omens are real, even if you presently do not perfectly understand the science behind it? Why?
2. Why do you think it is not always possible to directly verify the truth about certain facts (like omens) given in Vedic literatures? Does that make them any less factual?
3. As a devotee, how important should belief in omens be to you?

Language Activities
. . . to make you understand better!

FILL IN THE BLANKS

1. Warmongering materialists always create fighting without ______________.
2. Natural disturbances in Kali-yuga are due to the increase of ______________________ population.
3. According to verse 15 purport, the process of begetting good children is called ________________________.
4. Two inauspicious, impious planets mentioned in this chapter are ____________________ and ____________.
5. Among the two demoniac twins, _________________________ was older than __________________________.
6. Hiraṇyakaśipu and Hiraṇyākṣa were born from_____________.
7. When the two twin demons were born, claps of __________________ were heard, even without clouds.

8. Hiraṇyakaśipu received a benediction from ___________________.
9. Hiraṇyākṣa traveled the universe with a ________________ on his shoulder.
10. ____________________ is the deity of the waters, and his capital is known as ______________________.

MATCH THE SENTENCES

Match the first part of the sentence on the left with the second part of the sentence on the right to correctly finish the sentence:

1. Varuṇa predicted the falldown and death of	a. who had fallen into the material realm after offending the four Kumāras.
2. Hiraṇyākṣa carried a club on his shoulder and roamed throughout the universe	b. Hiraṇyākṣa after he would fight with Lord Viṣṇu.
3. When living outside of Vaikuṇṭha, one can sometimes feel scared,	c. which they believed made them almost immortal.
4. The demons were Jaya and Vijaya, the gatekeepers from Vaikuṇṭha	d. and everywhere in between marked the arrival of the demons.
5. The frightening and astonishing happenings across the earthly and heavenly planets	e. with a fighting spirit just to please Hiraṇyakaśipu.
6. After years of austerities, the twin demons received a special benediction from Lord Brahmā,	f. because only Vaikuṇṭha is free from anxiety.
7. Hiraṇyākṣa and Hiraṇyakaśipu were the instruments of the Lord in the whole episode,	g. and while walking they shook the earth at every step.
8. The terrible twins blocked the view of all the directions,	h. as Lord Kṛṣṇa had desired to battle in the earthly realms.

WHAT DO YOU THINK?

Set 1 – Tick the statements that you think are true. If any are false, write them correctly.

1. Hiraṇyākṣa and Hiraṇyakaśipu were Jaya and Vijaya, the gatekeepers from Indraloka who had fallen into the material realm after offending the four Kumāras.
2. The frightening and astonishing happenings across the earthly and heavenly planets and everywhere in between marked the arrival of a demon.
3. Hiraṇyakaśipu and Hiraṇyākṣa were not afraid of death by anyone within the three worlds.
4. Hiraṇyākṣa carried a club on his shoulder and roamed through the universe with a fighting spirit just to please Lord Kṛṣṇa.
5. Varuṇa is the lord of the aquatic creatures and the guardian of the upper regions of the universe where the demons generally reside.
6. The father of the twins, Prajāpati Dakṣa, named the younger twin Hiraṇyakaśipu and the older twin Hiraṇyākṣa.
7. When they saw that nobody could stop Hiraṇyākṣa, even the demigods went into hiding.
8. Fulfilling the purpose of this incarnation, Varāha, the incarnation of Lord Kṛṣṇa, would terminate the wicked and extend his grace to the virtuous.

Set 2 – Which of the following statements do you agree with and disagree with? Refer to the story summary and what you already know. Back up your argument with reasons.

1. The best way to overcome our fear is to approach an authority who can explain the matter and help solve our problems.
2. The four sage-sons of Lord Brahmā were afraid of the evil omens because they were responsible for the fall of Jaya and Vijaya to the material world.
3. People with demoniac mentality can become so powerful that no one in the universe can defeat them, and therefore they become immortal.
4. Lord Varuṇa refused to fight Hiraṇyākṣa because he had become old and no longer engaged in warfare.

WORD SEARCH

Find the words written below in the following table:

B	A	R	P	R	O	T	A	K	S	A	M	E
W	B	A	R	S	P	A	Y	D	E	M	E	R
I	O	M	E	N	S	M	X	A	M	A	S	I
C	O	R	D	I	A	P	N	G	E	T	I	O
R	N	E	I	W	S	L	A	R	A	S	A	C
E	A	P	C	T	A	S	K	O	R	R	R	O
D	E	L	T	R	F	R	O	G	D	E	P	M
A	I	M	S	A	R	A	O	B	L	T	A	B
C	O	I	C	M	A	C	E	A	E	N	U	A
G	I	S	A	T	I	S	F	Y	V	A	N	T
R	A	O	R	E	D	E	E	R	A	W	A	I
T	E	A	E	N	E	G	R	Y	R	I	N	L
E	F	S	D	A	H	A	T	Q	T	C	X	E
N	A	T	R	E	U	A	T	A	A	K	I	A
E	N	O	R	P	R	O	U	D	E	E	T	V
A	O	R	A	G	E	Q	M	I	P	D	E	R
G	D	A	R	E	A	N	X	I	E	T	Y	T

CRYPTOGRAM

Fill in the letters that correspond to the numbers below the blanks to solve the sentence:

A	B	C	D	E	F	G	H	I	J	K	L	M	N	O	P	Q	R	S	T	U	V	W	X	Y	Z
22	10	11	7	24	25	19	15	5	13	2	21	9	8	20	1	17	16	12	3	18	6	23	14	4	26

— — — —   — — — — — — — —   — — — — — —,
18 1 20 8   16 24 22 11 15 5 8 19   6 22 16 18 8 22

— — — — — — — — — —   — — — — — — —   — — — — — —
15 5 16 22 8 4 22 2 12 22   19 16 24 24 3 24 7   6 22 16 18 8 22

— — —   — — — — — — — — —   — — — — — — — — — —   — — —:
22 8 7   9 20 11 2 5 8 19 21 4   11 15 22 21 21 24 8 19 24 7   15 5 9

"—   — — — — — — —   — — — —,   —   — — — — — — — —
20   12 18 1 16 24 9 24   21 20 16 7   20   19 18 22 16 7 5 22 8

— —   — —   — — — — — —   — — — — — —,   — — —   — —
20 25   22 8   24 8 3 5 16 24   7 20 9 22 5 8   21 24 3   18 12

— — — — — —   — —   — — — — — — !"
24 8 19 22 19 24   5 8   10 22 3 3 21 24

ANSWERS

Understanding the Story: 1) d, 2) c, 3) c, 4) b, 5) a, 6) d, 7) b, 8) c, 9) a, 10) b

Fill in the Blanks

1. reason
2. demoniac
3. *garbhādhāna*
4. Saturn; Mars
5. Hiraṇyakaśipu; Hiraṇyākṣa
6. Diti
7. thunder
8. Lord Brahmā
9. club/mace
10. Varuṇa; Vibhāvarī

Match the Sentences

1) b, 2) e, 3) f, 4) a, 5) d, 6) c, 7) h, 8) g

What do you think?

Set 1

1. True
2. False. The frightening and astonishing happenings across the earthly and heavenly planets and everywhere in between marked the arrival of **the twin demons**.
3. True
4. False. Hiraṇyākṣa carried a club on his shoulder and roamed through the universe with a fighting spirit just to please **his brother, Hiraṇyakaśipu**.
5. False. Varuṇa is the lord of the aquatic creatures and the guardian of the **lower** regions of the universe where the demons generally reside.
6. False. The father of the twins, Prajāpati **Kaśyapa**, named the **older** twin Hiraṇyakaśipu and the **younger** twin Hiraṇyākṣa.
7. True
8. True

Set 2

1. Agree
2. Disagree. The four Kumāras were unafraid of the omens because they knew of the Lord's higher plan of destroying the demons and carrying out His pastimes.
3. Disagree. Even if demoniac people become powerful, they cannot become immortal, just as

Hiraṇyākṣa was killed by the Lord.

4. Disagree. Lord Varuṇa refused to fight Hiraṇyākṣa because he knew that he was not as powerful, but if he directed Hiraṇyākṣa to Lord Viṣṇu, then the Lord would defeat him.

Cryptogram

Solution Statement:

Upon reaching Varuṇa, Hiraṇyākṣa greeted Varuṇa and mockingly challenged him: "O Supreme Lord, O guardian of an entire domain, let us engage in battle!"

18
The Battle Between Lord Boar and the Demon Hiraṇyākṣa

STORY SUMMARY

Hiraṇyākṣa ran off in a frenzy after Varuṇa revealed to him the name of a suitable combatant – a rival supposedly equal in strength. That's all he really cared about. He paid no heed to Varuṇa's warning that his opponent, the Supreme Lord, would kill him in combat. Such was his pride and arrogance. He thought that he could conquer Lord Viṣṇu, who is known as Ajita, one who has never been conquered.

After finding out from Nārada Muni that the Supreme Lord was in the depths of the Garbhodaka Ocean, Hiraṇyākṣa reached the ocean, ready to attack his enemy. He took a few steps back, ready to run and plunge into the water's depths when something unexpected stopped him. It was the sight of a blue planet emerging from the water. Was it the earth? How was she coming up? The earth had been plunged to the bottom of the Garbhodaka ocean. How was it that she was rising by herself?

Hiraṇyākṣa watched suspiciously. His eyes widened when he saw that the earth planet was not emerging alone. She was resting on the tusks of an animal…what animal was this? Its snout was hairy and long and its eyes reddish.

The animal gradually surfaced. It was a boar – yet somehow dazzling with a charming appeal. It could be none other than the Supreme Personality of Godhead, Lord Varāhadeva.

Hiraṇyākṣa's suspense immediately turned into laughter, realizing this to be his supposed rival.

"Oh! An amphibious beast!" He spat maliciously.

Lord Varāha ignored him.

Hiraṇyākṣa shouted at the Supreme Lord: "This earth belongs to us demons! There is no way in this world that You will take the earth from me and not be hurt by me. I'm going to kill You and make my family very happy!"

Lord Boar continued to ignore him.

Hiraṇyākṣa tried to agitate the Lord and said, "When You fall dead and Your skull is smashed by the mace hurled by my very arms, Your devotees – the demigods and sages – will also die, just like a tree that can't live without its roots."

Lord Boar froze. These spiteful words concerning His dear devotees were hurtful, but He tolerated them, seeing that the earth on His tusks shivered and whimpered in terror. She had suffered enough at the hands of Hiraṇyākṣa. Lord Varāha, desiring to protect the earth, rose out of the water.

Hiraṇyākṣa raised his eyebrows. After not finding a suitable combatant for many years now, there was no way he was going to let this boar walk away.

Hiraṇyākṣa chased the Lord as He emerged from the water like an alligator chasing a mighty elephant. The demon's golden hair blew in the wind as He sped, and his fearful tusks glowed as he raised his mace ready to strike.

"How shameful You are, running away from a challenge!" Hiraṇyākṣa roared like thunder.

Lord Boar continued to ignore the demon as He carefully placed the earth on the surface of the water. She gasped, thinking she would again sink to the depths of the Garbhodaka ocean…but no, she was simply bobbing on the water. She sighed in relief and smiled at the Lord.

"Thank you, Lord Varāha," she whispered, "for energizing me with the ability to float."

Hiraṇyākṣa stopped in his tracks and watched with contempt.

The Lord smiled as Brahmā appeared in the sky riding on his swan carrier, accompanied by other demigods. While they showered flowers on the Lord, Brahmā praised Lord Varāha's heroic acts.

Hiraṇyākṣa could not wait any longer. He

flew towards the Lord, resounding a war cry.

The Lord turned around in rage, again cutting Hiraṇyākṣa short. "Yes! I am a creature of the jungle," He thundered, "and I'm here to hunt for dogs like you! I can never die. Do you think I am afraid of the loose talk of someone who can die? I'm staying right here. I have no place to go now that I have a powerful enemy.

"You are supposed to be a great commander, so give up your foolish talk and actually do something to fulfill your word to kill Me!"

Hiraṇyākṣa hissed and pounced on the Lord with his powerful mace, but the Lord moved slightly aside and dodged the blow.

Hiraṇyākṣa picked up his mace and turned to face the Lord. Biting his lip in fury, he brandished his mace about violently. Lord Boar sprang on the demon, aiming His mace

at the demon's brow, but alas, the demon blocked the blow.

In this way, the two combatants fought fearlessly, striking each other with their maces. They became more enraged as they smelled the blood of their injuries and looked like two powerful bulls fighting for the sake of a cow.

Brahmā and his followers watched the long fight. His patience was transforming to unease…then dread…then panic.

"My Lord," Brahmā called out, "this demon has been a bully to the demigods, Your devotees, the cows, and all innocent creatures. He's been unnecessarily harassing them and terrorizing them. Since he received a boon from me, he's been trying to fight everyone. Please, there's no need to play with this demon before killing him."

Brahmā continued with greater anxiety, "My Lord, the demoniac hour is coming. He'll be stronger. Please kill him. Look! The darkest hour of the evening is fast approaching. Please kill him and win victory for the demigods. The auspicious time *abhijit*, which is favorable for victory, has almost passed. For the sake of Your friends, please destroy this demon quickly and make the world peaceful again."

Themes and Key Messages

The following table summarizes the key messages and themes of this chapter. Use it as a quick reference guide to the verses listed. Can you find the listed verses in your *Śrīmad-Bhāgavatam*? Discuss each theme and message further with your teacher or friends. Can you think of examples in your own life that relate to these key messages?

Theme	Reference	Key Messages
Kṛṣṇa is the source of everything.	3.18.4–5	Kṛṣṇa is the root of all energies in the material and spiritual worlds. He is the source of everything. Demons also understand this, and they want to create a godless society to stop all activities of the Lord and His devotees. They do not realize that all such efforts will fail because Kṛṣṇa is supremely powerful. On the other hand, devotees take shelter of Kṛṣṇa and understand that satisfying Him through devotional service is the best way to satisfy the entire universe.
Kṛṣṇa has feelings.	3.18.6	Kṛṣṇa is as capable of feeling as we are. Kṛṣṇa is satisfied if someone offers Him a nice prayer, and He is dissatisfied if someone denies His existence or calls Him by ill names. Kṛṣṇa loves His devotees so much that to give them protection, He is ready to tolerate insulting words from the atheists.
Everything happens by the direction of Kṛṣṇa.	3.18.8	Demons cannot understand how the Lord floated the earth on the water, but devotees don't think this is very wonderful because they know that many millions of planets are floating in the air by the direction of the Supreme Lord and that everything in the universe moves by His direction.
We can overcome fear when we take shelter of the Lord.	3.18.7, 9, 12–13	Lord Varāha tolerated Hiraṇyākṣa's insults while He completed His task of delivering the earth from the depths of the ocean. He did this to show us that we should not be afraid of demons while performing our duty. Kṛṣṇa is the most powerful and He protects us from all demons who try to interfere with our duties in devotional service. No matter how powerful a demon may be, he is not powerful in front of the Lord and is destined to die.
Devotional service to the Lord is greater than worship of the demigods.	3.18.23	Demons sometimes worship the demigods to obtain power for their sense gratification. They misuse this power, become a source of trouble for everyone, and are destroyed by the Lord. Devotees of Kṛṣṇa, however, never ask Him for any favor for sense gratification. They are happy simply engaging in the transcendental loving service of the Lord.

Understanding the Story

Now it's time for you to check how well you understood the story by answering these multiple-choice questions. There can be more than one answer for each question. (Answers can be found at the end of the chapter.)

1. Why was Hiraṇyākṣa interested in fighting with Lord Viṣṇu even after being warned by Varuṇa?
   a) He was a fool and thought he could defeat the Lord because he had a strong body and powerful weapons, and he thought the Lord was his match.
   b) Lord Viṣṇu had invited him for a fight.
   c) Hiraṇyākṣa had defeated Lord Viṣṇu in the past.
   d) Hiraṇyākṣa had stolen Lord Viṣṇu's Sudarśana disc, so he expected to win.
2. Where was Hiraṇyākṣa seeking the Lord in order to fight?
   a) On the earth planet
   b) In the Garbhodaka ocean at the bottom of the universe
   c) On the sun planet
   d) In the heavenly planets
3. In which form did the Lord appear in the ocean before Hiraṇyākṣa?
   a) Matsya *avatāra* – fish incarnation
   b) As Lord Nārāyaṇa
   c) In His original form as Lord Kṛṣṇa
   d) Varāha *avatāra* – boar incarnation
4. What was Varāhadeva doing when Hiraṇyākṣa spotted Him in the ocean?
   a) He was resting on Ananta Śeṣa.
   b) He was sporting with aquatic animals.
   c) He was lifting the drowning earth on the tips of His tusks to rescue her from the deep waters.
   d) He was talking to Nārada Muni.
5. How did Hiraṇyākṣa address Varāhadeva when he saw Him?
   a) O Supreme Personality of Godhead!
   b) O amphibious beast!
   c) O pious one!
   d) O great sage!

6. When Hiraṇyākṣa dared the Lord to fight with him, what did Varāhadeva do with the earth that was resting on the tip of His tusks?
   a) Varāhadeva ignored Hiraṇyākṣa and carefully placed the earth on the surface of the water, giving her the ability to float.
   b) Varāhadeva tossed her back in the water to rescue her later and then fought with Hiraṇyākṣa.
   c) Varāhadeva put the earth back in her orbit.
   d) Varāhadeva began to fight with Hiraṇyākṣa while balancing the earth on the tip of His tusks.
7. How did Hiraṇyākṣa's react when he was ignored by Varāhadeva?
   a) He realized his mistake and returned home.
   b) He decided to attack Varāhadeva.
   c) He continued to ridicule the Lord with insulting words.
   d) He became quiet and waited for the Lord to finish what He was doing.
8. How did the demigods react to the fight?
   a) They did not care as they were busy enjoying on their heavenly planets.
   b) They showered flowers upon the Lord, happy that the Lord was going to protect them.
   c) They started throwing rocks at Hiraṇyākṣa.
   d) They got scared and began to hide in different planets.
9. How did Brahmā feel, watching the fight between Hiraṇyākṣa and Varāhadeva?
   a) He was happy that his benedictions could make a person so powerful.
   b) He felt guilty for giving a demon benedictions that made him so powerful that no one could fight him.
   c) He enjoyed watching a good fight.
   d) He did not care as this fight was not going to affect his position as Brahmā.
10. What did Brahmā advise Varāhadeva to do when the dark hour was arriving?
   a) To kill Hiraṇyākṣa immediately as the demon was good at trickery.
   b) To forgive Hiraṇyākṣa.
   c) To turn Hiraṇyākṣa into a rock.
   d) To give him a spiritual body and take him back to Vaikuṇṭha.

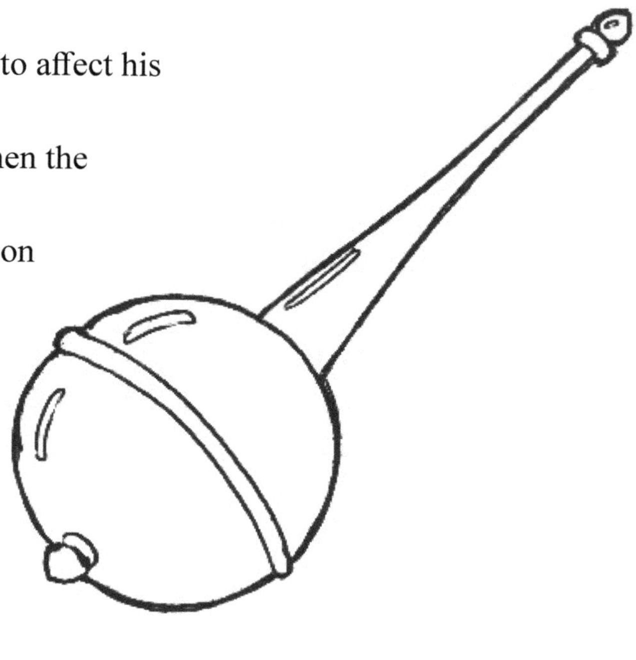

Higher-Thinking Questions

Now try to deepen your understanding of this chapter by delving into Śrīla Prabhupāda's purports and reflecting on the following questions:

1. How do demons perceive the incarnations of the Lord? And how should we understand the different forms of the Lord? See purport to verse 2.
2. Verse 8 explains that Lord Varāha placed the earth on the water and transferred His energy to her so that she could float on the water. How can you explain this miraculous act to materialistic people who may challenge it? See purport.
3. Śrīla Prabhupāda explains in the purport to verse 15 how a *yogī* or devotee deals with the deathblow. Write about any devotee whom you know or have heard about as to how they have dealt with their situation close to death. What did you learn from their example in relation to Śrīla Prabhupāda's description in this purport?
4. As described, Mother Earth is a personality who is a devotee of Kṛṣṇa. Hiraṇyākṣa tortured and exploited the earth in many ways, causing her unnecessary distress. In the modern world we see people who are exploiting Mother Earth in a similar way. List a few ways in which modern society is exploiting Mother Earth. How is she being affected?
5. What do you think is the solution to the environmental crisis we are facing?

ACTIVITIES

In this section you will find many exciting things to do. These activities will get you thinking, moving, drawing, and having loads of fun.

Artistic Activities

. . . to reveal your creativity!

EARTH PAPER- MÂCHÉ

You will need:

A round balloon, newspaper, flour and water, container for mixing the paper-mâché, spoon or stick to stir the glue, paint, paint brushes.

Description:

1. In a shallow bowl or basin, mix one part flour to two parts water to make a paste. Stir till the lumps are gone and the paste is smooth, and then add a few tablespoons of salt. Mix in the salt well.

2. Tear strips of newspaper about one inch wide; the length does not matter.
3. Blow up and tie off a round balloon.
4. Dip each strip of paper in the flour glue, wipe off the excess, and paste the paper strip around the balloon. Glue at least three layers on the balloon with all areas covered. Let it dry (at least overnight) after each layer. Let the globe dry completely (it may take a few days).
5. Now paint the paper- mâché globe with light blue paint. While it is drying, look at a map of the earth and then paint the continents, islands, and other details. You may even investigate how the earth looked in the past and draw the globe like that.

WANTED POSTER

Design and paint a wanted poster of Hiraṇyākṣa.

You will need:
Paper, pens, ruler, examples of wanted posters.

Description:
Look at some actual wanted posters for examples of layout and design. Make notes on Hiraṇyākṣa's appearance and crimes by referring to this chapter of *Śrīmad-Bhāgavatam*. Design and draw a wanted poster with a picture of Hiraṇyākṣa, his crimes, the reward, and any other relevant information.

Critical-Thinking Activities

. . . to bring out the spiritual investigator in you!

ATHEISTIC THEORIES

Śrīla Prabhupāda greatly desired that his followers defeat the atheistic way of thinking. In the diagram below are some of the common arguments non-believers make against God. Study them carefully. Then, in the circles, write down the possible reasons that a person could think this way about God. Lastly, in the adjacent blocks, write down how you would refute this argument (one example has been completed for you). Use this as a ready reference for convincing non-believers.

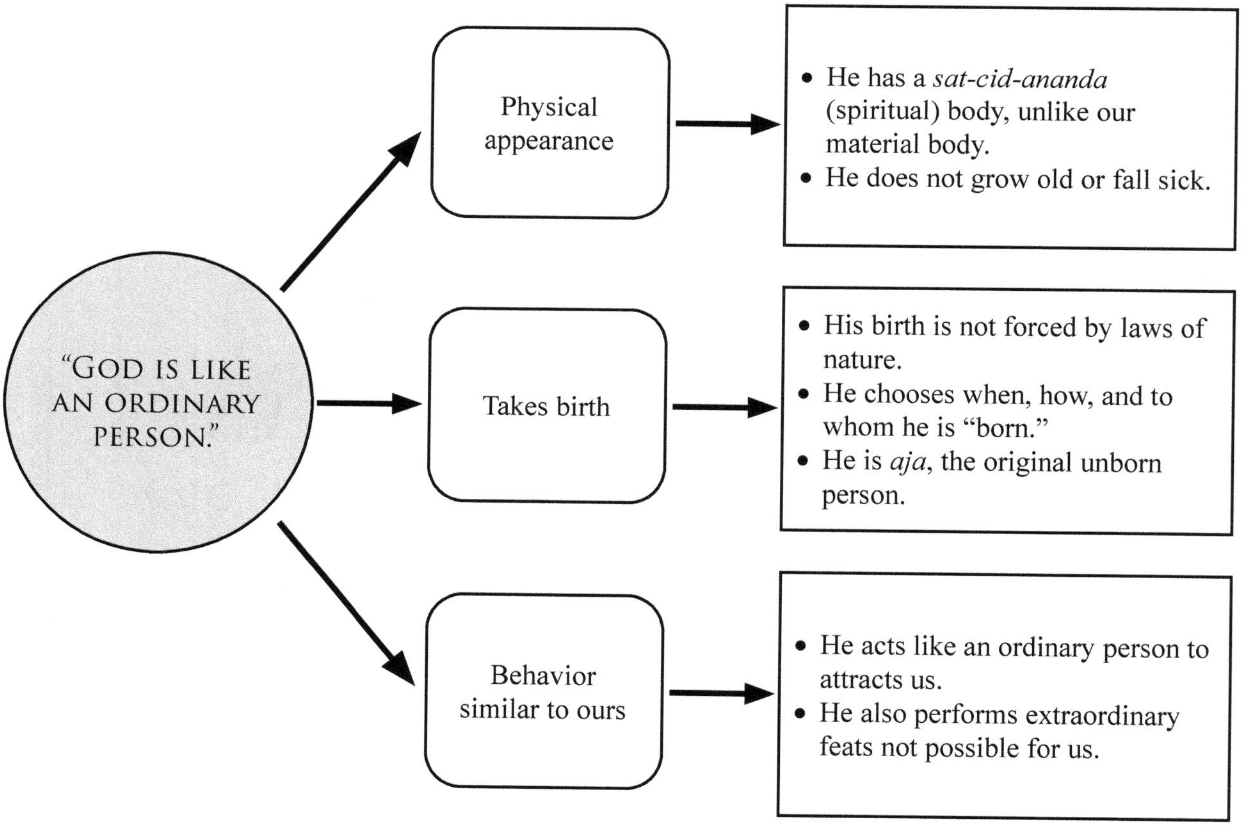

"GOD IS LIKE AN ORDINARY PERSON."
Physical appearance
• He has a *sat-cid-ananda* (spiritual) body, unlike our material body.
• He does not grow old or fall sick.
Takes birth
• His birth is not forced by laws of nature.
• He chooses when, how, and to whom he is "born."
• He is *aja*, the original unborn person.
Behavior similar to ours
• He acts like an ordinary person to attracts us.
• He also performs extraordinary feats not possible for us.

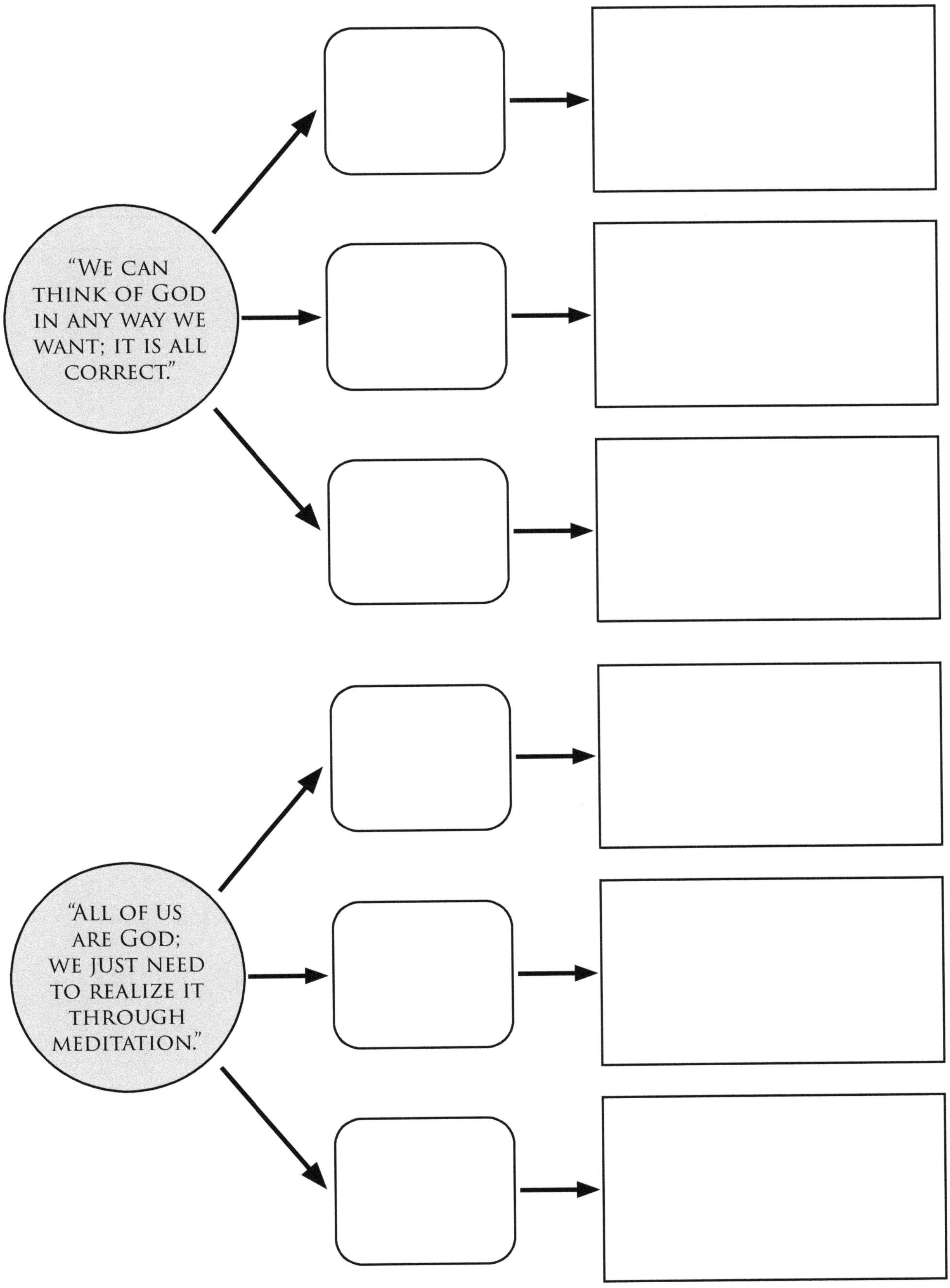
"WE CAN THINK OF GOD IN ANY WAY WE WANT; IT IS ALL CORRECT."
"ALL OF US ARE GOD; WE JUST NEED TO REALIZE IT THROUGH MEDITATION."

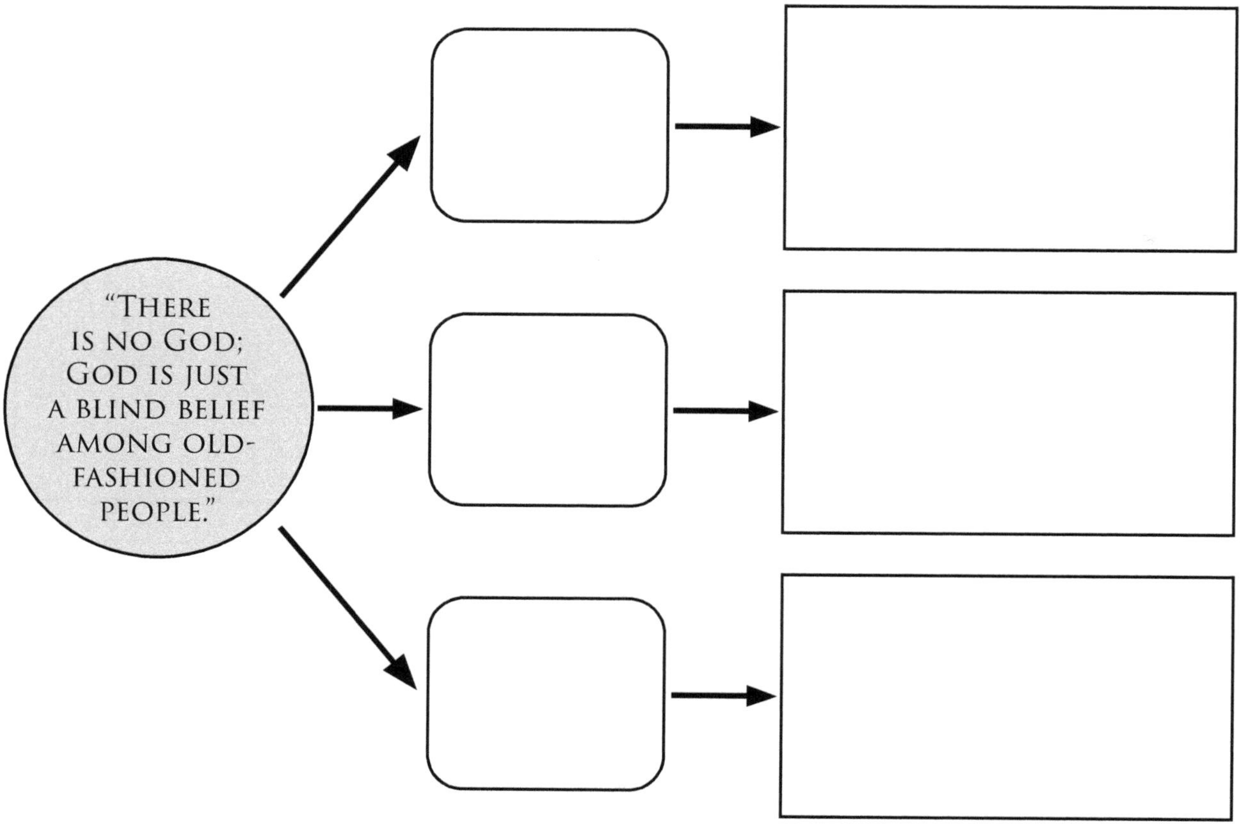

CHARACTER PROFILE

Learning Outcomes:
Recall at least three facts about the characters in this pastime.
Explain what the characters' main actions tell us about them.

Description: Choose one of the characters from this chapter listed below:

a) Hiraṇyākṣa
b) Lord Varāha
c) Lord Brahmā

First color the pictures on the next page and then complete their character profile on page 40, answering the questions about the six aspects of the character.

Depending on your age and ability, you can either draw or write your answers in the spaces provided below. (First discuss your answers in a group or with your teacher.)

What does the character look like? Draw a picture of the character here.

What does the character say?

What qualities are prominent in the character?

What does the character do?

Which other character is important to this character? Why is he important?

What problem or difficulty does the character face?

MATERIAL EPIDEMICS

An epidemic is something that spreads widely and quickly in a community or in the population. In the world today, materialism is an epidemic that has taken over. People are mostly interested in material gain and prosperity and not in spiritual development.

In this chapter we see how the demons are interested in the four objectives of human civilization for their own selfish purposes: religiosity, economic development, sense gratification, and liberation. Discuss these four stages of advancement of society with your teacher so you understand them better.

Then think about how each of them is used negatively for material purposes, e.g., destroying the planet, exploiting others, and hindering spiritual life for anyone. Describe how each stage can be used for selfish purposes and give examples of each.

1. **Religiosity** –

2. **Economic Development** –

3. **Sense Gratification** –

4. **Liberation** –

Theatrical Activity
. . . to bring out the actor in you!

BATTLE BETWEEN LORD VARĀHA AND HIRAṆYĀKṢA

In this activity you will act out one of three scenes from the battle between Lord Boar and Hiraṇyākṣa.

Description:

Read the three scenes below:

1. Before the battle
2. During the battle
3. After the battle

Each scene has a set of sequential activities performed by Lord Varāha and Hiraṇyākṣa. And some have Lord Brahmā, Maitreya, and Sūta Gosvāmī's words as well.

Choose one of the scenes below. Act out the part of all the characters, of Lord Varāha, Lord Brahmā, and Hiraṇyākṣa. While speaking each part, be conscious of the different moods of the characters. In places where you have to mime or act without speaking, make sure to use proper facial expressions and body language. You can use simple props, like a helmet, lightweight globe, mace, and flower garland. You may choose a partner to enact the battle scene. After you enact your scene, the audience can guess whether the scene was before, during, or after the battle.

Scene 1: Before the Battle

Hiraṇyākṣa: O amphibious beast! The earth has been plunged into the lower regions, and now it belongs to us. You may be the Lord of the demigods, but I will not let You take planet earth from me without a battle!

Lord Varāha lifts planet earth from the water to His tusks and starts walking.

Hiraṇyākṣa: Are You a coward who is not ashamed of running away from a challenge?

Lord Varāha places the earth on the surface of the water and transfers His own energy to her so she can float.

Lord Varāha: We are creatures of the jungle, and We are searching after hunting dogs like you.

Scene 2: The Battle

Lord Varāha: You may be proud of your so-called strength and you think you can end My life, but tell Me, what becomes of a loser who cannot keep his promise? How will you face the world when you will be defeated by Me? Give up all your foolish talk and slay Me if you dare!

With his mace Hiraṇyākṣa aims a powerful blow at the Lord's chest. Lord Varāha dodges the blow by moving aside and then strikes the demon. They continue to strike each other, enraged and desirous of victory.

Lord Brahmā: My dear Lord, there is no need to play with this arrogant demon who always harasses everyone. He is very good at trickery and is most wicked. His death has been predestined by You, so please, better kill him at once without delay and establish peace in the worlds.

Lord Varāha: Sudarśana *cakra*!

Lord Brahmā: May victory attend You! Kill him!

Hiraṇyākṣa hisses like a serpent.

Hiraṇyākṣa: You are slain!

He flings his mace towards the Lord.

Lord Varāha (knocks down the demon's mace with His left foot): Take up your weapon and try again, eager as you are to conquer Me.

Hiraṇyākṣa roars, picks up the mace, and throws it again. Lord Varāha catches the mace.

Lord Varāha: My beloved Sudarśana can disperse all your magical forces.

Hiraṇyākṣa runs to embrace the Lord to crush Him, but he always finds the Lord outside the circle of his arms. So he strikes the Lord with his hard fists. The Lord slaps him under the ear. The demon's body begins to wheel, and he falls down dead.

Scene 3: After the Battle

Lord Brahmā: Oh! Who could meet such a blessed death? While beholding the Lord, this crest jewel of Diti's sons has cast off his mortal coil.

Sage Maitreya: After thus killing the most formidable demon Hiraṇyākṣa, the Supreme Lord Hari, the origin of the boar species, returned to His own abode where there is always an uninterrupted festival.

Sūta Gosvāmī: This most sacred narrative gives extraordinary merit, wealth, fame, longevity, and all the objects of one's desire. On the field of battle, it promotes strength. One who listens to it at the last moment of his life is transferred to the supreme abode of the Lord, O dear Śaunaka.

Language Activities

. . . to make you understand better!

FILL IN THE BLANKS

1. Another name for Viṣṇu is__________________, meaning one who has never been conquered.
2. Less intelligent persons deride the transcendental form of the Lord as ____________________________.
3. For a dutiful man, there is nothing to ____________________________________ _.
4. The law of ________________ works under the control or direction of the Supreme Lord.
5. The Lord tolerated Hiraṇyākṣa's ill words to show the ____________________ that they do not need to be afraid of the demons while discharging their duties.
6. When Mahārāja Parīkṣit ruled the earth, the earth was called ____________ -*varṣa*.
7. The fight between the Lord and Hiraṇyākṣa is compared to a fight between __________________________ for the sake of a cow.
8. ______________________ means full independence in Sanskrit and is exclusive to the Lord.

WHO FITS THE CLUE?

Read the sentence clues in the table below and state which personality would make both sentences true.

Sentence Clues	Personality
The incarnation of Lord Kṛṣṇa as a boar. He gave the earth the ability to float on water for her own protection.	
He is born from the navel of the Supreme Personality of Godhead. The four Kumāras are his sons.	
The brother of Hiraṇyakaśipu. After years of austerities he received a special benediction from Lord Brahmā, which he believed made him almost immortal.	
She assumed the form of a cow at the beginning of Kali-yuga and was in tears when she prayed to Lord Brahmā. She was rescued from the depths of the water by Kṛṣṇa in the form of a transcendental boar.	

INFERRING QUESTIONS

Which questions do you agree with and disagree with, using what the author says and what you know. Back up your argument with reasons.

1. Lord Varāha tolerated Hiraṇyākṣa till He finished His task of delivering the earth from the depths of the ocean. From this we learn that when faced with difficulty, we should try to ignore it for as long as possible.
2. Hiraṇyākṣa knew that Kṛṣṇa is the source of everything.
3. Lord Varāha had to fight with Hiraṇyākṣa for a long time because the powerful demon could not be defeated immediately.
4. It was important for Lord Varāha to destroy Hiraṇyākṣa before the demoniac hour arrived, because after that it would have become impossible to do so.

ANSWERS

Understanding the Story: 1) a, 2) b, 3) d, 4) c, 5) b, 6) a, 7) b, 8) b, 9) b, 10) a

Atheistic Theories *(Potential Answers)*

1. We can think of God in any way we want:
   a) God is a product of human imagination. ➞ There are many great persons and saints who have witnessed and experienced the presence of God, like Jesus Christ, Mohammed, and many saints in the Vedic tradition, like the Six Gosvāmīs, the *ācāryas* in the Vaiṣṇava *sampradāyas*, and Śrīla Prabhupāda. They cannot be lying or imagining God's existence because they give similar descriptions of God, although some are more complete than others.
   b) Many scriptures represent God in different ways. ➞ Different scriptures may give different descriptions of God according to the kind of people it is addressing; for example, just as one who does not know the alphabet cannot understand higher subjects of language, one who does not know the basics of God realization cannot understand higher topics of God. So certain scriptures give a basic understanding of God while the Vedic scriptures give a complete account of God's personal form, which is the highest and most complete understanding.
   c) All paths lead to the same destination. ➞ This is not true; there may be longer paths to the same destination, or some paths may lead to a completely different destination depending on the desire and knowledge of the traveler; someone may even get lost on the way without a proper map. Similarly, according to our desires, we follow a certain spiritual path, but that doesn't mean that we will get the same result.

2. We are God; we just need to realize this through meditation:
   a) We are spirit, one with God and the universe. ➞ Although we are spirit, we are minute compared to the Supreme Spirit; our power is insignificant, and we are conditioned living beings prone to the miseries of birth, death, old age and disease. Therefore, we cannot be God.
   b) Through meditation we can experience our divinity. ➞ This may be true because we are a small fragment of the Divine Absolute Being. We are finite whereas He is infinite. Some kinds of meditation can only give a partial understanding of who we are, and because we have an imperfect mind and imperfect senses, we cannot understand who we are in essence unless we approach a perfect source of knowledge. The Vedic scriptures

give us the process of *mantra* meditation by which we can understand God's supremacy and our personal relationship with Him.

c) We have forgotten that we are God. → God is perfect; He knows past, present, and future and certainly cannot forget anything. Also, God is always God; He is the origin of everything otherwise He would not be God. If we are God, then how can "not-God" become God?

3. There is no God:
   a) We cannot see God. → God cannot be seen with the material senses; we need to become spiritually qualified and obtain spiritual vision; God is not so cheap as to appear on our order.
   b) God is a creation of the fearful. → The Vedic literatures teach us to love God, not to fear Him. Therefore, He can easily be approached with love and devotion.
   c) How can an all-loving God create suffering in this world? → We are responsible for our own suffering due to past sinful activities or *karma*. Although God does not like to see us suffer, He fulfills our desires to enjoy separately from Him, which causes our own suffering. However, He creates various ways by which we can become free of suffering forever. He comes as different incarnations to attract us to Him and take us back to His abode where there is no suffering, and He gives us the process of devotional service by which we can be liberated from miserable material life.

The Material Epidemic *(Potential Answers)*

1. **Religiosity** – A person can follow religious principles and rules only to gain fame and prestige or to attain wealth, power, or dominion. Using religion for these reasons creates hypocrisy, corruption, and perversion.

2. **Economic Development** – Corporate businesses take over small businesses to make millions and billions of dollars, while exploiting the workers, land, and natural resources. Family men cheat in business to make surplus cash to provide excess things for their family. People slaughter animals to make profit while wasting resources (grains and water) to breed livestock.

3. **Sense Gratification** – Persons who kill and eat meat for the pleasure of the tongue, take intoxicants, and eat more than is required while exploiting the earth's resources, e.g., using non-reusable plastic for convenience and creating many businesses to facilitate sinful activities.

4. **Liberation** – Persons who adhere to impersonal philosophy, who abandon religion, and do not following sense regulations, e.g., taking intoxicants and engaging in illicit sex to experience "something spiritual."

Fill in the Blanks

1. Ajita; 2. material; 3. fear; 4. gravitation; 5. demigods; 6. Bhārata; 7. bulls; 8. *svarāṭ*.

Who Fits the Clue?

Lord Varāha; Brahmā; Hiraṇyākṣa; the earth

Inferring Questions *(Potential Answers)*

1. Disagree. The Lord ignored Hiraṇyākṣa because He wanted to save the earth, but as soon as He placed the earth in safety, He dealt with Hiraṇyākṣa appropriately. In order to give protection to His devotee, the earth, He was ready to tolerate insulting words. The Lord was also not fearful because He had nothing to fear and was conscious of His duty to save the earth. Similarly, depending on the circumstances, we may ignore or tolerate a person or situation, but in general we deal with the situation. (See purports to verses 6 and 7.)
2. Agree.
3. Disagree. Lord Varāha could have killed Hiraṇyākṣa immediately but to fulfill His desire to fight and as part of His pastimes, he continued to fight with the demon.
4. Disagree. Lord Varāha could have killed Hiraṇyākṣa at any time.

19

The Killing of the Demon Hiraṇyākṣa

STORY SUMMARY

Lord Brahmā had just appealed to the Lord to end the fight and vanquish the demon Hiraṇyākṣa before the impending dark hour dawned. Lord Boar, Varāha, glanced lovingly at Brahmā and laughed heartily, acknowledging his sincere prayer.

The Lord then turned towards Hiraṇyākṣa with narrowed eyes. He sprung at the demon, aiming His mace at the demon's chin. Hiraṇyākṣa struck the oncoming mace with his own, sending the Lord's mace whirling in the sky.

The fighting stopped.

The sight was not to be missed.

All looked on in awe and reverence. How could a whirling mace that had just left the hand of its combatant be so captivating? It was incomprehensible…but it just was.

This was Hiraṇyākṣa's opportunity. At this moment, his enemy had no weapon. Hiraṇyākṣa could end the fight. He could strike his unarmed foe and win the battle.

But he stepped back. He placed his mace on his shoulder and smiled haughtily, waiting for Lord Varāha to ready himself again. What was Hiraṇyākṣa doing? Was he abiding by the laws of combat, not to strike an unarmed opponent? The demon who followed no laws

but his own was deciding now to follow a rule. A pretender of righteousness. What was he trying to achieve by doing this? Invoke anger in his opponent? If so, it was working.

As the Lord's whirling mace fell to the ground, the demigods and *ṛṣis* cried in alarm. Seeing their anxiety, Varāha invoked His spinning disc with razor-sharp edges – His Sudarśana *cakra*. Suddenly their solemn cries turned to startled muttering. They had just realized that Varāha was none other than the Supreme Personality of Godhead!

"Victory to you, oh Lord!" they all hailed. "Please don't play with this demon anymore. Finish him off now!"

Hiraṇyākṣa hissed in contempt. He leapt into the air, mace overhead, roaring: "You are slain!"

The Lord chuckled as He lifted His left foot and playfully knocked the mace from the demon's grasp. It thudded clumsily to the ground.

"Pick up your weapon and try again," the Lord taunted him with a smile. "I'll wait."

Hiraṇyākṣa growled as he picked up the mace, keeping his eyes locked on the Lord. He roared and hurled the mace one more time at Varāha. Standing rooted to the ground, the Lord caught the mace with graceful ease.

Hiraṇyākṣa's jaw dropped.

Never before had he faced such an opponent.

"I think you dropped this," said Varāha, again smiling and offering the mace back to the demon.

Hiraṇyākṣa was humiliated. There was no way he was going to accept his weapon back from his enemy. Scowling, he invoked his flaming trident instead. Without a second thought, he desperately hurled the fiery trident towards the Lord. Within moments, however, the Lord's disc sliced the trident to pieces.

Hiraṇyākṣa, now roaring wildly like an untamed beast, charged at the Lord and struck Varāha's chest with his hard fist. The Lord was not at all shaken just as an elephant would hardly notice when struck with a wreath of flowers. Then the demon instantly vanished.

All was quiet.

The onlookers searched the eerie sky with pure dread. It seemed like the calm before a storm.

What was the demon planning now? Was he going to use his most fearful weapon – dark magic? Surely, this would cause the end of the universe as they knew it.

Well, Hiraṇyākṣa did use dark magic and caused terror with his tricks. He caused fierce winds to blow from all directions. Dust and hailstorms darkened the world, large boulders hurtled across the sky and landed in all directions as if shot by canons, and the sky rained pus, hair, blood, stool, urine, and bones.

If that wasn't fearsome enough, Hiraṇyākṣa's army surfaced. Naked demonesses shrieked wildly as they roamed the universe. Oh, they looked so terrifying with their loosened hair and tridents. And then an infantry of ruffian Yakṣas and Rākṣasas marched along on foot and on horses, elephants, and chariots, chanting fearful slogans.

The world was filled with utter horror. All except for Lord Boar. Unnerved, He simply released His *cakra* again, and all the magical forces melted into oblivion.

Meanwhile, Diti, Hiraṇyākṣa's mother, felt a shudder in her heart. She remembered the prophecy of her husband Kaśyapa, and blood streamed from her breasts. This was a sure sign. Her son would soon be no more. However evil her son had been, he was still her child.

Hiraṇyākṣa reappeared before the Lord, breathing heavily in rage. Lunging himself towards Varāha, he tried to crush the Lord with his embrace. But the Lord simply appeared outside of his embrace. How was that possible?

Wild with frenzy, Hiraṇyākṣa finally beat the chest of the Lord again and again.

Lord Varāha, not affected in the slightest, simply slapped the demon across the ear.

And that was it.

Hiraṇyākṣa's body wheeled through the sky before landing on the ground. His eyes bulged out of their sockets. With arms and legs broken and hair scattered, he fell down dead.

Brahmā and the others rushed to see the demon's body lying lifeless on the ground. Although his spirit had left, the glow of his face had not yet faded. His tusks were still fearful, and he was still biting his lip.

Brahmā smiled and said, "Who could meet such a blessed death. This demon was struck by the foot of the Lord, which *yogīs* meditate upon to gain freedom from their material bodies. Hiraṇyākṣa will now surely return to his position in Vaikuṇṭha."

The demigods addressed the Lord: "We feel better now that this terrifying demon is no more. You have assumed the form of a boar, in pure goodness, for maintaining the world. We are now at ease and devoted to Your lotus feet. All glories to You!"

As the demigods, headed by Brahmā, praised the Lord, He returned to His own abode where there is always a festival.

Vidura was delighted to hear this pastime from Maitreya Ṛṣi.

Anyone who hears this story, tells this story, or even enjoys this story of the killing of Hiraṇyākṣa will no longer have to suffer the results of sinful activities. Such persons will achieve great wealth, fame, a long life, and everything they wish for. If they engage in battle, they will have great strength, and if they listen to this story at the last moment of their life, they will immediately return to the spiritual world.

Themes and Key Messages

Please go through this table of themes and key messages, with corresponding verses, and discuss each topic further.

Theme	Reference	Key Messages
Kṛṣṇa cannot be bound or measured by any material calculations.	3.19.24	Hiraṇyākṣa wanted to embrace the Lord to crush Him, thinking he could capture the Lord by his material power. However, the Lord cannot be captured or measured except through pure love, just as Mother Yaśodā could bind baby Kṛṣṇa with her pure love in the Dāmodara-*līlā*. For the sake of His devotees, Kṛṣṇa takes on His deity form and even agrees to live in a box so we can always serve Him and be happy!
Kṛṣṇa is supremely powerful.	3.19. 25–26, 32	Although Hiraṇyākṣa was a mighty demon, Lord Varāha crushed him with absolutely no effort. The Lord is so powerful that He is called *adhokṣaja*, which means "that which is beyond the measurement of our senses." When we are afraid, we should remember this and take shelter of Kṛṣṇa and seek His protection.
Simply by the touch of the Lord, one is very fortunate.	3.19.27–28	When Hiraṇyākṣa was killed by the Lord, his body glowed and did not fade like an ordinary dead body. Just by having contact with the Lord, even the demons are fortunate and are liberated, which takes the *yogīs* may lifetimes of meditation to achieve. Similarly, if we meditate on the Lord's form at the time of death, we can be liberated and go to the kingdom of God.
It is important to hear about the Lord and His devotees and to hear from authority.	3.19.32–34, 37–38	There is no difference between Kṛṣṇa and His pastimes. Therefore, when we hear stories of Kṛṣṇa, it is the same as associating with Him directly, and we become qualified to join Him in the spiritual world after leaving this material body. But we can truly relish the Lord's pastimes if we hear them from an authorized source, from the spiritual master or from a devotee in disciplic succession (*paramparā*). We also get spiritual benefit from hearing about Kṛṣṇa's devotees.
We should be grateful to the Lord.	3.19.35–36	Kṛṣṇa provides us with everything we need, from the air we breathe to the delicious *prasāda* we eat. When we realize this and serve Kṛṣṇa with gratitude, He becomes very pleased. Those who are ungrateful are compared to rogues and thieves because they enjoy the gifts of God without recognizing or acknowledging the Lord.

Understanding the Story

Now it's time for you to check how well you understood the story by answering these multiple-choice questions. (Answers can be found at the end of the chapter.)

1. What is the benefit of hearing the story of Lord Varāha and Hiraṇyākṣa?
   a) We will never have any suffering in the material world.
   b) We will have extraordinary merit, wealth, fame, longevity, and ultimately be promoted to the abode of the Lord.
   c) We can become powerful like Hiraṇyākṣa in our next life.
2. Why did Lord Varāha laugh heartily when Brahmā requested Him to kill Hiraṇyākṣa instantly?
   a) Lord Varāha wanted to enjoy His pastime of killing demons and so wanted to prolong His fight with Hiraṇyākṣa.
   b) Lord Varāha was thinking Brahmā as insignificant, so how could he give any advice to Him?
   c) Lord Varāha was pleased because Brahmā's prayers were made with love, and the Lord accepted his prayer to kill the demon.
3. What weapons did Lord Varāha and Hiraṇyākṣa use when they began their fight?
   a) Sudarśana *cakra*
   b) Sword
   c) Mace
4. What did Hiraṇyākṣa do when he saw the Lord was without any weapons?
   a) He knew the rules of combat, so he waited for the Lord to get another weapon.
   b) He ran towards the Lord and hit Him on the chest.
   c) He declared victory over the Lord and began chasing the demigods.
5. Which weapon did Lord Varāha get next after His mace fell on the ground?
   a) Another mace
   b) Trident
   c) Sudarśana *cakra*

6. What was the reaction of the demigods when they saw the Sudarśana disc revolving in Lord Varāha's hand?
   a) They were scared that the disc would destroy the entire creation.
   b) They cheered the Lord, feeling confident that He would win the battle.
   c) They were not interested in the outcome of the battle as they felt safe sitting in their airplanes.
7. What was Hiraṇyākṣa's reaction when he saw the Sudarśana disc in Lord Varāha's hand?
   a) Out of great anger he attacked Lord Varāha with his mace.
   b) He got scared as he knew the Sudarśana disc would kill him.
   c) He was not affected by the Lord's disc as he was confident of his victory.
8. When Lord Varāha knocked down Hiraṇyākṣa's mace and offered the mace back to him, what did Hiraṇyākṣa do?
   a) He took the mace and struck the Lord again.
   b) He got his trident and hurled it at the Lord.
   c) He insulted the Lord.
9. What happened after the Lord tore Hiraṇyākṣa's trident to pieces with His Sudarśana disc.
   a) Hiraṇyākṣa got scared and ran away.
   b) Hiraṇyākṣa began roaring loudly and striking the Lord's chest.
   c) Lord Varāha killed Hiraṇyākṣa with His Sudarśana disc.
10. How was the Lord reacting towards Hiraṇyākṣa's constant attacks?
    a) Lord Varāha felt bored as Hiraṇyākṣa was insignificant compared to His might.
    b) Lord Varāha became angrier with each attack from Hiraṇyākṣa.
    c) Although seemingly angry, Lord Varāha enjoyed the attacks just as a father enjoys a playful wrestle with his son.
11. How was Hiraṇyākṣa going to benefit from this fight?
    a) By winning this fight he could become the Supreme Lord.
    b) If he got killed in this fight, he would take birth in the heavenly planets.
    c) He was helping the Lord in His pastime and would go back to Vaikuṇṭha after the Lord killed him.
12. How did Lord Varāha kill Hiraṇyākṣa?
    a) He cut off Hiraṇyākṣa's head with His Sudarśana disc.
    b) He slapped Hiraṇyākṣa on his ear, which killed him.
    c) He choked Hiraṇyākṣa with His hands.

Higher-Thinking Questions

Now try to deepen your understanding of this chapter by delving into Śrīla Prabhupāda's purports and reflecting on the following questions:

1. Verse 1 purport explains that the devotees and the demons pray. How are their prayers different? Can you think of some examples in *śāstra* and in today's world of praying to advance in sinful activities?
2. Verse 16 and 17 explains how the Lord enjoys fighting with His devotee. The analogy is given of a father having a mock fight with his child. Explain how this analogy relates to the Lord's fighting with His devotee. How is this related to the fight between Lord Boar and Hiraṇyākṣa?
3. Verses 37 and 38 state that if you hear the story of Lord Varāha with attention, you will receive many benedictions and your love for Lord Kṛṣṇa will grow. However, we need to hear from a bona fide source. Why is it important to hear the activities of the Lord from a pure devotee instead of the impersonalist philosopher? See verse 37 purport.
4. In the fight between Lord Varāha and Hiraṇyākṣa we see that when the club from the hand of Lord Varāha fell, Hiraṇyākṣa, although a demon, did not attack Lord Varāha because He was unarmed. The demon followed the law of single combat. How would you contrast this with behavior in Kali-yuga where *dharma* is at its lowest? (Hint: Satya-yuga stood on the four legs of *dharma*; no one would even think of doing something which was against *dharma*.) However, even though Hiraṇyākṣa followed moral codes, why do you think his behavior was still against *dharma*?
5. The purport to verse 24 explains how Lord Kṛṣṇa can be captured by the devotees but not by demoniac people. Explain in your own words how a devotee can capture Lord Kṛṣṇa who is unconquerable.
6. The purport to verse 31 explains that Lord Boar is the origin of the boar species. Why is the Lord praised in this form as a boar although in the material world a boar or a pig is considered abominable?
7. Explain the term "*avatāra*" as described in verse 31 purport.

ACTIVITIES

In this section you will find many exciting things to do. These activities will get you thinking, moving, drawing, and having loads of fun.

Action Activity . . . to get you moving!

KṚṢṆA'S ANIMALS

Play the following game based on verses 31 and 35 in which the Lord is described as the origin and protector of all species of life.

Learning Outcomes:

1. All species of life come from Kṛṣṇa. When He gives us a particular body, we act in the way that body is meant to act.
2. In whatever body we are, we can serve Kṛṣṇa, just as Gajendra, the king of elephants, took shelter of the Lord.

You will need:

1. A picture of Kṛṣṇa.
2. A bowl.
3. Lots of different toy animals. Include as many as possible – birds, mammals, fish, insects, or even dinosaurs. You may use pictures instead or write the names of animals on pieces of paper.

Description:

1. Place all the toy animals or pieces of paper in the bowl and place the bowl at Kṛṣṇa's

feet. This shows that all the different species of life come from Kṛṣṇa.

2. Now close your eyes and take turns to pick one of the animals or pieces of paper from the bowl. Whichever animal you pick, you have to act like that animal until your next turn. (Act like the animal just as if Kṛṣṇa has given you that body.)
3. When you pick an animal from the bowl, you have two more tasks:
   a) Act out a way for that animal to do some devotional service for Kṛṣṇa; for example, an elephant can carry heavy loads in Kṛṣṇa's service or a cow can offer her milk to Kṛṣṇa.
   b) Think of a devotee in the *Bhāgavatam*, *Rāmāyaṇa*, or *Mahābhārata* who had this animal's body and tell the name aloud.
4. Everyone in your group takes turns to choose an animal and perform the tasks while the rest of the group watches until your next turn when you "reincarnate" into a different animal specie.
5. At the end of the game everyone gets their human form back and uses his or her body for the devotional service of hearing and chanting Hare Kṛṣṇa!

Analogy Activity . . . to bring out the scholar in you!

MILK TOUCHED BY A SERPENT

Śrīla Prabhupāda gives the analogy in verse 33 purport of milk being poisoned by a serpent's touch, which illustrates that when the topics of the Lord are recited by impure persons, they can have "poisonous" effects.

Illustrate a snake poisoning pure milk. Try to add all the elements from the analogy, such as the devotees drinking the poisonous milk, the pure milk, an authorized distributor of pure milk, etc.

Be creative! Then answer the questions below to fully understand the analogy:

1. Who is the snake in the analogy?
2. What is the milk?
3. What does the snake's poison represent?
4. How is it dangerous to drink such "poisoned milk"?
5. How can we preserve the purity of the milk and maintain healthy Kṛṣṇa consciousness?

Artistic Activity
. . . to reveal your creativity!

VARĀHA AND HIRAṆYĀKṢA MASKS

What you will need: Thin card or paper plates, scissors, string, pens, paints or crayons, paintbrush, glue, decorative materials

Description:

1. See "Resources" at the end of this chapter for templates of the two faces. You may copy these on paper plates or cardboard as an oval shape, the size of your face.
2. Cut out eyes, a nose, and a mouth.
3. Paint the outlines of the eyes and other features and paint or color the face.
4. Make a helmet or crown, using more cardboard. Paint and decorate it with gold beads, sequins, glitter, or other decorative materials using glue. Glue on tusks, a mustache, or a beard for Hiraṇyākṣa if you like from cardboard or felt. Add tusks for Lord Varāha, a crown, or jewelry. Be creative!
5. Make a hole on either side of the completed masks through which you can insert a piece of string to tie it up.
6. Now enact the roles of Hiraṇyākṣa and Lord Varāha using your masks. Or enact the poem at the end of this chapter.

Introspective Activity

. . . to bring out the reflective devotee in you!

GRATITUDE

Śrīla Prabhupāda explains in verse 36 purport that every living entity should be grateful to the Lord for everything He has given us. It is by His grace that we have the necessities of life and the gift of Kṛṣṇa consciousness.

Do the following activity and answer the questions to develop the quality of gratitude:

- Have you ever thanked the Lord for water or warm sunshine? Or for anything else?
- Why do you think we should be grateful to the Lord?
- Why shouldn't we take the Lord's benedictions for granted? (Hint: Śrīla Prabhupāda compares ungrateful people to rogues and thieves.)

Sometimes when we are grateful for all the good things in our life, we feel more positive and don't focus on the difficulties. Therefore, it is important to develop this wonderful quality of gratitude.

In the table below, write a minimum of three things that you are grateful to the Supreme Lord for every day for a week.

Day of the Week	Things I am grateful for

Critical-Thinking Activity

. . . to bring out the spiritual investigator in you!

BEHAVIOR OF DEMONS AND DEVOTEES

In the previous few chapters, we see how Hiraṇyākṣa displayed demoniac qualities and behavior. As devotees, we know that a devotee would have acted differently in similar situations.

The table below contains some action points from the pastime and Hiraṇyākṣa's behavior in that situation. In the third column fill out the quality that the action comes from. Then, think of how a devotee would have reacted in the same situation, and due to what quality. Then answer the questions that follow. (The first one has been done for you.)

Action	Hiraṇyākṣa's Behavior	Hiraṇyākṣa's Qualities	Devotee's Behavior	Devotee's Qualities
Attitude towards the demigods	Hiraṇyākṣa drives away the demigods from heaven	Pride due to being powerful	Cooperates with and respects the demigods	• Humble • Respectful • Grateful to the demigods and the Lord • Responsible in using power/ position properly
Relating with a weaker person	Hiraṇyākṣa challenges Varuṇa			
Understanding the position of the Lord	Hiraṇyākṣa ignores Varuṇa's warning			

Action	Hiraṇyākṣa's Behavior	Hiraṇyākṣa's Qualities	Devotee's Behavior	Devotee's Qualities
Behavior on coming face-to-face with the Lord	Hiraṇyākṣa taunts Varāhadeva			
On being challenged by the Lord	Hiraṇyākṣa fights Varāhadeva			
Knowledge about the position of the Lord	Hiraṇyākṣa tries to crush Varāhadeva			

Writing Activities . . . to bring out the writer in you!

NEWS REPORT

Description: The demigods have asked you to write a news report on the battle between Lord Varāha and the demon Hiraṇyākṣa to present to the celestial assembly who did not witness the fight.

First, read a few short news articles (from ISKCON NEWS, *Back to Godhead* magazine, or a daily newspaper) to become familiar with some of the language techniques news reporters use in their writing (a few listed below). Then use the News Story – Writing Draft (below) to help you plan your report before you start writing.

A. Features of News Articles

While you are reading a news article, see if you can identify the following features:

- A catchy headline
- A byline: name of writer and place of incident
- Opening paragraph, providing information on the "Five W's": what, where, when, why, and who; and how
- A quote by someone involved in the story or a witness
- The tense of the article: past tense or present tense?
- Powerful words/verbs to portray action
- A photo included with a caption

B. News Story – Writing Draft

Use this writing draft to help you plan your news story. Then write a news story based on this draft.

1. List the main events in the story.
2. Create a catchy headline for your story. Include a byline.
3. Write a quotation from someone in the story or a witness to an event in the story.
4. List the "5 W's": Who, What, Where, When, Why, and How.
5. Draw a picture (this will be the photo) to capture the main event. Include a caption. (Sketch an idea here to redo in final form with the final news report.)
6. Write a conclusion that sums up the report.

BIOGRAPHY OF HIRAṆYĀKṢA

Description: Write a biography of the demon Hiraṇyākṣa. A biography is a written account of the series of events that make up a person's life.

Your first task is to research Hiraṇyākṣa's life. You can use some of the prompts below to guide you:

- Date and place of birth
- Family background and events leading to birth
- Adjectives to describe him
- Examples from his life that illustrate these qualities
- Lifetime accomplishments if any
- Major events that shaped or changed his life
- How his life has impacted future generations
- Would the world have been a better or worse place if he hadn't lived? How and why?

Remember to add illustrations and a cover page to make the biography complete.

Language Activity
. . . to make you understand better!

FIVE ITEMS OF DEVOTIONAL SERVICE

Listed below are the five items of devotional service recommended by Śrī Caitanya Mahāprabhu. Give examples of each. Where would you perform these activities? What times of the day? With whom would you perform them? Why?

Serving the Devotees of the Lord:

Chanting Hare Kṛṣṇa:

Hearing *Śrīmad Bhāgavatam*:

Worshiping the Deity of the Lord:

Living in a Place of Pilgrimage:

P O E M

Because of a curse from the Kumāras four
After stopping them at the door
Jaya and Vijaya for their next births three
lived as demons not devotees

Forced to leave the land of beauty
To fulfill a higher duty
For it was Kṛṣṇa who wanted to fight
But only with devotees of great might

So from the place of love of God
To the land of tears and sod
They transformed in body and in face
Fearsome forms holding a mace

The first time he took birth
Hiraṇyākṣa stole the earth
Lord Varāha then did appear
At this the fearful demon jeered

Then took place a fearsome fight
To which the demigods gasped in fright
But the Supreme Lord defeated him
(To beat Kṛṣṇa your chance is slim)

Just two more demon births to take
To rectify their Vaiṣṇava mistake

RESOURCES

Template 1: Lord Varāha

Template 2: Hiraṇyākṣa

ANSWERS

Understanding the Story: 1) b, 2) c, 3) c, 4) a, 5) c, 6) b, 7) a, 8) b, 9) b, 10) c, 11) b, 12) b

Milk Touched by a Serpent

1. *Who is the snake in the analogy?* The nondevotee or impure person who does not know the conclusion of the scriptures.

2. *What is the milk?* The narration of the pastimes of the Lord.

3. *What does the snake's poison represent?* The Lord's pastimes contaminated by the wrong interpretation.

4. *How is it dangerous to drink such "poisoned milk"?* If you hear from someone who does not know the conclusive truth of the scriptures, you can become contaminated by their wrong conclusions. For example, the Māyāvādī or impersonalists deny the personal feature of the Lord and their conclusion is that the Lord's form is *māyā* or imaginary.

5. *How can we preserve the purity of the milk and maintain healthy Kṛṣṇa consciousness?* We have to hear the Lord's pastimes from an authorized source, pure devotees who learn and transmit spiritual knowledge through *paramparā*, or disciplic succession.

Behavior of Demons and Devotees *(Potential Answers)*

Action	Hiraṇyākṣa's Behavior	Hiraṇyākṣa's Qualities	Devotee's Behavior	Devotee's Qualities
Relating with a weaker person	Hiraṇyākṣa challenges Varuṇa	Pride due to being powerful	Respectful to superiors and merciful to subordinates	• Humble • Compassionate • Respectful • Grateful to the Lord for what he has

Action	Hiraṇyākṣa's Behavior	Hiraṇyākṣa's Qualities	Devotee's Behavior	Devotee's Qualities
Understanding the position of the Lord	Hiraṇyākṣa ignores Varuṇa's warning	• Pride due to being powerful • Ignorance of the Lord's prowess	Understands the position of the Lord and is subordinate to the Lord	• Knowledge of the Lord's position and his own • Humble • Willing to surrender in love
Behavior on coming face-to-face with the Lord	Hiraṇyākṣa taunts Varāhadeva	• Pride due to being powerful • Ignorance of the Lord's prowess	Offers his respects, prayers, worship, and service to the Lord	• Knowledge of the Lord's position and his own • Humble • Willing to surrender in love
On being challenged by the Lord	Hiraṇyākṣa fights Varāhadeva	• Faith in one's own ability and strength • Ambition to be the greatest • Pride • Ignorance of the Lord's position and prowess	Refrains from any kind of confrontation with the Lord (e.g., Jāmbavān, after realizing Kṛṣṇa's true position, refrains from fighting Lord Kṛṣṇa in Canto10)	• Knowledge of the Lord's position and his own • Love and servitude towards the Lord
Knowledge about the position of the Lord	Hiraṇyākṣa tries to crush Varāhadeva	• Ignorant of the Lord's position and prowess • Pride • Envy	Has full knowledge about the position of the Lord	Possesses transcendental knowledge and acts upon that knowledge

***Five Items of Devotional Service** (Potential Answers)*

Serving the Devotees of the Lord:

1) Serving *prasādam* for the Sunday feast at the temple with other devotees. Why? To cultivate humility and a service attitude.
2) Offering a drink of water to a devotee who comes to your house or doing some other menial service to a devotee to practice selflessness, awareness, and devotion.

Chanting Hare Krishna:

1) Chanting *japa* in the morning before the sun rises, ideally with other devotees or alone in a quiet, sacred place. It is better in the morning because it is more peaceful and easiest to chant.
2) Performing *kīrtana* with other devotees at any time to deepen devotional practice and share the holy name with others.

Hearing Śrīmad-Bhāgavatam:

1) Reading *Śrīmad-Bhāgavatam* or other important scriptures in the morning at the temple or in a quiet place is recommended in *śāstra*. Reading with other devotees helps you focus your day on Kṛṣṇa and alleviates the influence of *māyā*.
2) Listening to *Śrīmad-Bhāgavatam* at the temple or to a class online; you can listen alone for inspiration and contemplation.

Worshiping the Deity of the Lord:

1) Performing or witnessing the *ārati* of the Deities at home or at the temple every morning. This is a good start to the day and will help you remember the Lord during the day.
2) Offering the Deity *bhoga* before meals to please the Lord and sanctify the food you take (*prasāda*).

Living in a Place of Pilgrimage:

1) Visiting or living in a holy place or the holy *dhāmas* like Vṛndāvana or Māyāpur to focus on devotional life.
2) Visiting or living in a temple, also for the above reasons.
3) Making your home a temple.

20
Conversation Between Maitreya and Vidura

STORY SUMMARY

The trees of Naimiṣāraṇya stood tall and grand, living just to serve the large gathering of sages. Their branches extended to support the varieties of singing birds and give cooling shelter to the great sages. These saintly persons were eager to hear more from Sūta Gosvāmī, who had heard the *Śrīmad-Bhāgavatam* from Śukadeva Gosvāmī when he had spoken it to Mahārāja Parīkṣit on the banks of the Ganges. How fortunate the learned sages, headed by Śaunaka Ṛṣi, felt to hear first-hand from Sūta Gosvāmī.

Sūta Gosvāmī had just explained to them how Lord Varāha had saved the earth and placed it carefully back in orbit ready for Manu to rule. But now Sūta waited. He gave a chance to the sages to dwell on the wonderful pastime of Lord Varāha, the first boar incarnation that took place at the time of Svāyambhuva Manu. Peace filled the air. Not an empty peace – a peace infused with thoughts of the Supreme Lord.

The sages wanted to know more. They all looked at each other before resting their eyes on Śaunaka Ṛṣi who so far had asked Sūta Goswami the questions on their behalf. Śaunaka also felt a thirst to hear more.

"Dear Sūta," he began, "what did Svāyambhuva Manu do after Lord Varāha placed the earth back in orbit? What did Manu do to show the path of liberation? And what else did Vidura ask Maitreya? I have no doubt that they must have spoken about many more pastimes of the Lord. Our thirst to know more about these pastimes can never be satiated. Please tell us more!" A murmur of agreement spread across the crowd of sages.

"Vidura was delighted to hear of Varāha," replied Sūta. "He then wondered more about Lord Brahmā's creation. Maitreya had explained how the *prajāpati* – the progenitors – were created, but he hadn't yet explained further. Vidura wanted to know more. How were the living entities created after this? How did the *prajāpatis* develop the universe to what it is now? Did the *prajāpatis* evolve the creation with their wives or did they each serve alone? Or did they all serve together?"

Sūta Gosvāmī continued to narrate the conversation between Vidura and Maitreya.

Maitreya smiled at Vidura's eager questions as he contemplated where to start.

"My dear Vidura," he began, "do you remember I explained earlier how the elements, the senses, and sense objects were made?"

"Yes," replied Vidura as he tried to recall what he had heard. "Weren't they made from the false ego of the living entities?"

"Correct!" exclaimed Maitreya. "And from the ego evolved many groups of five principles."

"Oh yes!" Vidura chimed in, remembering everything clearly now. "Material nature, or *prakṛti*, which consists of three modes, generates four groups of five. The first group is the gross or elementary elements: earth, water, fire, air, and ether; the second is the subtle elements or sense objects: sound, touch, form, taste, and smell. The third is the five sense organs: eyes, ears, nose, tongue, and skin. The fourth is the five working senses: speech, hands, feet, anus, and genitals;

and the last is the five deities who control these divisions."

"Excellent!" Maitreya beamed at his disciple. "But now, nothing more could be created without Lord Viṣṇu's help. So with the help of His energy, a shining egg was produced – a universal bubble. It lay on the waters of the Causal Ocean for over a thousand years in a lifeless state. Then Garbhodakaśāyī Viṣṇu entered it and lay on its waters.

"Then, as you know, eventually a lotus sprouted from His navel with Lord Brahmā in its whorl. He was the first living entity. The Supreme Personality of Godhead entered his heart, and because of this, Brahmā was able to use his intelligence to create.

"Now, Brahmā first created the five coverings of ignorance of the living entities from his shadow. As a result, the living entities forgot who they were, who Lord Kṛṣṇa was, and felt that they were their bodies and nothing more. Brahmā was a good-hearted devotee of the Lord. Knowing this "ignorance" to be his first creation made him quite disgusted. He immediately threw off his shadow, his subtle body made of ignorance. Suddenly Yakṣas and Rākṣasas appeared. Like a pack of ravishing wolves, they sprang for the shadow, which had taken the form of night, and wanted to claim it for themselves. This night is also the cause of hunger and thirst, so feeling hungry and thirsty, they ran

to Lord Brahmā, ready to devour him. He looked ever so delectable."

Vidura grimaced. Maitreya continued to narrate what happened next.

The Yakṣas and Rākṣasas glared at Brahmā. "Let's eat him up!"

"Let's not spare him!"

Brahmā held up his hands and shouted, "Don't eat me! I'm your father. I created you. You're meant to protect me!"

They stopped in their tracks and reluctantly retreated.

Brahmā let out a sigh of relief before focusing on his next creation – the demigods. He awarded them the form of daytime, which they graciously accepted. Unlike the Yakṣas and Rākṣasas, who were born from the creation of night (the quality of ignorance), the demigods were born from the creation of day (the quality of goodness).

Then, from his buttocks, Lord Brahmā gave birth to the demons. The demons looked at their father. Crooked, perverted smiles appeared on their faces. What were they thinking? They crept towards him.

"Let's enjoy his body," one said in a sickening tone.

"Oh yes… let's!" the others agreed, laughing uncontrollably.

Brahmā laughed at his sons' ridiculous words.

They couldn't be serious.

No. They were serious. Their advances were lusty. This was absurd.

"You can't possibly be serious…" he faltered.

Panic ran through his veins. There were too many of them. What could he possibly do? Run. Run as far and fast as he could.

He ran to his only shelter. "Lord, protect me!" he called.

"Cast off this impure body of yours!" ordered the Lord.

Immediately, Brahmā knew what to do. The impure body the Lord was referring to was his passionate thinking. His mind had been contaminated by passion when he created the demons. It was this passionate mentality he needed to get rid of. Without further ado, he ripped away his passionate thoughts and threw them up in the air. Before his eyes, they turned into twilight.

Watching this, the demons didn't see twilight. They saw something else – an attractive, alluring damsel. Now they wanted to enjoy her and nothing else.

"Oh, beautiful girl, who are you?" they asked with as much respect as they could conjure. "Look at you, bouncing that ball. Oh, tie up your beautiful dark tresses…they are distracting us." And they seized her. In this way they took possession of the twilight, thinking it to be the young beauty they desired.

Lord Brahmā laughed and then produced the Gandharvas and Apsarās from his own loveliness, which took the shining form of the moonlight. Then Brahmā created the ghosts and fiends from his laziness, and as they stood before him naked with their hair scattered, he felt it best to give them the form of yawning and drooling in one's sleep.

Brahmā then continued to cast off different

mentalities, which took on different forms and which were used to create different living beings that took possession of these forms. From his navel Brahmā created the invisible forms of the ancestors, which evolved from his own invisible form. And then he created the Siddhas and Vidyādharas from his ability to be present but not seen. The Kimpuruṣas and Kinnaras were created from his reflection in water. They took possession of this shadowy form cast off by Brahmā, which was the auspicious time of dawn.

Then one day, Brahmā was in a sullen mood. You know that feeling when you're trying your best, but it doesn't feel like it's enough? Well, even our creator, Brahmā, felt like this. He lay on the ground, feeling sorry for himself. Creation was just taking too long.

"No, I must continue," he told himself after some time. "I must give up this mood."

Lifting himself up, he discarded the mood. The hair that dropped from this body turned into snakes and slithered away.

Eventually, he felt some accomplishment. This mood from his mind produced the Manus, the fathers of mankind. Brahmā gave them his own human form, and with this they promoted the welfare activities of the universe. Everyone who was created earlier congratulated Brahmā for this creation.

From his austere penance and devotion, Brahmā then created the sages as his beloved sons. To each of them he gave a part of his own body, which was characterized by deep meditation, mental concentration, supernatural power, austerity, and renunciation.

Themes and Key Messages

Please go through this table of themes and key messages, with corresponding verses, and discuss each topic further.

Theme	Reference	Key Messages
If we hear the pastimes of Kṛṣṇa, it is just like bathing in the Ganges, for it can free us from all sinful reactions.	3.20.5	Ganges water can purify us because it comes from the lotus feet of the Lord. Similarly, the topics of the Lord can also purify us and free us from sinful reactions. The water of the Ganges, the narrations of the Lord's pastimes, and the Lord's words in the *Bhagavad-gītā* are all on the absolute platform, and if we take shelter of any one of them, it is equally good.
When the Lord descends to this earth, He takes on a form by His own internal energy.	3.20.8, 12	The Lord assumed the form of a boar by His own potency, not by the external, or material, energy. The Māyāvādīs claim that the form of the Lord is covered by *māyā*. This is not true because *māyā* is under the Lord's control. She can only cover the ordinary living entities – not the Supreme Lord. The conditioned souls are forced to accept a particular body by material laws, but the Lord was not forced to accept the form of a boar. The form of the Lord, therefore, is not material even though the material creation comes from Him.
The creative power of every living entity is not his own; it is only by the grace of the Lord that one can create.	3.20.17	The Lord, as the Supersoul within Brahmā, gave him the intelligence to create. Similarly, there are many scientists and great workers in this material world who are very creative, but they can only create by the grace of the Supreme Lord.
The Lord manifests in innumerable divine forms to satisfy His devotee.	3.20.25	There are innumerable forms of the Lord and all are eternal and transcendental, but if a devotee is inclined to worship the Lord in a particular form, He is happy to manifest that form for the pleasure of His devotee.
The Lord in our hearts guides us on how to get out of dangers and approach Him with devotion.	3.20.28	Lord Brahmā created many living beings and conditions by the state of his mind, and when they gave him distress, the Lord instructed him to cast off his body – which meant his subtle body, his contaminated mind. When he followed the Lord's advice, he was able to create good things. Similarly, when we surrender to the Lord like Brahmā did, the Lord can direct us how to relieve our distress and rediscover our love for Him.
One who is attracted by the beauty of Rādhā and Kṛṣṇa cannot be attracted by the false beauty of this material world.	3.20.30–37	The demons were attracted to the beautiful damsel and desired to enjoy her. They were so infatuated that they could not understand that she was just a combination of flesh and blood. A godly person, on the other hand, is full of knowledge and understands that material enjoyment is limited whereas spiritual happiness never ends. When he is attracted to the Lord, he is not attracted to anything in this material world.

Higher-Thinking Questions

Now try to deepen your understanding of this chapter by delving into Śrīla Prabhupāda's purports and reflecting on the following questions:

1. Review the five types of coverings of ignorance introduced in verse 18. Describe two of them and give personal examples of these types of ignorance that you have experienced in your life.
2. Explain the differences between the demons and the demigods as described in the purport of verse 31. What do the demigods understand that the demons do not? Can you find any similarities between the two?
3. What do you think it means when Lord Brahmā, out of disgust with his creation, "threw off his subtle body"? Refer to verse 28 and purport. What example is used to explain this concept? What lesson do you learn from this incident about the condition of the mind?
4. Under what conditions do ghosts and hobgoblins attack living entities? What is the result of this attack mentioned in verse 41 purport?
5. Verse 43 purport describes the occasion of *śrāddha* for the departed soul. What is the purpose of this ceremony and why is it unnecessary for devotees?
6. This chapter mentions a shining egg, which lies on the Causal Ocean for a thousand years. What is this shining egg? See verse 15.
7. In verse 12, Maitreya explains how the three modes of material nature and the unseen activity of the living entities create the material universe. How exactly does this happen? What does Śrīla Prabhupāda say is the actual cause of material creation?
8. The Manus promote the welfare activities of the universe. Would you be willing to take on this responsibility? What do you think are the pros and cons in being a Manu? What role does it emulate in modern government?

ACTIVITIES

In this section you will find many exciting things to do. These activities will get you thinking, moving, drawing, and having loads of fun.

Analogy Activity . . . to bring out the scholar in you!

POWERFUL LORD BRAHMĀ

> "Just as a highly posted manager is almost as independent as the owner of a firm, Brahmā is described here as independent because, as the Lord's representative to control the universe, he is almost as powerful and independent as the Lord."
> (*SB* 3.20.17, purport)

Exercise 1:

This analogy compares Lord Kṛṣṇa to the owner of a firm and Lord Brahmā to the head of the firm. Śrīla Prabhupāda also explains that Lord Brahmā is so powerful that he is as good as the owner of the firm.

1. Which "firm" do you think the analogy is referring to?

   ____

2. Why do you think Lord Brahmā has been given so much power by Lord Kṛṣṇa?

   ____

3. Does this analogy illustrate that Lord Brahmā is as independent as the Lord because he uses this power as he likes? Explain.

   ____

Exercise 2:

Now that you have studied the primary and secondary creation in some detail, you know something about the different aspects that Lord Brahmā is in charge of within the universe. Listed below are some key words that indicate a manager's responsibilities as we know in today's world. With your group, discuss how Lord Brahmā performs these duties by relating each one to his responsibilities in creation. Also think about how he can make his own decisions regarding these aspects, which makes him look powerful and independent.

Introspective Activity
. . . to bring out the reflective devotee in you!

SIX MENTALITIES OF THE MIND

In this chapter we see how Brahmā "casts off different bodies" to create different grades of living beings. Śrīla Prabhupāda explains in the purport to verse 28 that this means that he gave up those mentalities (habits and thinking) of the mind and purified himself.

Śrīla Bhaktivinoda Ṭhākura, in his song "*Anādi Karma Phale*," tells us that we usually have six impure mentalities of the mind we need to get rid of. They are lust, anger, greed, envy, illusion, and madness.

In the table below are these six "bodies" that we need to "cast off" to purify ourselves. In the columns provided, write down what will happen to our minds when we "accept these bodies" and when we "cast them off."

Body	When I accept this body	When I cast this body
 Lust		

Body	When I accept this body	When I cast this body
 Anger		
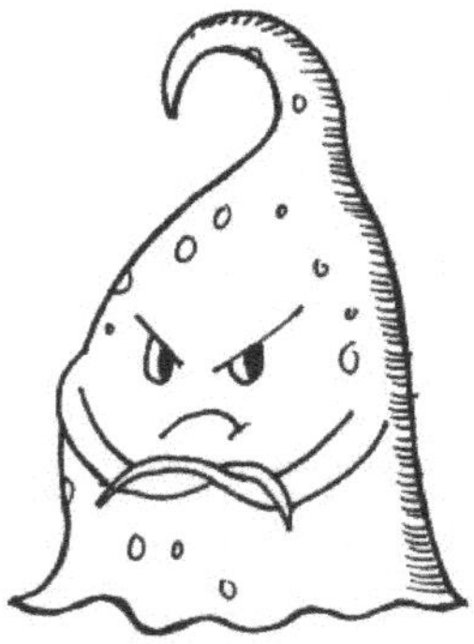 Envy		
 Greed		

Body	When I accept this body	When I cast this body
 Illusion		
 Madness		

What can you conclude from this exercise?

Critical-Thinking Activity

. . . to bring out the spiritual investigator in you!

DROPPING OF LORD BRAHMĀ'S BODY

In verse 28 purport, Śrīla Prabhupāda describes how "the continual dropping of Lord

Brahmā's body by Lord Brahmā himself is not referring to his actually giving up his body. Rather, Lord Brahmā is giving up a mentality. Mind is the subtle body of the living entities." Notice how in the story, each time Lord Brahmā gave up his body, he was able to create something. In this activity, you will be listing each mentality Lord Brahmā gave up and the result from that mentality.

Example:

Mentality: Laziness and lack of cleanliness
Result: Ghosts and fiends

Directions: Read the summary carefully and identify as many mentalities that Lord Brahmā gave up in the process of creation, along with the results of those mentalities. Some are a little tricky!

Mentality:
Result:

Mentality:
Result:

Mentality:
Result:

Mentality:
Result:

Mentality:
Result:

Mentality:
Result:

Mentality:
Result:

Mentality:
Result:

Mentality:
Result:

Language Activities

. . . to make you understand better!

FOUR GROUPS OF FIVE

The primordial matter, or *prakṛti*, which consists of the modes of material nature, generates four groups of five.

Directions: Fill in the diagram below with the information given in verse 13 or in the story summary. Begin with the name of each group on the top line and then list the items 1 to 5 of each group.

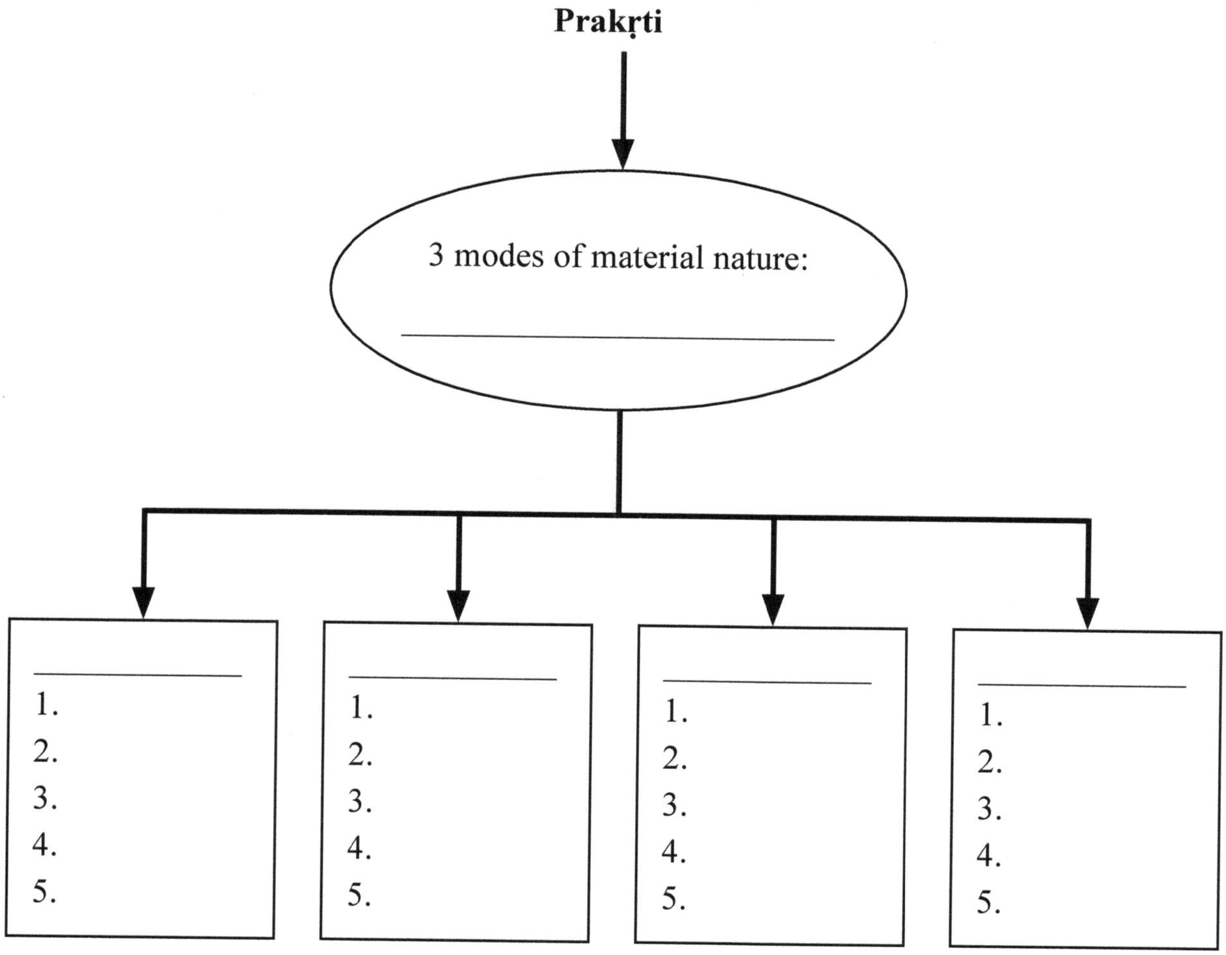

FIVE TYPES OF IGNORANCE

Directions: Match the correct phrase in the box to the specific type of ignorance listed below. Then describe or give an example of each type. This could be a personal experience and/or an example Śrīla Prabhupāda gives in verse 18 purport.

Thinking death is the end

Ignorance of the soul

Madness for material enjoyment

Anger and envy

Illusion of bodily conception

1. **Mahā-moha:** ______________________________

____

2. **Andha-tāmisra:** ______________________________

____

3. **Tāmisra:** ______________________________

____

____

4. **Moha:** ______________________________

____

5. **Tamas:** ______________________________

____

WHAT DO YOU THINK?

Set 1 – Tick those statements that you think are correct. If false, write the correct sentence.

1. Captivated, the demons seized the woman who represented the evening twilight of knowledge.
2. From his own invisible form Lord Brahmā then created the hosts of Sādhyas and Pitās who took over the invisible body.
3. Overpowered by compassion and thirst, the demons ran towards Brahmā and yelled, "Spare him! Do not eat him!"
4. The demons, who had run after Brahmā, began to imagine this form of twilight as a beautiful damsel due to their own renounced desires.
5. From Lord Brahmā's hands, ferocious serpents and Nāgas manifested with their hoods expanded.
6. However, out of surprise with his creation, Lord Brahmā threw away this subtle body of ignorance, and it turned into nighttime.
7. Finally, once Brahmā felt the object of his life had been accomplished, he manifested the demigods from his mind, who promote the welfare activities of the universe.
8. The Lord commanded: "Brahmā, you must cast off this body of yours!"

Set 2 – INFERRING QUESTIONS

Which questions do you agree with and disagree with, using what the author says and what you know? Back up your argument with reasons.

1. After Lord Brahmā created the demons from his buttocks, the demons immediately ran towards him to jump on him with their material desires. We can infer that this reaction from the demons was due to some karma from a past life that Lord Brahmā was now experiencing. Otherwise, there would be no reason for demons to try and harm Lord Brahmā.
2. In the beginning of this chapter, Maitreya again describes the beginning of the material creation, although it has been thoroughly described in previous chapters. Here we can understand that Maitreya needed to review the story of creation again to get to his next point, Lord Brahmā's creation.

CROSSWORD

Across

4. Refers to the ignorance of the soul
5. Lord Brahmā gave birth to these from his buttocks
6. Heavenly musicians
7. A word used for anger and envy
9. Hearing the transcendental pastimes of the Lord is as purifying as bathing in this river
10. A name for those who eat

Down

1. The Sanskrit term for "illusion of bodily conception"
2. The demons imagined this form of Brahmā as a beautiful damsel
3. Those who are man eaters, or who do not protect
8. Heavenly dancing girls

ANSWERS

Powerful Lord Brahmā

Exercise 1:

1. The universe 2. Lord Brahmā was a qualified personality; he is a responsible devotee of the Lord who uses his powers to serve the Lord. The Lord also does not want to be involved personally with the creation, so He uses His best agents to do this important service. 3. No, it means that he understands the mood of the Lord and works according to that, although he looks like he makes his own decisions.

Exercise 2:

Lord Brahmā had the "project" of completing the secondary creation. He had specific things to create, which means he had "goals." He puts "systems" and "rules" in place, like the rules of karma, laws of Manu, etc., to ensure the universe runs smoothly without chaos. He makes sure things function nicely according to the plan and ensures "dilemmas" are solved (e.g., helping Mahārāja Priyavrata to come back and take charge of the kingdom SB.5.1). He deals with "emergencies" properly (e.g., asking Dhruva Mahārāja to stop killing so many Yakṣas *SB*. 4.10). He takes care that the population of the universe is undisturbed (e.g., He prays to the Lord to incarnate when he cannot solve the problems in the universe) and ensures that the purpose of the universe in fulfilled by producing the "results" (preaching and making devotees). He does all this according to the will of the Lord, not independently, although it seems so.

Six Mentalities of the Mind *(Potential Answers)*

- Lust:
  - By accepting, I want to enjoy in the material world, forget Lord Kṛṣṇa, increase my attachment, and don't realize how it is harming me.
  - By casting off, I try to understand my position as the Lord's servant, serve the Lord, understand why we should not run after things in the material world, and experience happiness.
- Anger:
  - By accepting, I become disturbed, frustrated, dissatisfied, go away from Kṛṣṇa.
  - By casting off, I become calm, satisfied, able to understand clearly, and please Kṛṣṇa.
- Greed:
  - By accepting, I desire more and more, become dissatisfied and unhappy, frustrated, angry, disturbed, and forget Kṛṣṇa.
  - By casting off, I become satisfied and happy, focused on understanding Kṛṣṇa, and don't desire more than I need to live.

- Envy:
  - By accepting, I become dissatisfied, worried, stressed, greedy, and lose focus on Kṛṣṇa.
  - By casting off, I become peaceful, satisfied, friendly, appreciative, and grateful to Kṛṣṇa for what I have.
- Illusion:
  - By accepting, I lose track of the truth and develop the bad qualities mentioned above.
  - By casting off, I become happy and peaceful and can see things as they are.
- Madness:
  - By accepting, I lose track of the truth and develop the bad qualities mentioned above.
  - By casting off, I become happy and peaceful and can see things as they are.
- Conclusion: *Anarthas* pull us down and take us away from Lord Kṛṣṇa, while pure habits bring us closer to Him and make us peaceful and happy.

Dropping of Lord Brahmā's Body

Mentality: Subtle body of ignorance
Result: Nighttime; Yakṣas and Rākṣasas

Mentality: Subtle body of goodness
Result: Daytime; the demigods

Mentality: Passion
Result: Demons from his buttocks, evening twilight when the day and night meet.

Mentality: Loveliness, laughter, and moonlight
Result: Gandharvas and Apsarās

Mentality: Ability to become invisible
Result: Siddhas and Vidyādharas (with the form of Antardhāna)

Mentality: Brahmā's admiration and reflection
Result: Kimpuruṣas and Kinnaras

Mentality: Worry and his hair
Result: Serpents and Nāgas

Mentality: Accomplishment and his own human form
Result: Manus

Mentality: Devotion and sense control
Result: The great sages

Four Groups of Five

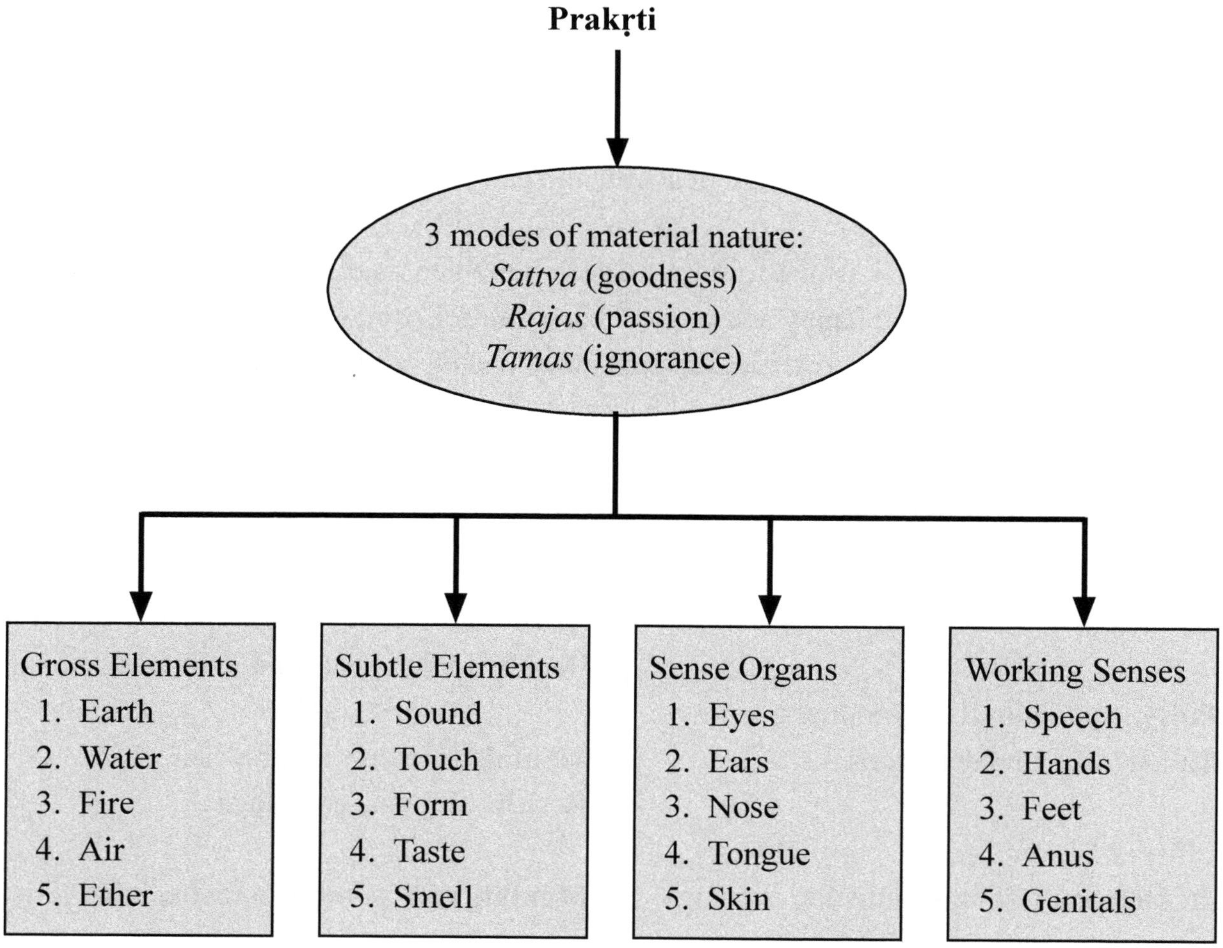

Five Types of Ignorance *(Potential Answers)*

Mahā-Moha – Madness for material enjoyment

Example: People in this age of Kali are mad after acquiring possessions for material enjoyment.

Andha-tāmisra – Thinking death is the end

Example: Atheists tend to think this body is the self and everything ends when the body dies.

Tāmisra – Anger and envy

Examples: Getting angry when our desires are not fulfilled and not being happy when others are happy.

Moha – Illusion of bodily conception
Example: A mentality of "I am this body and everything belonging to this body is mine."

Tamas – Ignorance of the soul
Examples: Thinking the body to be the self (not knowing that we are the soul) and being bereft of spiritual knowledge.

What do you think?

1. **False:** Captivated, the demons seized the woman who represented the evening twilight of ignorance.
2. **True**.
3. **False:** Overpowered by **hunger** and thirst, the demons ran towards Brahmā and yelled, **"Spare him not! Eat him all!"**
4. **False:** The demons, who had run after Brahmā, began to imagine this form of twilight as a beautiful damsel due to their own **passionate** desires.
5. **False:** From Lord Brahmā's **hair**, ferocious serpents and Nāgas manifested with their hoods expanded.
6. **True**.
7. **False:** Finally, once Brahmā felt the object of his life had been accomplished, he manifested the **Manus** from his mind, who promote the welfare activities of the universe.
8. **True**.

Inferring Questions

1. Disagree. The demons ran after Lord Brahmā due to their material (sexual) desires. There is no mention at all about Lord Brahmā's *karma* or past lives, therefore this is not the reason why the demons attacked him.
2. Agree.

Crossword

Across: 4. tamas; 5. demons; 6. Gandharvas; 7. tāmisra; 9. Ganges; 10. Yakṣas
Down: 1. moha; 2. twilight; 3. Rākṣasas; 8. Apsarās

21
Conversation Between Manu and Kardama

Story Summary

"Tell me more about Svāyambhuva Manu," Vidura prodded. "As far as I remember, he had two sons called Priyavrata and Uttānapāda…and three daughters?"

"Yes, that's right," answered Maitreya.

"Oh, I think I remember their names." Vidura looked up, trying to concentrate. "Aha! Ākuti who married Ruci. Prasūti who married Dakṣa and…ah yes!" He snapped his fingers, beaming. "Of course. Devahūti! She married Kardama Muni. How many children did they have?"

Vidura's enthusiasm always made his spiritual master smile.

"Well, it all started when Brahmā ordered the great sage Kardama Muni to beget children," began Maitreya. "But Kardama Muni was an ascetic. How was he to find a wife and have a family? Well, he turned to the person that could undoubtedly help him, of course. He turned to Lord Viṣṇu."

"How?"

"Well, he performed ten thousand years of penance on the banks of the river Sarasvatī."

Vidura's eyes widened in disbelief. "Ten…thousand…years?"

"Ten thousand years," confirmed Maitreya, "and oh, his trance of devotion pleased Lord Viṣṇu so much that He appeared directly before the sage."

"He stood right in front of Kardama Muni?"

"Yes! Well…more in mid-air, on the shoulders of Garuḍa – His eagle carrier. Oh Vidura, Lord Viṣṇu dazzled with a bright effulgence. He was such a captivating sight. He glanced about, smiling, His lotus face framed with shiny dark locks of curly hair. He held a conch, disc, and mace in three of His hands and a white lily in the fourth. He wore a garland of white lotuses and water lilies. And to see this garland against His bluish hue, to see it encircling the Kaustubha gem on His chest…and then contrasting with His golden attire that shone like lightning…it was worth waiting ten thousand years for such a sight."

Maitreya described what happened next.

Kardama Muni immediately fell to the ground, offering obeisances. Then kneeling and feasting his eyes on the Lord's alluring form, he folded his hands in prayer.

"My power of sight is now fulfilled," he said, mesmerized. "Advanced yogīs have to take many births of deep meditation to see You, yet You've given me Your mercy, dear Lord, by being present before me.

"All living beings are bound by the rope of satisfying their desires. Deprived of intelligence, they worship Your feet to attain temporary pleasures of the senses, and yet You bestow Your mercy even upon them. In the same way, desiring to marry, I too seek shelter at Your lotus feet to satisfy my material desire. Please, Lord, give me a wife whose qualities and character will match mine, for You are like a desire tree."

Lord Viṣṇu looked at the sage with an affectionate smile. The Lord replied, "I knew what was in your mind, dear Kardama, so I've already arranged for this. There is no frustration for living entities that serve me with devotion like you.

"The righteous emperor Svāyambhuva Manu rules the earth. The day after tomorrow, he will arrive here with his queen Śatarūpā to see you. They have a grown-up daughter, with delicate black eyes, who is searching for a husband. She has good character and good qualities and is compatible with you. Her parents are coming here to present her to you. This young princess is the one you have been desiring all these years, dear Kardama, and she is soon to be yours. She will readily serve you, and together you will have nine daughters who will later also marry sages and have children."

Kardama smiled in appreciation.

"By following My orders," continued the Lord, "offering Me the fruits of your acts, and showing compassion to all living entities, your heart will be cleansed. You will attain self-realization, and finally, you will come to Me."

Kardama nodded. Yes, there was nothing more he wanted than to live this life in service to his dear Lord.

Finally, Lord Viṣṇu said, "I will then

incarnate as your son and I will instruct your wife Devahūti."

At this, the sage stood up, shocked. Did he hear right? The Supreme Personality of Godhead would take birth as his very own son? He opened his mouth to speak, but the Lord was already leaving to return to Vaikuṇṭha. Garuḍa's wings reverberated the hymns of the Sāma Veda as they swished and glided through the sky, higher and higher, back to the spiritual abode.

The sage watched the Lord and His carrier disappear into the sky. He was now alone and again aware of his surroundings. On the banks of the river Sarasvatī, where he had resided for thousands of years and performed austerities, now appeared a lake. He sipped some of its water in his palm and sipped it again…and again. It was unexpectedly sweet – as sweet as nectar – for this lake was formed from the Lord's tears of compassion for the sage. It thus became known as Bindu-sarovara.

The sage waited on these newly formed banks for Manu to come.

Meanwhile, Svāyambhuva Manu, with his dear wife and daughter, mounted their glorious chariot and traveled the earth before reaching the hermitage of Kardama Muni just as Lord Viṣṇu had foretold.

On the banks of Bindu Sarovara they looked around and admired their surroundings. The shore was decorated with trees and creepers, bearing fruits and flowers of all seasons. Amidst the beautiful groves of forest trees, birds sang sweet melodies, intoxicated bees hummed, proud peacocks danced, and cuckoos joyfully cried, "Cuckoo! Cuckoo!" Roaming deer skipped through the woods, boars rummaged through the leaves, porcupines scuttled along, and gavayas, elephants, baboons, lions, monkeys, mongooses, and even musk deer roamed about freely.

Svāyambhuva Manu and Devahūti entered the sage's sacred hermitage and saw him sitting there, having just performed a fire sacrifice and offered oblations into it. Kardama's body shone brilliantly. Although he was dressed in rags and was engaged in severe penances for a long time, he did not appear emaciated, for the Lord had cast His affectionate sidelong glance on him and Kardama had heard the nectar flowing from the Lord's moonlike words.

The sage looked up, his eyes large like lotus petals. He stood up to receive his guests. He was tall. With his matted hair and soiled ragged garments, he looked like an unpolished gem.

Immediately, the emperor bowed before him. Kardama Muni greeted him with a benediction by raising his right hand and honored the King before offering him a sitting place.

Remembering the Lord's words, Kardama spoke to the King sweetly: "Dear Manu, you tour the world to protect the innocent and destroy the miscreants as the representative of Lord Hari. If you didn't mount your chariot, if there weren't fierce sounds by the twanging of your bow, if you didn't roam the world leading an army making the earth tremble, the laws of the Lord would be broken by rogues and rascals. All obeisances unto you!

"I must now ask why you've come to these banks. Whatever your purpose may be, we shall carry it out without hesitation."

Themes and Key Messages

The following table summarizes some of the key messages and themes of this chapter. Use it as a quick reference guide to the verses listed and discuss each theme and message further with your teacher or friends.

Theme	Reference	Key Messages
Without devotion, nothing can be perfect.	3.21.6–8	The Lord revealed His personal form to Kardama Muni not because of his ten thousand years of *yoga* practice and meditation but because of his devotion to please the Supreme Lord through his meditation and practices. Therefore, any practice needs devotion to get any beneficial result. Thus, Kṛṣṇa consciousness or *bhakti-yoga* is the direct method to achieve real success in spiritual life.
The perfection of *yoga* is to see the Supreme Personality of Godhead in His eternal form.	3.21.9–12	By performance of *yoga,* Kardama Muni saw the Supreme Lord as He is. There was no point in seeing an imagined form of the Lord after practicing for so many years. Therefore, the perfection of *yoga* is not voidness or impersonalism but to see the personal form of the Lord. By performing Kṛṣṇa conscious activities, we can eventually see the form of Kṛṣṇa directly.
If one worships the Supreme Lord even with material desires, he will gradually become a pure devotee and have no more material hankering.	3.21.15–17, 21	Whether a devotee is full of desires, has no desire, or desires liberation, he should worship the Supreme Lord, who fulfills everyone's desires. Kṛṣṇa, being very kind, engages the devotee in loving service to Him, and so the devotee gradually becomes purified. Even if we desire material enjoyment, we should enjoy under the direction of the Lord or the Vedas, which will gradually elevate us to a higher platform of spiritual realization.
By hearing and chanting about the Supreme Lord, we become freed from the cycle of birth and death. 	3.21.17	*Saṁsāra,* or the repetition of birth and death, is like a forest fire. This fire can only be extinguished by water from a cloud. The cloud is the mercy of the Lord or the spiritual master. Therefore, when we take shelter of Kṛṣṇa by hearing and chanting about Him, He gives us His mercy, and we are freed from material existence.
In all circumstances we must take shelter of the Supreme Personality of Godhead and depend completely on His decision.	3.21.28, 30	If we pray to the Supreme Lord in every stage of our lives, everything will be done very nicely and suitable to our heart's desire. Kardama Muni desired only a wife, but because he was a devotee of the Lord, the Lord selected a wife who was a princess. Thus, Kardama Muni got a wife beyond his expectation. If we depend on the choice of Kṛṣṇa, we will receive benedictions greater than we desire. Therefore, we must perform all activities in Kṛṣṇa consciousness.

Higher-Thinking Questions

Now try to deepen your understanding of this chapter by delving into Śrīla Prabhupāda's purports and reflecting on the following questions:

1. In verse 2 purport Śrīla Prabhupāda explains that *Śrīmad-Bhāgavatam* is also a history of the great rulers of the universe and that people may benefit by studying their histories. How do you think they will benefit?
2. In verse 14 Kardama Muni mentions how only those of less intelligence worship the Lord's feet to achieve temporary pleasures, for even the hellish beings can attain these pleasures. What are the temporary pleasures Kardama Muni is talking about? Name two temporary pleasures you have experienced.
3. Then, despite condemning persons who approach the Lord for material enjoyment, Kardama Muni expressed that he desired to marry a girl of like disposition. He could have asked this benediction from Umā, the demigoddess who fulfills such desires, but He approached the Supreme Lord. What is the advantage of approaching the Lord to fulfill one's material desires? (Hint: See purport to verse 15.)
4. Śrīla Prabhupāda also raises the question in verse 16 purport that if Kardama Muni was advanced in spiritual life, why didn't he ask the Lord for liberation even after seeing and experiencing the Lord? What do you think Kardama Muni teaches us by his example?
5. In the purport to verse 15 Śrīla Prabhupāda also describes the differences between marriage nowadays to the marriages in the Vedic culture. Describe how two people were arranged to marry in the Vedic system. (Refer also to verses 27 and 28.)
6. Why do you think the time factor cannot affect the lifespan of the devotees? (See verse 18.)
7. Explain the analogy of the spider and its web from the purport to verse 19.
8. What are the two branches of the Sāma Veda as described in verse 34 purport and what is its essence? The Sāma Veda is heard when Garuḍa flaps his wings. Who can hear this and see the Lord and Garuḍa flying to Vaikuṇṭha? Explain his qualifications.
9. Why did Kardama Muni, who was a great sage, offer his obeisances to the King despite holding a higher position than the King? (Refer to verse 51 purport.)
10. Describe the reciprocal relationship between the *brāhmaṇa* and *kṣatriya* classes described in verse 56 purport. Do you see this example in our current day and age (the executive branch of government with saintly people)? How has it changed? Do you think it is possible to restore such a relationship?
11. In the age of Satya-yuga, there were only one or two kings who presided over the whole earth planet. What were their duties? Refer to the purport of verses 52–54.

ACTIVITIES

In this section you will find many exciting things to do. These activities will get you thinking, moving, drawing, and having loads of fun.

Analogy Activity . . . to bring out the scholar in you!

AN UNPOLISHED GEM

"Svāyambhuva Manu approached and saw him to be somewhat soiled, like an unpolished gem." (*SB* 3.21.45–47)

In this analogy Kardama Muni is being compared to an unpolished gem. To understand this better, let us first understand the difference between a polished and an unpolished gem.

1. Research and explain the main difference between a polished and an unpolished gem.

____

____

____

2. Next, read the purport to verses 45–47 and explain the main reason why Kardama Muni was compared to an unpolished gem.

____

____

____

3. In the table below, write down some characteristics of Kardama Muni that made him appear like an unpolished gem. Make sure you include his spiritual qualities (that made him appear so bright) as well as the external appearance that made him look somewhat covered.

Qualities that made Kardama Muni a real 'gem':	
Qualities that made Kardama Muni look somewhat "unpolished":	
Qualities that show despite his unrefined external looks:	

4. What are some important lessons you learn from this analogy and your analysis?

____

____

____

Introspective Activities
. . . to bring out the reflective devotee in you!

PURIFYING THE SENSES

Verse 13 describes that the perfection of the senses is to use our senses in the service of the Lord, which will purify them completely. In the purport Śrīla Prabhupāda explains that this is what *bhakti-yoga* means: to engage our senses in relationship to the Lord.

Directions: Either from this chapter or from your own knowledge, describe how you can purify each sense below by using it in the service of the Lord.

Sight:

Hearing:

Taste:

Touch:

Smell:

EVERYTHING FOR KṚṢṆA

In verse 17 purport Śrīla Prabhupāda describes that although Kardama Muni understood that the highest goal of life is to be liberated from this material world through pure love for Kṛṣṇa, the sage still asked for a wife. This is because no matter what desire we have or what duty we need to perform (like Kardama Muni), material or spiritual, we should always seek help, guidance, and blessings from Kṛṣṇa. In any circumstance we should take shelter of Him and somehow dovetail our desires to serve Krsna. In this story Kardama Muni got married and together with his wife served the Lord with devotion. In time his desires were purified, and he only desired Krsna's service, so much so that he eventually renounced his family and exclusively served the Lord.

Directions: Choose five of your desires (spiritual or material). For the material desires see how they can be used in Krsna's service thereby spiritualizing them. Then write a prayer for each. Try to follow the process of 1) offering obeisances, 2) glorifying the Lord, and then 3) asking for help in a humble state of mind.

Example: *"Oh Lord Kṛṣṇa, please accept my humble obeisances. All glories to Your lotus feet. You are the Supreme Personality of Godhead, the cause of all causes! You have come to protect us and give us Your shelter. Please help me to do well in my studies and be able to use that to serve You. I cannot do this by myself."*

Now you try!

1)

2)

3)

4)

5)

Critical-Thinking Activities
. . . to bring out the spiritual investigator in you!

APPROACHING THE LORD WITH MATERIAL DESIRE

In this chapter we see how Kardama Muni approached Lord Viṣṇu and asked Him to kindly find him a suitable wife. In the *Śrīmad-Bhāgavatam* we read many times that we should not ask for anything material (i.e. something for our own enjoyment) from the Lord. And yet we see here that Kardama Muni asked for a good wife.

Tamāla and Vraja, two students of the *Śrīmad-Bhāgavatam*, were asked to write down their thoughts about whether one should ask the Lord for anything material or not. They were also asked to support their ideas with proper evidence from scriptures. Here are their notes:

Tamāla's Notes:

It is all right to have material desires because we are not pure devotees. And it is fine to approach the Lord with our desires:

One with many desires, no desires, or desire for liberation should worship the Lord. (SB 2.3.10)

Kardama Muni and Dhruva worshiped the Lord with material desires, but the Lord was never angry with them. Instead He fulfilled their desires and purified them of all material desire.

It is better to ask for the Lord's help than approaching the demigods or trying by ourselves without His blessings.

We should, however, follow the injunctions of the Vedas, or God's laws, to carry out our material duties and desires.

Vraja's Notes:

Srimad-Bhagavatam often emphasises that one should not seek anything from the Lord for one's pleasure; rather, we should only desire to serve Him for His pleasure. (SB 1.2.6 - unmotivated service)

Dhruva Maharaja realized that he should not have worshiped the Lord for a kingdom. Prahlada Maharaja also did not want anything in return from the Lord for his service.

We also see this in the highest devotional service of the gopis. They simply loved Krsna and never wanted anything in return from Him.

Material benedictions from the Lord do not last, but spiritual benedictions last forever.

Do you think one of them is more correct than the other? Discuss with your teacher and group and come to a proper conclusion. Then refer to the potential answers at the end of this chapter.

PENANCE IN DEVOTIONAL SERVICE

Kardama Muni performed penance on the bank of the river Sarasvatī for ten thousand years. During that period, the sage worshiped the Lord through devotional service in yogic trance. The Supreme Lord was pleased with Kardama Muni and showed His transcendental form to him, which can be understood only through the Vedas.
Let us meditate on this topic:

- What does "penance" mean?
- What are the results of performing penance? Why should it be done for many years?
- Do you think it is possible to do this kind of penance in this age of Kali? Why or why not?
- Explain why this kind of penance is not recommended in Kali-yuga?
- Describe a list of penances in devotional service suitable for Kali-yuga? Explain why they are suitable.
- What should be the mood or motive behind all penances or austerities?

THE EIGHTFOLD YOGA SYSTEM

Verse 4 purport describes Kardama Muni as a *mahā-yogī*, a great mystic, and Princess Devahūti as a *yoga-lakṣaṇa*, very advanced in the performance of the eightfold *yoga* system (*aṣṭāṅga-yoga*).

Directions:

1. List the eight divisions of the *yoga* system (refer to verse 4 purport).
2. After self-realization, what are the additional eight perfectional stages called? Refer to verse 12 and earlier chapters in Canto 3.
3. In verse 12 purport Śrīla Prabhupāda explains that achieving such material success

in *yoga* is not the perfection or the ultimate goal. What does he describe as the ultimate goal?

4. Do you think it is possible to practice this eightfold *yoga* system today? Explain.
5. Why do you think that it is not possible to get the same results from performing the *yoga* postures (*haṭha-yoga*) that people do today?
6. Śrīla Prabhupāda concludes that the danger of this *yoga* system is that one can fall down because of becoming attracted to material power. How is *bhakti-yoga* superior?

PIOUS AND IMPIOUS LIVING ENTITIES

Verse 40 describes that on the shores of the holy lake Bindu-sarovara are "pious trees and creepers and birds and animals."

According to the descriptions in this chapter, identify whether the following living entities in the table below are pious or impious and by what mode of material nature (goodness, passion, or ignorance) they are influenced. Then give a reason why you think so.

Living Entity	Pious or Impious	Mode
Crow 		
Magpie 		
Swan 		
Pine tree 		

Living Entity	Pious or Impious	Mode
Snake 		
Apple tree 		
Dove 		
Scorpion 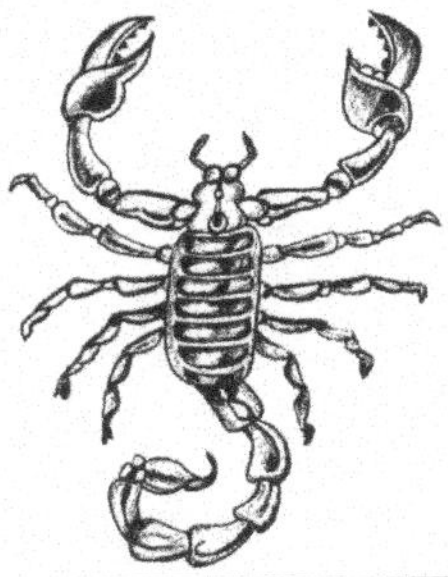		

Now come up with three additional animals, birds, trees, or any other living entity that are either pious or impious and give a reason why you think so.

ANSWERS

An Unpolished Gem *(Potential Answers)*

1. The luster of a polished gem shows easily since it is cut in a way to expose the shine whereas an unpolished gem, which is directly from the mine, is not cut or polished but has a similar luster.
2. Although Kardama Muni looked unkempt externally, dressed in rags and had matted locks, the luster of his spiritual austerity made him look bright. He had just seen the Supreme Lord face to face and had heard the sound vibrations from the Lord's mouth; therefore, he did not appear emaciated like most *yogīs* but appeared lustrous and healthy.
3. Refer to answers in the purport and discuss further with your teacher and friends.
4. When we associate with the Lord and chant His holy names, we become purified and are lustrous and healthy. Even though a devotee may not have a beautiful appearance externally or may not dress in beautiful clothes, he is "gemlike" with saintly qualities; therefore, we should not judge a devotee just by external appearances.

Approaching the Lord with Material Desire *(Potential Answer)*

Discuss both viewpoints clearly. Both are valid arguments, but Tamāla's notes describe mixed devotional service (with material desire) and Vraja's notes describe pure devotional service (with no material desire). The two arguments can be reconciled – while it is allowed to ask the Lord for something in the beginning stages (the Lord also states that four kinds of people worship Him – *catur-vidhā bhajante māṁ – BG* 7.16), we should understand that the ultimate goal is pure devotional service, that is, to serve the Lord without expecting anything in return.

The Eightfold Yoga System

1. *Yama:* control of the senses; *Niyama:* strict following of the rules and regulations; *Āsana:* practice of the different sitting postures; *Prāṇāyāma:* control of the breath; *Pratyāhāra:* withdrawing the senses from sense objects; *Dhāraṇā:* concentration of the mind; *Dhyāna:* meditation; *Samādhi:* self-realization.
2. Yoga-*siddhis*:
   aṇimā: becoming smaller than the smallest; *laghimā:* becoming lighter than the lightest; *mahimā:* becoming bigger than the biggest; *prāpti:* ability to be anywhere or acquire anything from anywhere; *īśitā:* ability to control nature; *vaśitā:* ability to bring others under control; *prākāmya:* ability to attain whatever one desires; *kāmāvasāyitā:* ability to do the impossible.
3. To see the Supreme Personality of Godhead in His eternal form as Kardama Muni did.
4. No. It is a very difficult process that is not possible to perform in this age where people are

short-lived, not disciplined or austere, lazy, and dull in mind and senses.

5. Just performing *haṭha-yoga* for a few minutes or hours cannot give the results of *aṣṭāṅga-yoga*, which requires many years of performance, extreme discipline and control of the senses, and arduous practices.
6. *Bhakti-yoga* requires that one only accept the necessities of life to maintain the body and soul together; thus, *bhakti-yogīs* do not become enamored by material power and can focus on the real goal, which is to achieve love for Kṛṣṇa and go back to Him. In this way, they attain everlasting spiritual happiness instead of the material happiness of other *yoga* systems. *Bhakti-yoga* is also easy to perform in this age and doesn't require any strict rules and regulations.

Pious and Impious Living Entities

Crow	→	Impious	→	Mode of ignorance
Magpie	→	Impious	→	Mode of ignorance
Swan	→	Pious	→	Mode of goodness
Pine tree	→	Impious	→	Mode of ignorance
Snake	→	Impious	→	Mode of passion
Apple tree	→	Pious	→	Mode of goodness
Dove	→	Pious	→	Mode of goodness
Scorpion	→	Impious	→	Mode of passion

22
The Marriage of Kardama Muni and Devahūti

Story Summary

Kardama Muni stood silently, anticipating the Emperor's response.

The Emperor, Svāyambhuva Manu, sat on a *kuśa* grass mat offered by the *brāhmaṇa*. He scanned the hermitage approvingly before gazing at Kardama Muni with loving admiration. He was humbled by the words of the sage.

"Dearest Kardama," began Manu, "we have both come from the universal form of the Lord. While the *kṣatriyas* have come from the Lord's arms, the *brāhmaṇas* have come from His face. Therefore, we the *kṣatriyas* are meant to protect the *brāhmaṇas* while the *brāhmaṇas* protect us by instructing us in Vedic knowledge. In this way, our Lord ensures we are all protected.

"You have protected me from ignorance by clearly describing the duty of a king who yearns to protect his subjects. Now all my doubts have been resolved. How fortunate I am to have heard your pure words. How fortunate I am to have touched my head to your lotus feet.

"O great sage, now please listen to my prayer. I am troubled by affection for my daughter. You see, she's looking for a suitable husband, and the moment she heard of you from Nārada Muni, she fixed her mind upon you. Ever since, she has been meditating on your character, good qualities, wisdom, handsome appearance, youthfulness, and other virtues. Therefore I humbly request you to accept her as your wife."

Kardama Muni smiled at these words.

Hastily, the King added, "It's not honorable to reject an offering even if you're detached, what to speak of if you actually want such a gift. And I've heard you desire a suitable wife like my daughter. She is the fulfillment of your prayers, so please accept her."

"Certainly!" answered Kardama. "I'll surely accept her. Your daughter has not yet married nor given her word to anyone, therefore our marriage according to the Vedic system can take place. Besides, who in their right mind wouldn't accept her? She is so beautiful that the luster of her body outshines the dazzling ornaments she wears."

Devahūti bit her lip and looked down. Blushing, she inched behind her father.

"I have heard of her glories," Kardama continued. "I have heard that Viśvāvasu, the famous Gandharva, fell from his celestial airplane when he saw this young maiden playing with a ball on the roof of the palace. So what wise man wouldn't accept her, the ornament of womanhood, the beloved daughter of Svāyambhuva Manu, and sister of Uttānapāda?"

The Emperor smiled.

"I have one condition though," said Kardama Muni. "After I give her children, I shall renounce everything and lead the rest of my life in devotional service to the Supreme

Personality of Godhead. After all, He is my highest authority and the goal of my life."

Kardama Muni became silent and smiled, thinking of Lord Viṣṇu, the Lord with a lotus in His navel.

Manu turned to look at his queen. She smiled with an approving nod. He then turned toward his daughter Devahūti. She had been peering at the sage who had captured her mind.

There was no mistaking it. His queen and the princess had made their decision.

"So be it!" pronounced the Emperor as he gently placed Devahūti's soft, delicate hand in the palm of Kardama.

He had now given his daughter to the sage.

Overjoyed, Queen Śatarūpā gave valuable presents, such as jewelry, clothes, and household articles in dowry to the bride and bridegroom.

Manu was relieved. He had found a suitable match for his daughter. She was happy, which made him happy. Yet, he couldn't help but feel an impending separation from his daughter. He choked up. She had been under his care all her life. He had protected and loved his daughter from the day she was born. His own little princess was no longer under his protection. Tears trickled down his cheeks as he watched her with her

new husband surrounded by their wedding gifts. Manu embraced her, his tears drenching her hair.

"My dear mother, my dear daughter!" he cried repeatedly.

They both remained in the comfort of each other's embrace as their tears expressed what was impossible to say.

Then wiping his tears, clearing his throat, and straightening his royal gown, Manu spoke to the sage: "My dear Kardama, I must take your permission to leave now."

Kardama brought his palms together and bowed to the King.

Manu and his queen boarded their chariot and waved a final goodbye to their daughter. The wings of the chariot spread out and ascended into the sky. They marveled at the beautiful prosperous hermitages of the sages on the banks of the river Sarasvatī.

Before long, the chariot arrived home. As it encircled Brahmāvarta from the sky, the subjects gazed upwards in excitement. They greeted the Emperor with songs, prayers, and musical instruments.

The chariot then landed in the city of Barhiṣmatī. This was an incredibly special city, rich

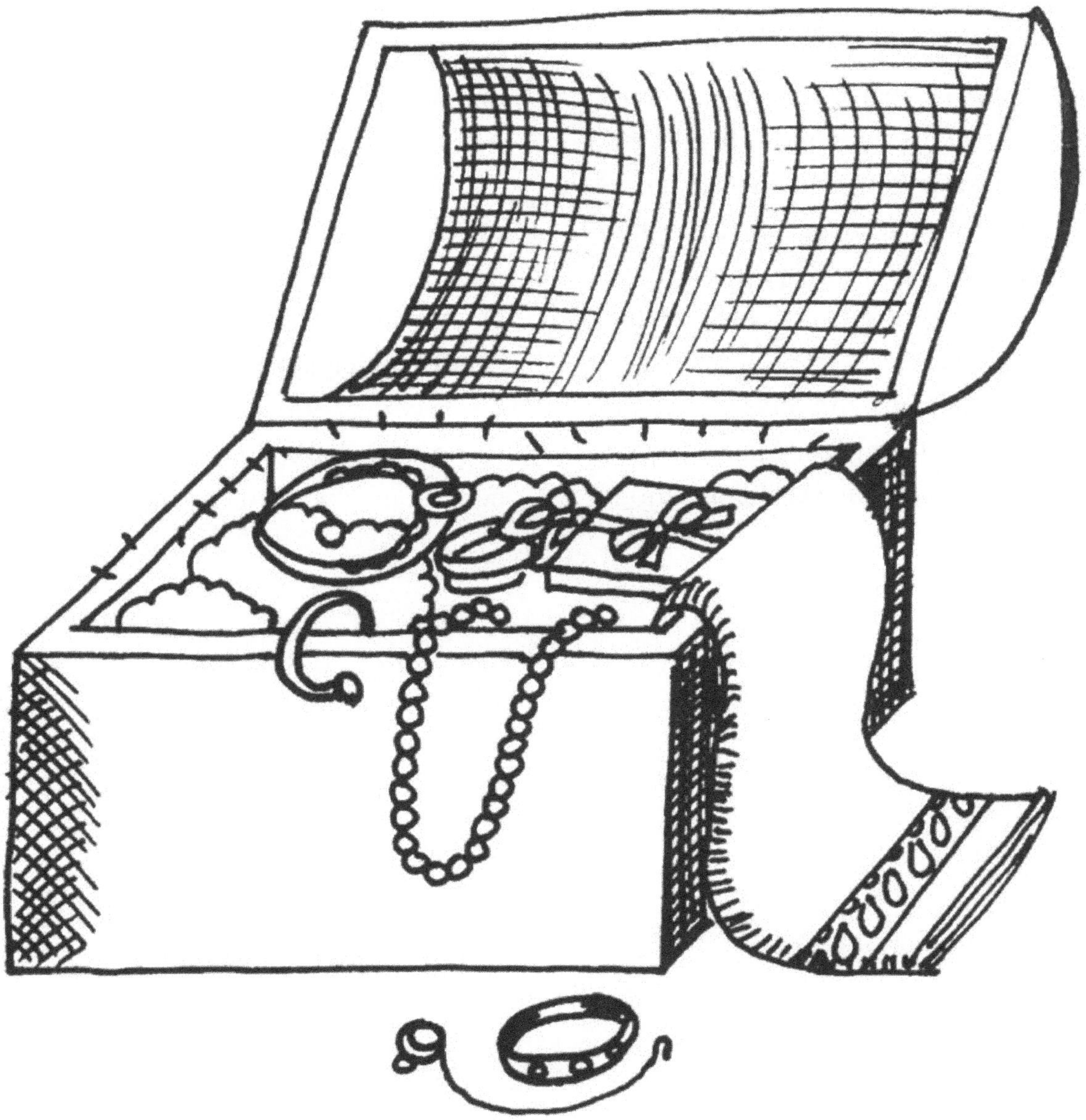

with all kinds of wealth for a unique reason. Strands of Lord Varāha's hair had fallen in this city, and from the hair, *kuśa* grass had grown. The sages had worshiped Lord Varāha with this sacred green grass after He had killed Hiraṇyākṣa.

Manu first sat on the *kuśa* grass and worshiped the Lord before entering his palace. His palace radiated a spiritual atmosphere in which the three miseries of material existence could not be present.

For many years thereafter, the Emperor enjoyed life with his wife and subjects and fulfilled his desires without being disturbed by irreligion. This was because he was a saintly king and enjoyed material happiness in a Kṛṣṇa conscious atmosphere. Thus, he did not become degraded.

Celestial musicians and their wives sang of the reputation of Emperor Manu. Out of compassion he would answer the questions of his subjects, teaching them the duties of different classes of men at various stages of life. Early every morning, he would listen to the pastimes of the Supreme Personality of Godhead with a loving heart.

He lived a long life, which was not spent in vain, for he was always hearing, remembering, writing down, and chanting the pastimes of the Lord. He passed his time, which lasted 71 cycles of the four ages (71 x 4,320,000 years) always thinking of the Lord and absorbed in devotional service. Therefore, he never had to take birth again.

Maitreya concluded the story. He gazed at Vidura, who had been listening with rapt attention. The *ṛṣi* continued: "So how can anyone under the shelter of devotional service ever experience bodily miseries?

"My dear Vidura, I have spoken of the wonderful character of Svāyambhuva Manu; now let me speak of Devahūti – his daughter."

Themes and Key Messages

The following table summarizes some of the key messages and themes of this chapter. Use it as a quick reference guide to the verses listed and discuss each theme and message further with your teacher or friends.

Theme	Reference	Key Messages
If the *brāhmaṇas* and *kṣatriyas* cooperate with each other, the Lord is pleased and protects them.	3.22.2–4	The *brāhmaṇas*, created from the Lord's face, are meant to protect the *kṣatriyas* by giving them spiritual knowledge and instruction. The *kṣatriyas* are created from His arms to protect the *brāhmaṇas*. If the *brāhmaṇas*, the head of society, are protected, then the whole society flourishes, materially and spiritually. When both social orders (*varṇas*) cooperate with each other, the Lord protects them through His energies. Similarly, if all *varṇas* and *āśramas* cooperate fully, then the Lord is pleased and He protects them.
By even a moment's association with a saintly person, we can become liberated from material entanglement.	3.22.5–7	To be blessed by the holy dust of the lotus feet of a great devotee (*mahātmā*) is the perfection of spiritual life because by the association and blessings of a *mahātmā*, one can also become a *mahātmā*. Therefore, we should hear with open ears from the spiritual master or *mahātmā* and follow his instructions faithfully.
A *gṛhastha* is a householder who remains with his family for spiritual advancement, whereas a *gṛhamedhī* is a householder who simply satisfies his senses.	3.22.11	The duty of a wife is to help her husband in household duties, and the duty of a husband is not to satisfy his senses but to help his family in spiritual life. Thus *gṛhastha* is an *āśrama*, a spiritual social order meant for spiritual advancement. Svāyambhuva Manu offered his daughter to Kardama Muni with this intention.
One should not remain married for one's entire life but should eventually retire to fully dedicate oneself in the service of the Lord.	3.22.19–20	Kardama Muni had a desire to marry, but he didn't want to be a householder throughout his life. He wanted to follow the Vedic principles, which encourage that one should first follow *brahmacārya* (celibate life) to develop spiritual character and qualities, then accept a wife and have children, and ultimately renounce to dedicate himself fully to the Lord in the *sannyāsa* or *paramahaṁsa* stage. Kardama Muni preferred to devote himself to the Lord and to get a child only for that purpose, not to get many children like cats or dogs that served no purpose.
One is not affected by material miseries if one is Kṛṣṇa conscious.	3.22.32, 36–37	Svāyambhuva Manu created an environment of Kṛṣṇa consciousness so that the miseries of material life could not enter. Because of his devotion to the Lord, he transcended the three modes of material nature (goodness, passion, and ignorance) and was not affected by miseries. Therefore, for a devotee, there is no difference between heaven and hell because in any condition he can remember and serve the Lord. By taking complete shelter of the Lord's lotus feet, he is not disturbed by any miseries due to the mind, body, or natural disturbances.
Vedic principles are designed in such a way that one can be guided to fulfill material desires and at the same time be liberated and go back to Godhead.	3.22.33–35	Manu enjoyed material happiness in a Kṛṣṇa conscious atmosphere and therefore was not dragged to lower stages of life. Similarly, if we can create a Kṛṣṇa conscious atmosphere as depicted in the scriptures by chanting the holy names and worshiping the Deity, then in spite of our material enjoyment, we can make spiritual advancement and gradually give up material attachments and desires.

Understanding the Story

Now it's time for you to check how well you understood the story by answering these multiple-choice questions. There can be more than one answer for each question. (Answers can be found at the end of the chapter.)

1. Who were created from Lord Brahmā's face?
   a) *Śūdras*
   b) *Brāhmaṇas*
   c) *Kṣatriyas*
2. What are the qualities of *brāhmaṇas*?
   a) They are austere, averse to sense gratification, and possess knowledge and mystic power.
   b) They possess mystic power and are addicted to sense gratification.
   c) They are austere, rigid in following rules, and are good speakers.
3. How was the *kṣatriya* order created?
   a) From the thousands of arms of the Supreme Being
   b) From the hairs of the Supreme Being
   c) From the mouth of the Supreme Being
4. From whom did Devahūti learn about Kardama Muni?
   a) Dhruva Mahārāja
   b) Svāyambhuva Manu
   c) Nārada Muni
5. What were the qualities of Devahūti?
   a) Extremely beautiful, humble, and chaste
   b) Extremely beautiful, chaste, but proud of her father's kingdom
   c) Extremely beautiful, chaste, and attached to her family

6. What was Kardama Muni's one condition to marry Devahūti?
   a) He would leave home and take up full-time devotional service to Lord Viṣṇu after he had children with Devahūti.
   b) He would dedicate his entire life in serving her and his family.
   c) He would be given a place in the royal family.

7. What was special about Svāyambhuva Manu's kingdom, Barhiṣmatī?
   a) All the trees in this city produced gems and gold instead of fruits and flowers.
   b) Lord Varāha dropped his hair in this city after defeating the great demon Hiraṇyākṣa.
   c) This was a flying city created by Kardama Muni's mystic powers.
8. What was the lifespan of Svāyambhuva Manu?
   a) One million years
   b) Hundred million years
   c) A *manvantara* era (4,320,000 x 71 years)

Higher-Thinking Questions

Now try to deepen your understanding of this chapter by delving into Śrīla Prabhupāda's purports and reflecting on the following questions:

1. King Svāyambhuva Manu explains in verses 1 to 3 how the *brāhmaṇa* class was created from the face of the Lord's universal form and the *kṣatriya* class from His arms. What is the purpose of both classes and how do they protect each other?
2. What is Svāyambhuva Manu referring to when he says that one who rejects an offering [marriage] and then begs a boon from a miser loses his reputation and is thus humbled by neglect from others? Why was it important that Kardama accepted Devahūti as his wife? What were some good reasons to accept her? Refer to verses 9 and 13 purports.
3. What are the considerations for marrying a woman according to Vedic standards? Refer to verse 15 purport.
4. List the different classes of Vedic marriages from verse 16 purport. What marriages are now forbidden in Kali-yuga and why?
5. Describe the two types of sons born of good fathers and give examples in your own life or from *śāstra* for each type. Refer to verse 19 and purport.
6. Explain the condition Kardama Muni laid before Svāyambhuva Manu before he agreed to marry his daughter. Why was this so important to him? See verse 19 purport.
7. It is said that Devahūti only heard about the sage from Nārada Muni and from that moment was fixed upon whom she was to marry (See verse 10 purport). What lessons can you extract from Devahūti's exemplary behavior?
8. Why was Svāyambhuva "relieved of his responsibility" and yet felt feelings of separation for his daughter in verses 34 to 35 and purports? Then explain why a woman is never independent and how she is always protected in the Vedic culture.
9. Why do you think Svāyambhuva Manu could enjoy all the riches and material enjoyment that his kingdom and family offered and still be transcendental to the three modes of nature? See verses 33 to 34 purports.

ACTIVITIES

In this section you will find many exciting things to do. These activities will get you thinking, moving, drawing, and having loads of fun.

Analogy Activity . . . to bring out the scholar in you!

STALE AND TASTELESS FOOD

"As freshly prepared food is very tasteful but if kept for three or four hours becomes stale and tasteless, so the existence of material enjoyment can endure as long as life is fresh, but at the fag end of life everything becomes tasteless, and everything appears to be vain and painful. The life of Emperor Svāyambhuva Manu, however, was not tasteless; as he grew older, his life remained as fresh as in the beginning because of his continued Kṛṣṇa consciousness. (*SB*. 3.22.35, purport)

In this purport Śrīla Prabhupāda explains how our sense of enjoyment changes as we age. When we are young, we like to enjoy ourselves in many ways, but as we grow older, the same things do not feel as much fun anymore. They begin to feel stale and boring, and therefore older people who do not cultivate finer tastes may become morose in their old age.

Śrīla Prabhupāda also says that this is not true for devotional activities. For one who is serving Kṛṣṇa, the activities of devotional service feel joyful at all stages of life, even in old age.

Exercise 1:

1. Read the analogy carefully. What is compared to food in the analogy and why?
2. Why do you think that devotional activities do not get stale or tasteless?

Exercise 2: Survey

You can practically test the conclusion of this analogy through the survey in the Resources section at the end of this chapter (see Resource 1).

Choose two groups of devotees: one group of three to four devotees between 15 to 18 years old and another group of three or four devotees over sixty years old. Photocopy and give them the following survey to fill out (they can answer anonymously if they choose):

With the help of your *Bhāgavatam* class teacher, evaluate the two groups of surveys. What do you find? Record your observations and conclusions. *(See if you came up with the same conclusion in the answer section of this chapter.)* Share experiences or examples with your teacher or class to reinforce the conclusion.

Artistic Activity
. . . to reveal your creativity!

HORSE AND CHARIOT

In this activity you will make a chariot and horse to remind you of Svāyambhuva Manu's flying chariot.

What you will need: Template (under Resources at the end of this chapter), glue, card, scissors, two toothpicks, cellotape, eight beads with a hole to fit tightly through the toothpick, string or ribbon.

As you follow the directions below, please look at the picture of the completed chariot to get a clearer idea of what to do.

Directions:

1. Print the template at the end of this chapter (see Resource 2), glue it onto some card, and cut out.
2. Follow directions on the template to glue the foldable tabs.
3. With cellotape fasten your two toothpicks underneath the base of the chariot as your axle.
4. Put a bead on the end of each stick, then screw on the wheel, and then glue a bead on the end, making sure the wet glue does not touch the wheel or it won't turn.
5. Now poke two holes in the front of your chariot and thread your string through one hole, then around the horse and back through the other hole on the chariot.
6. Now you have a horse and chariot with moving wheels.

Introspective Activity

. . . to bring out the reflective devotee in you!

QUALITIES THAT QUALIFY

Devahūti is very beautiful, but she also has other qualities that make her qualified to marry Kardama Muni.

- Think of other women in *Śrīmad-Bhāgavatam* who are similarly very qualified and name some of their qualities.
- Which of their qualities do you admire the most?
- Choose one of these that you would like to develop. Can you think of ways you can do that?

Similarly, think about the qualities of Kardama Muni:

- Why does Manu think Kardama Muni would make a suitable husband for his daughter?
- Which of his qualities do you admire the most?
- Choose one of these that you would like to develop. Can you think of ways you can do that?

Critical-Thinking Activity
. . . to bring out the spiritual investigator in you!

THE PROTECTION OF WOMEN

Directions: Śrīla Prabhupāda explains that women should always be protected in the three stages of their life. In the table below list the three stages of a woman's life. Then describe each stage, who is responsible for her at that stage, and how they protect her.

A Woman's Life

Stage 1:	
Stage 2:	
Stage 3:	

KṚṢṆA IN THE CENTER

Directions: Svāyambhuva Manu enjoyed material life in Kṛṣṇa consciousness and therefore was liberated from the material world. How did he do it? List the different activities he performed that centered his life on Kṛṣṇa and briefly describe how this helped his Kṛṣṇa consciousness.

Manu's Activities	How did it help his Kṛṣṇa consciousness?

Writing and Oral Activities

. . . to bring out the writer and speaker in you!

TELEVISION NEWS REPORT: VEDIC CULTURE

In this chapter we get a glimpse of many wonderful aspects of Vedic culture in the past. Here are a few:

- Vedic culture was a culture of respect. Society highly respected the *brāhmaṇas* because of their spiritual advancement. The *brāhmaṇas* also respected the *kṣatriyas* who protected them.
- Marriages were arranged by the elders.
- When matching a boy and girl, the couple had to be similar in nature, family, and culture.
- Women were treated with great care and were always protected.

- The husband did not remain with his family for his entire life but retired to fully dedicate himself to the Lord's service.
- Kings did not forget their relationship with Kṛṣṇa and were not attached to material enjoyment.

Imagine you are a television news reporter who has been sent to Svāyambhuva Manu's kingdom. You've just witnessed the conversation between Manu and Kardama Muni as in this section of the *Bhāgavatam*. Your job is to make a three- to five-minute news report for an audience that does not know about Vedic culture and ways.

Choose one element from the different cultural aspects and exchanges we find in this chapter and make a news report about it for your channel. Make sure you think about the following:

- What aspect you are going to present.
- What information you have about the topic in this chapter.
- What additional details you want to gather from other parts of the *Bhāgavatam* to make your presentation more complete.
- How the aspect you are presenting had an impact on the larger society in Vedic times; for example, how remaining God conscious rather than greedy about possessions helped people become simple, selfless, satisfied, etc.
- What modern society can learn from it.

Now write your script for the news report, first introducing your topic. Remember to include quotes, pictures, video clippings, interviews (you may have others play the part of characters from the chapter), etc. Finally, record your news item and present it to your study group.

ESSAY: QUALITY AND CULTURE VS. WEALTH

Directions: Write an essay about the importance of quality and culture over wealth and material possessions. Refer to purport of verse 13.

Make sure to answer the following questions:

- Why does quality and culture take precedence over wealth and material possessions?
- How would maintaining culture and quality of life benefit Devahūti, the princess of the emperor of the entire universe?
- If Svāyambhuva Manu had given more importance to wealth than quality and culture, how would it have affected Devahūti?
- To conclude, what do you personally think about wealth versus quality? Do you think wealth is more important, or quality? Explain.

Language Activities

. . . to make you understand better!

WHAT IS THEIR DHARMA?

Directions: Match the words in the box below (people in society) with the descriptions of their occupations.

Śūdra	Gṛhastha	Woman	Father
Children	Every living entity	Vānaprastha	Vaiśya
Kṣatriya	Brāhmaṇa	Brahmacārī	King

1. He has the responsibility to find suitable matches for his children. ______________
2. Truthfulness is most important to him. ______________
3. Protects the *brāhmaṇas*. ______________
4. Shyness and chastity are their greatest strengths. ______________
5. Serves the Lord. ______________
6. Reproduces and provides for community. ______________
7. Preaches to society. ______________
8. Builds a spiritual foundation for the rest of his life. ______________
9. Takes care of parents when they grow old. ______________

10. Leads a country to develop God consciousness. ______________________
11. Distributes goods to society. ______________________
12. Serves others. ______________________

FILL IN THE BLANKS: THE SPIRITUAL MASTER

Directions: Choose the correct words from the box to fill in the blanks below.

execution	spiritual master	aural	perfect	
Bhagavad-gītā	service	ability	instruction	capacity
māyā	duty	artist	Śrīla Rūpa Gosvāmī	

1. ______________________ has given directions, in his *Bhakti-rasāmṛta-sindhu,* on how to accept a bona fide spiritual master and how to deal with him.
2. First, the desiring candidate must find a bona fide ______________, and then he must very eagerly receive instructions from him and execute them.
3. Because everyone is under the delusion of __________ and is forgetful of his prime duty, Kṛṣṇa consciousness, a saintly person always desires that everyone become a saintly person.
4. One should receive the transcendental message by______________ reception.
5. ______________ makes it clear that one can attain the highest perfection of spiritual life simply by offering ___________ according to his ___________ , just as Arjuna served Kṛṣṇa by his ability in the military art.
6. Arjuna offered his service fully as a military man, and he became ___________.
7. Similarly, an ___________ can attain perfection simply by performing artistic work under the direction of the spiritual master.
8. One has to receive the message of the spiritual master regarding how to act in one's ______________, for the spiritual master is expert in giving such instructions.
9. This combination, the instructions of the spiritual master and the faithful ___________of the instruction by the disciple, makes the entire process perfect.
10. The faithful execution of the instruction, which he receives from the spiritual master, is the only ___________ of a disciple, and that will bring him perfection.

CROSSWORD

Across:

2. A person who hoards wealth and spends as little money as possible.
4. The power or right to give orders, make decisions, and enforce obedience.
5. A male child or offspring.
7. To refuse something.
9. They are created from the Lord's thousand arms. (Answer spelled phonetically)

Down:

1. An eloquent, skilled public speaker.
3. They are created from Lord Brahmā's face.
6. A person or thing that generates something.
8. Heavenly place where the Lord dropped His hair after killing the demon Hiraṇyākṣa.
10. A gentle feeling of fondness or liking.

RESOURCES

Resource 1: Survey

Leisure Activities Versus Devotional Activities
Questionnaire

1. What leisure activities do you enjoy in your free time?

   ....

2. What devotional activities do you enjoy?

   ....

3. Do you still enjoy the leisure activities you used to as a child or when you were younger? What do you still like and what don't you like anymore?

   ....

   ....

4. What devotional activities do you still enjoy since you were younger?

   ....

5. Do you think your relationship with Kṛṣṇa has deepened as you continue with the same devotional service?

   ....

RESOURCES

Resource 2: Template – Horse and Chariot

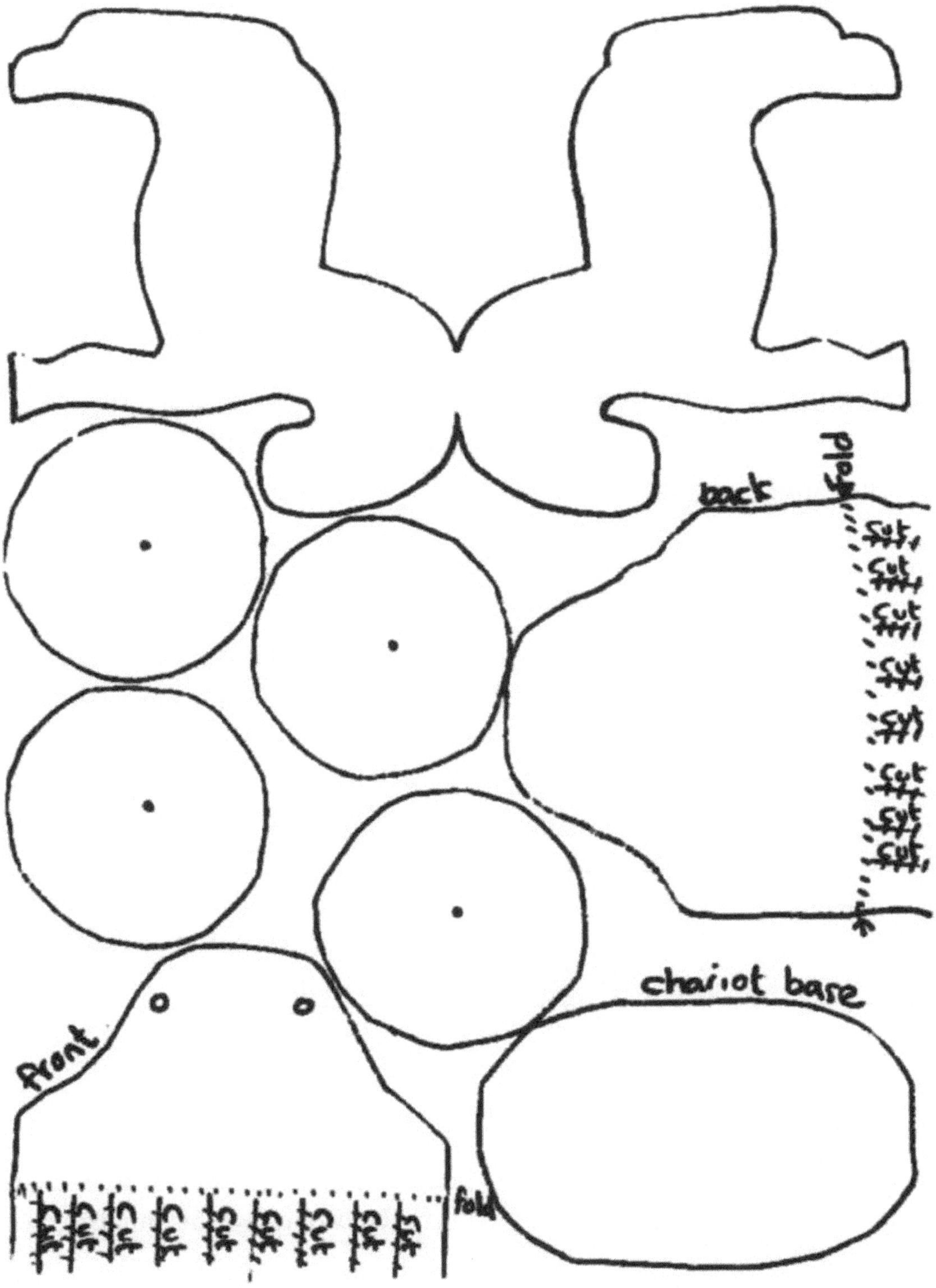

ANSWERS

Understanding the Story: 1) b, 2) a, 3) a, 4) c, 5) a, 6) a, 7) b, 8) c

Stale and Tasteless Food

Exercise 1:

1. Material enjoyment is compared to food. Just as food goes stale after a while, material enjoyment does not last.
2. Devotional activities are spiritual and give everlasting satisfaction and happiness. The more one performs devotional service, the more "fresh" and relishable it is.

Exercise 2 – Survey: The results of the survey would likely indicate that younger and older devotees have different interests or leisure activities, while they have at least some similar devotional interests. The results may also indicate that although devotees may change their leisure activities when they grow older, they enjoy devotional activities at all ages; devotional service feels ever fresh to them. Thus, we can conclude that activities of sense enjoyment go stale after a while, while devotional activities are always enjoyable.

The Protection of Women

Stage 1: Childhood to marriage	The father is responsible. He provides a home and all her necessities and finds her a suitable husband.
Stage 2: Marriage till retirement	The husband is responsible. He provides her with children and all necessities, such as good house, clothing, etc.
Stage 3: Retirement till death	The sons (or daughters) of the mother are responsible. They provide shelter, all necessities in her old age, and help her in her spiritual life.

Kṛṣṇa in the Center

Manu's Activities	How did it help his Kṛṣṇa consciousness?
Chanted and meditated on Lord Viṣṇu.	This helped to keep his mind always on the Lord.

Manu's Activities	How did it help his Kṛṣṇa consciousness?
Only talked about the Lord and His pastimes.	This helped to purify his speech, spend his time wisely, and keep his mind always on the Lord.
Wrote down the Lord's glories and pastimes.	This helped him reflect on the Lord and his realizations of the Lord.
Woke up to the musical glories of the Lord.	This helped start the day with thoughts and sounds of the Lord.
Fell asleep listening to the glories of the Lord; held *Bhāgavatam* class and *kīrtana* before bed.	This helped to end the day with Kṛṣṇa in the mind and heart.
Engaged in temple worship and programs, such as *mangala-ārati* and morning *kīrtana*.	This helped him and his family maintain Kṛṣṇa consciousness, which enriched his spiritual and material environment; it also helped him set an example for the citizens of the importance of temple worship and devotional service.
Had children in a Kṛṣṇa conscious environment.	This helped him carry out his duty as a Prajāpati, helped to purify his desires, and helped his children learn the goal of life.

What Is their Dharma

1. Father; 2. *Brāhmaṇa*; 3. *Kṣatriya*; 4. Woman; 5. Every living entity; 6. *Gṛhastha*; 7. Vānaprastha; 8. Brahmacārī; 9. Children; 10. King; 11. *Vaiśya*; 12. *Śūdra*.

Fill in the Blanks: The Spiritual Master

1. Śrīla Rūpa Gosvāmī; 2. spiritual master; 3. *māyā*; 4. aural; 5. *Bhagavad-gītā*; service; ability; 6. perfect; 7. artist; 8. capacity; 9. instruction; execution; 10. duty

Crossword

Across: 2. miser; 4. authority; 5. daughter; 7. deny; 9. *kshatriyas*

Down: 1. orator; 3. *brāhmaṇas*; 6. generator; 8. Barhiṣmatī; 10. affection

23
Devahūti's Lamentation

STORY SUMMARY

Devahūti was in her new home, in a simple village hut, with her newly wedded husband. Gone were her days of being a princess. Instead of the songs of professional royal musicians, she heard the rippling waters of the river Sarasvatī. Instead of the hustle of the palace attendants and ministers, she heard the rustling of the leaves from the forest trees, and instead of the familiar voices of her friends and family, she simply heard the chirping of the birds. Nothing else.

She had left the comforts of royalty to get married to a sage. But he was no ordinary sage. He was Sage Kardama, renowned for his magnanimity, austerity, *yogīc* power, humility, and extraordinary devotion to the Lord. He was the one she had sought, the one whom, after hearing his glories from Nārada Muni, she had resolved to marry. And now here she was. Wife of the illustrious Kardama Muni. Gratitude instantly radiated through every cell of her body.

Bringing her palms together, she spoke to her husband for the very first time: "My dear lord, how may I serve you?"

From this day on, Devahūti's resolved to live a life of service to her husband. She served him with great love, intimacy, and respect. She always spoke sweet words and worked diligently to please her husband. Never did she consider herself – so selfless was her service.

After many years of austerity and devoted service, Devahūti grew weak and emaciated. Kardama Muni was pleased with his wife's constant loving service, but he noticed she was withering away. He was overwhelmed by love and compassion for his wife.

"You've neglected your own body for me," Kardama finally said.

Devahūti smiled bashfully.

"I'm overwhelmed and pleased with your excellent service," continued the sage. "You have neglected your own body to use on my behalf. O respectful daughter of Svāyambhuva Manu, the Lord has blessed me in my many years of austerity, meditation, and Kṛṣṇa consciousness. Although you haven't experienced these achievements, I shall offer them to you because of your service to me. Mark my words when I say that there's nothing more precious in this world than the Lord's grace.

"My dear Devahūti, what is the use of enjoyments other than the Lord's grace? All material achievements are temporary. Because of your devotion to your husband, you will now enjoy transcendental gifts."

Devahūti was satisfied hearing the words of her wise husband. She smiled shyly and replied, "I know that you have achieved perfection and are the master of mystic power because you are protected by *yogamāyā*, the Lord's divine nature. But when we got married you promised…you promised you would give me children."

She looked up at him now. "I'm ready."

The sage smiled.

Devahūti stepped back, ashamed of her haggard appearance. She said, "Being a master of the mystics, oh lord, please revive my emaciated body and conjure a house for us."

The sage nodded and turned to face a clearing. Closing his eyes and silently muttering a *mantra*, he slowly brought his hands together. A small spark popped out of nowhere and hovered midair. It grew bigger and bigger, expanding into a structure which took the form of a bejeweled mansion – with wings! It was massive. Domes of sapphire crowned with gold pinnacles stood out above the diamond walls, which were set with rubies, making it appear as eyes. The golden entrance gates swung open to reveal grand doors bedecked with diamonds. The palace had seven stories with emerald floors and coral daises.

Devahūti tiptoed into the gigantic, opulent mansion. She saw flags, festoons, tapestries, and artistic work everywhere; wreaths of flowers decorated with the sweet humming of bees; and real and artificial swans and pigeons singing their songs throughout the palace.

Even the sage was astonished to see all this.

Devahūti couldn't even remember living like a princess. For so long she had lived a

life of austerity alongside her husband – her clothes were muddied and hair matted. She wasn't beautiful enough to occupy such an extravagant home.

Kardama, who had also been peering into the wonderful palace, sensed his wife's anxiety.

"You seem afraid," he said, smiling at her. "First bathe in the sacred Bindu-sarovara Lake and then mount this aerial mansion. This lake fulfills all desires."

Devahūti obeyed her husband and walked to the lake. She saw her reflection in the clear waters. Her body was coated with a thick layer of dirt, and her breasts were discolored. Not bearing to see herself any longer, she closed her eyes and dove into the lake, which contained the sacred waters of the Sarasvatī.

Underwater, she smelt fresh lotuses. Opening her eyes, she smelled a house and a thousand young damsels, as fragrant as lotuses, who rose to greet her with folded

hands.

"We are your maidservants," they said. "Tell us what we can do for you."

"I'm… I'm…" Devahūti didn't know what to say.

The young girls knew immediately what she desired. Giggling, they took her into the house where they bathed her with valuable oils and ointments, dressed her with fine, spotless cloth, and decorated her. They fed her the most nutritious foods and drink. When she was well and ready, they placed a mirror before her. Looking into the mirror, she didn't recognize her own reflection. Her body glowed, freed from all dirt. She wore costly robes, a beautiful garland and necklaces, bangles, tinkling anklets, and a jeweled golden girdle around her hips.

Devahūti smiled and was surprised to see beautiful teeth. Looking closer at her face, she saw how charming her eyebrows now were and how her dark curling tresses of hair

framed her face – no longer matted.

She was excited to show her husband.

Just at the thought of her husband, Devahūti and the maids were immediately transported to the sage. Raising his eyebrows approvingly, Kardama took her hand and they all boarded the mansion.

At his will, the mansion flew up into the air and traveled to the pleasure valleys of Mount Meru and other gardens where they spent many years enjoying themselves, coasting throughout different planets as they desired. Although served by a thousand Gandharva girls and seemingly attached to his wife, Kardama Muni did not lose his glory. He was self-controlled. Coursing through the air in that great and splendid aerial mansion, he surpassed even the demigods who were not free to move anywhere without restriction.

What cannot be achieved easily for someone who has taken shelter at the Lord's lotus feet?

After showing his wife the universe and its wonders, the great sage Kardama with his wife returned to his hermitage. He divided himself into nine personalities to give pleasure to Devahūti. In this way they continued to enjoy each other's company for many years – so much so that Devahūti didn't realize how much time was passing. A hundred autumns passed like a brief span of time.

Before long, the sage gave her nine charming and fragrant baby girls whom she gave birth to on that very day. It was time for Kardama to leave home according to the condition set at their marriage.

Devahūti smiled externally, but her heart was agitated and distressed. Scratching the ground with her toe, her head bent down, she fought back her tears as she spoke.

"You've fulfilled all your promises," she admitted, "but I'm scared. Please make me fearless. My daughters will get married and leave me one day. Who will instruct me and give me solace when you leave home as a *sannyāsī*?

"We wasted so much of our time enjoying ourselves, neglecting to cultivate knowledge of the Supreme Lord. Not knowing your divine position, I have loved you. Let this love for you rid me of all fear. Association for sense gratification binds us to this material world, but association with a saintly person, even without knowledge, can liberate a person.

"Anyone whose work does not elevate him to religious life, anyone whose religious activities do not make him renounced, and even if one is renounced but does not perform loving devotional service to the Supreme Lord, must be considered dead, even though he is breathing.

"I have been cheated by *māyā*, because although I obtained your association, I did not seek liberation."

Themes and Key Messages

Please go through this table of themes and key messages, with corresponding verses, and discuss each topic further.

Theme	Reference	Key Messages
If a girl gets a good devotee husband, her life becomes successful.	3.23.1–2	In Vedic times girls were taught to select a husband not based on riches or material opulence for sense gratification but based on whether he was a devotee of the Lord. If her husband is a Vaiṣṇava, she shares the results of his devotional service because of her service to him. She also serves her husband with intimacy and sweet words. This reciprocation of love and service is ideal householder life.
The greatest achievement of human life is to achieve the grace of the Lord, love of God.	3.23.7–8	Caitanya Mahāprabhu said, "*premā pumartho mahān*": to achieve love of Godhead is the highest perfection of life. This grace of the Lord was achieved by Devahūti when she satisfied her husband, who was a great devotee. He willingly gave her the Lord's grace, love of God, which can destroy all fear and the disease of hankering and lamenting.
Children born of good parents are expansions of the parents' good qualities.	3.23.10–11	Kardama Muni and Devahūti possessed all good qualities and were spiritually enlightened; therefore their children would be glorious. Devahūti wanted to have a son of the same qualities as her highly qualified husband, and by her devotion to her husband, her desire was fulfilled. Lord Kapiladeva, the Supreme Lord Himself, would be born from her.
Nothing is difficult to achieve when determined devotees take shelter of the Supreme Personality of Godhead.	3.23.41–44	For Kardama Muni nothing was impossible. He could travel in an aerial mansion to places and planets in the universe that not even the demigods could enter. He could do the impossible not because he was a great mystic *yogī*, but because he was a great devotee of the Lord. He was therefore more glorious than a *yogī*. However, even though a perfect *yogī* can travel throughout space, he cannot be compared to the Supreme Lord. A *yogī*, like Kardama Muni, can only expand himself up to nine times whereas the Lord can expand Himself unlimitedly.
The duty of the superior is to give fearlessness to the subordinate.	3.23.51–52	The responsibility of the husband is to give his wife fearlessness, which is freedom from the fearful situations in material life. He can only do this by giving her Kṛṣṇa consciousness, which will free her from repeated birth and death. Similarly, a father, mother, or spiritual master must be able to free their dependents from the miseries of life, the cycle of birth and death. Even when a husband leaves home and renounces everything at the end of his life, he entrusts his wife to his children, who take care of her needs and help her further in spiritual life.
Even if a person unknowingly associates with the Lord or a saintly person, he can be liberated.	3.23.54–55	Lord Kṛṣṇa had many enemies, but they were all liberated because of their association with Him. Just as if someone goes toward fire knowingly or unknowingly, he becomes warm, similarly, if one associates with a saintly person, he gets immense benefit, just as Devahūti received from serving and associating with her saintly husband. Therefore, Sri Caitanya Mahāprabhu emphasized that the association of great saintly persons is most important to advance in spiritual life.

Higher-Thinking Questions

Now try to deepen your understanding of this chapter by delving into Śrīla Prabhupāda's purports and reflecting on the following questions:

1. How does a wife in Vedic marriage behave toward and think of her husband as described in verses 4 to 8 purports, and what then does she achieve? Explain.
2. In verse 8 Kardama Muni explains that one should not simply try to enjoy the material world but receive the Lord's grace. What is the Lord's grace, and why do you think it is superior?
3. If you had the opportunity to enjoy material life like Devahūti and Kardama Muni, traveling the universe, would you take the time to enjoy or would you simply engage in loving service of the Lord? Honestly explain your reason.
4. Why didn't Kardama Muni lose his glory by being attracted to his wife, Devahūti? (Hint: see verses 38 and 42 and purports)
5. Śrīla Prabhupāda explains in his purport to verse 39 that even though Kardama Muni enjoyed with his wife for many, many years in the area of Mount Meru, where many demigods enjoy sensual pleasures, he was praised by great devotees? Why is this so?
6. We learn from verse 43 that even from the time of Kardama Muni, people were aware that the planets were round with different features and opulences. These features were experienced by Kardama Muni and Devahūti in their travels. Why does Śrīla Prabhupāda describe Kardama as a perfect *yogī*? Is it just a matter of doing *yoga* postures and meditation? Explain.
7. What do you think Devahūti is indirectly asking her husband Kardama Muni when she asked, "Who will give me solace after your departure as a *sannyāsī*?"
8. How can a husband or spiritual master liquidate his debt to his dependents? Why is he indebted to them in the first place? See verse 52 purport.
9. What other great sages can you think of that had the *yogic* power to travel around different universes? Name two. See verse 43 purport.
10. Princess Devahūti, who was the daughter of King Svāyambhuva Manu, was so dedicated to the service of her husband that she completely neglected her physical body, wearing only rags and matted hair. Did this diminish her fame in any way as the King's daughter? Do you think the King would be ashamed if he saw her like this? Explain. Refer to verses 4–5 and purports.
11. Verse 56 implies that greater than work is religious life, greater than religious life is renunciation, and greater than renunciation is devotional service to the Supreme Lord. Why do you think this is so? Why is a person considered a dead body if he doesn't come to devotional service? See purport.
12. Why does Devahūti think that she has been cheated by the illusory energy? See verse 57 and purport.

ACTIVITIES

In this section you will find many exciting things to do. These activities will get you thinking, moving, drawing, and having loads of fun.

Artistic Activity

. . . to reveal your creativity!

AERIAL MANSION MOBILE

What you will need: Cardboard, paper, pens, paint or other coloring materials, glue, decorations, string

Description:

- Read the story summary and verse descriptions in this chapter and take detailed notes of the description of the aerial mansion that Kardama Muni created.
- Draw your mansion design on paper. Paint or color it in.
- Cut out your mansion and glue it onto cardboard. Then glue jewels, sequins, glitter, or other decorations onto the mansion.
- Secure the cardboard mansion with string so it can hang mid-air.
- Suspend it to the ceiling or wall so it acts like a mobile.

Critical-Thinking Activities
. . . to bring out the spiritual investigator in you!

THE PURPOSE OF ALL ACTIVITIES

"Anyone whose work is not meant to elevate him to religious life, anyone whose religious ritualistic performances do not raise him to renunciation, and anyone situated in renunciation that does not lead him to devotional service to the Supreme Personality of Godhead, must be considered dead, although he is breathing." (*SB* 3.23.56)

Kardama Muni fulfilled his promise to Devahūti and was about to leave to dedicate himself fully to spiritual life, but Devahūti wanted her husband to give her fearlessness first. She felt she had wasted her time by neglecting to cultivate knowledge of the Supreme Lord.

Devahūti lamented her position and realized that she had failed to understand Kardama Muni's advancement in spiritual realization. She recognized that she was attached to her husband for sense gratification, which could not give her liberation from material entanglement.

She understood that we should not work simply for sense pleasures but follow religious principles. But this alone is not enough. We have to associate with saintly persons and become renounced from worldly pleasures and attachments. But this too is not the highest stage. She recognizes that we have to serve the Lord with devotion to achieve success – liberation from material bondage.

Let us meditate on this topic by answering the questions below:

1. Identify the engagements that are common to animals and humans.
2. From this analysis, why do you think activities of people should lead to religious life?
3. What is the result of engaging in religious life?
4. Now make a list of activities performed by nondevotees and devotees.
5. Discuss what are the intentions or motives behind each of their activities.
6. What is the result of activities for sense gratification?
7. What is your understanding of the words "liberation," "material bondage," and "renunciation"?
8. Explain why activities performed for sense gratification cause material bondage.
9. Discuss why religious activities must lead to renunciation.
10. Explain why it is useless if renunciation does not lead to devotional service to the Supreme Lord.

AN IDEAL HUSBAND AND WIFE

This section of the *Bhāgavatam* illustrates nicely the qualities of an ideal husband and wife.

Devahūti has been described as a chaste wife.

- What does being a chaste wife mean? Describe some of a chaste wife's qualities and activities. (See verses 1 to 3)
- The table below lists some women who are famous as chaste women in Vedic history. Find out what chaste qualities or actions they are glorified for and write them in the space on the right.

Pārvatī Devī 	
Gāndhārī 	
Sāvitrī 	
Rukmiṇī 	

Draupadī 	
Sītā 	
Mandodarī 	

- As understood from the table above, we see that chaste women have gone to great lengths and made great sacrifices to please their husbands. What lesson can we learn from this?
- This chapter also describes the activities of Kardama Muni, who behaved like a perfect husband. What is the greatest quality of a husband that Kardama Muni possessed?
- Śrīla Prabhupāda says that it is the duty of a husband to protect his wife. In what ways did Kardama protect Devahūti?

- Kardama Muni gave two of the greatest blessings a husband can give a wife. Read verse 7 and find out what these blessings were. Why were they the greatest blessings?
- What lessons can we learn from Kardama Muni's dealings with Devahūti?

STORY ELEMENTS

Directions: After analyzing the story summary, determine the different story elements below.

1. Who are the characters in this summary?
2. State the different places in which this story takes place.
3. What are the problems?
4. How are the problems solved?

Writing and Language Activities

. . . to make you understand better!

COMPARE AND CONTRAST

Directions: In this activity compare the marriage and personalities of Kardama Muni and Devahūti with Kaśyapa Muni and Diti using the Venn diagrams below.

To compare both couples, think of the following questions:

- What are their similarities? (List these in the overlapping part of the circles.)
- What are their differences? (List these in the outer part of the circles.)
- Who does Kardama Muni/Kaśyapa Muni worship?
- Who was the father of Diti/Devahūti?
- How did Diti/Devahūti respect her husband?
- Who did Diti/Devahūti give birth to?

Kardama Muni **Kaśyapa Muni**

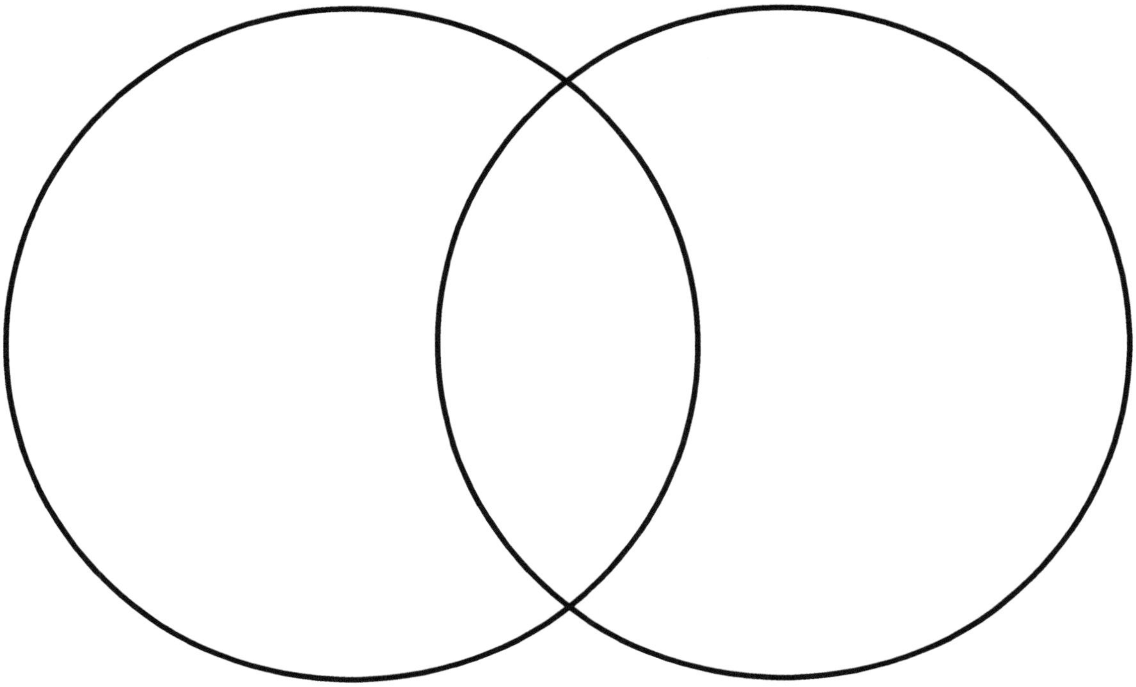

Devahūti **Diti**

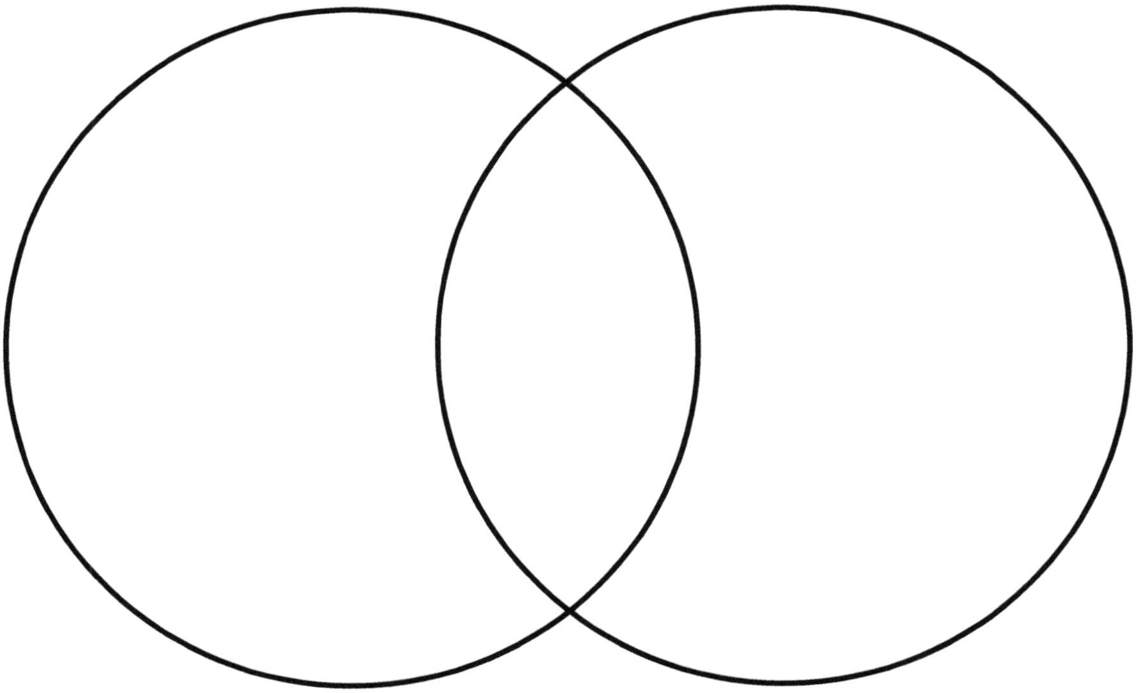

ESSAY

Now, write a short essay about the main differences and similarities between the two couples. How was their *gṛhastha* life successful or unsuccessful? To conclude, write three basic lessons you learned from their stories.

STORY QUIZ

Directions: Use the chapter summary to answer the questions below.

1. After serving her husband so nicely, what did Devahūti expect from him?

   ____

2. What did Devahūti neglect while she was serving her husband?

   ____

3. What did Devahūti give up while serving her husband?

   ____

4. What did Kardama Muni feel when he noticed how weak Devahūti grew by serving him?

   ____

5. What did Devahūti ask Kardama Muni for?

   ____

6. How many children did Devahūti bear at this point?

   ____

7. What did Kardama produce with his mystic powers?

   ____

8. What were the floors of their mansion made from?

   ____

9. How many stories high was the mansion?

   ____

10. Why was Devahūti displeased when she saw this grand mansion?

    ____

11. What lake did Devahūti dive into?

    ____

12. What did Devahūti do for her husband to suddenly appear before her?

    ____

ANSWERS

The Purpose of all Activities

1. The engagements that humans and animals have in common are eating, sleeping, mating, and defending.
2. If humans don't engage in religious life and simply remain busy with eating, sleeping, mating, and defending, they are no different from animals.
3. One gets pious credits and becomes regulated in sensual pleasures. Following the Vedic injunctions gradually elevates one to the next stages of advancement, to renunciation, then to devotional service.
5. Nondevotees perform activities simply to enjoy their senses while devotees perform activities to give pleasure to Kṛṣṇa's senses.
6. Sense gratification performed without regard for Vedic injunctions results in further entanglement in the material world. One becomes absorbed in lust and greed and is never satisfied. The result is rebirth in the material world.
7. "Liberation" means to become free from material bondage – to become free from repeated birth and death in the material world. There are various kinds of liberation but regaining one's spiritual identity in the spiritual world as a servant of God is the highest. "Material bondage" means to be attached to this world and to be trapped in the cycle of birth and death. One is also attached to seeking material pleasures and therefore cannot be liberated. "Renunciation" means to be detached from material pleasures and family ties and free from the desire to enjoy the material world. Simply giving up one's possessions while still remaining attached and attracted to sense pleasures is not true renunciation.
8. When one only enjoys the senses, one becomes a slave to the senses. He becomes so attached to working for material gain and sensual pleasures that he is not interested in the spiritual purpose of life. Therefore, he continues in the cycle of birth and death to satisfy his material desires. He becomes bound to the material world.
9. If a person performs religious activities just to fulfill his material desires, he is also bound to the material world. If he performs religious activities according to the Vedic injunctions to advance in spiritual life, he gradually renounces material enjoyment. Without renunciation of material pleasures and desires, he has to come back to the material world to fulfill them.
10. If one is renounced but does not perform devotional service to the Lord, it is useless because simply being renounced does not satisfy the soul. Only when we connect with the Lord in love and devotion are we completely satisfied and happy. Thus Devahūti describes someone who is renounced but not engaged in devotional service to be dead. The true purpose of life is not fulfilled.

An Ideal Husband and Wife

- A chaste wife means one who is pure and loyal to her husband.
- Devahūti's qualities: She served her husband with great love; she understood the desires of her husband; she served her husband with intimacy, respect, control of the senses, and sweet words; she worked diligently to please her husband, giving up lust, pride, envy, greed, sinful activities, and vanity.

Table:

Pārvatī:	She remained loyal to her husband in spite of her father's criticism; she even sacrificed herself when her husband was insulted.
Gāndhārī:	She blindfolded herself when she married the blind king, Dhṛtarāṣṭra.
Sāvitrī:	She brought her husband back from Yamarāja's kingdom by her devotion and loyalty.
Rukmiṇī:	She was completely dedicated to Lord Kṛṣṇa's service and was so attached to Him that at her request, Kṛṣṇa kidnapped her from her wedding.
Draupadī:	She remained loyal to her husbands through all their trials and hardships.
Sītā:	She followed her husband Rāma to the forest and served him faithfully.
Mandodarī:	She was faithful to Rāvaṇa and always gave him good counsel.

We learn from these examples that a chaste woman has many good qualities that make her loyal; we also learn that a woman may need to sacrifice or go out of her comfort zone to create a happy family (such an act, however, when done with love, does not feel like a great sacrifice; in Vedic times women willingly and happily took it up).

Kardama Muni:

- He was a pure devotee of the Lord.
- He protected devahūti by treating her affectionately, giving her blessings in return for her service, understanding her mind, providing her with whatever she desired, giving her children.
- His two blessings: freedom from fear, freedom from lamentation.
- By these blessings he shared his spiritual achievements with devahūti, and she became realized simply by her service to him.
- We learn the qualities of an ideal husband and devotee of the lord.

Story Elements

1. Maitreya and Vidura; Kardama Muni and Devahūti; maidservants
2. Kardama Muni's hermitage; Bindu-sarovara Lake; the aerial mansion; the pleasure groves

of Mount Meru; celestial planets such as Vaiśrambhaka and Mānasa-sarovara Lake.

3. First problem: Devahūti becomes very weak and emaciated from selflessly serving her husband. She has an unfulfilled desire to have children.
   Second problem: Kardama Muni is leaving home after giving her children; Devahūti does not have a son who will protect her and give her transcendental knowledge once her husband leaves.
4. Kardama Muni solves the first problem by giving Devahūti material comforts and children to satisfy her desires. The second problem will be solved in the next chapter when Kardama gives Devahūti the Supreme Lord Kapiladeva as her son.

Compare and Contrast

Similarities between Kardama Muni and Kaśyapa:

- *Brāhmaṇas*
- Austere
- Devoted
- Married (*gṛhasthas*)
- Gave children to their wives
- Satisfied their wives
- Children were powerful historical personalities

Differences:

Kardama Muni

- Was devoted strictly to Lord Viṣṇu
- Had only one wife, Devahūti
- Completely self-controlled
- Gave his wife the Supreme Lord, Kapiladeva, as her son

Kaśyapa Muni

- Was devoted to Lord Viṣṇu but also worshiped Lord Śiva
- Had 13 wives, the daughters of Dakṣa
- Was obligated to his wife Diti to fulfill her sexual desires
- Gave his wife Diti two great demon sons, Hiraṇyākṣa and Hiraṇyakaśipu, and an exalted grandchild, Prahlāda Mahārāja

Similarities between Devahūti and Diti:

- Princesses/daughters of a great King/Prajāpati
- Very chaste and devoted to their husbands
- Eager to have children
- Devotees
- Married

Differences:

Devahūti

- Daughter of Svāyambhuva Manu (a greater king than Dakṣa)
- Never disobeyed or was impatient with her husband
- Received the Supreme Lord as her son
- Received transcendental knowledge at the end of her life

Diti

- Daughter of King Dakṣa
- Became impatient with her husband, Kaśyapa Muni
- Bore two demons as a result of her impatience
- Didn't receive transcendental knowledge in a pleasant way
- Received Prahlāda Mahārāja as her grandson

Story Quiz

1. She expected great blessings and/or children; 2. Her body; 3. She gave up lust, pride, greed, sinful activities, and vanity; 4. Compassion; 5. For children; 6. Nine daughters; 7. An aerial mansion; 8. Emerald with coral daises; 9. Seven stories high; 10. She did not feel comfortable entering due to her emaciated appearance; 11. Bindu-sarovara Lake; 12. She simply thought of him.

24

The Renunciation of Kardama Muni

STORY SUMMARY

Chaste, dutiful Devahūti stood before her husband Kardama Muni. She fought back her tears, apprehensive of his imminent departure, regretful that she hadn't made use of his association, and fearful of being alone after her daughters were married.

Kardama Muni observed her and remembered the words of Lord Viṣṇu, who had appeared before him many years ago on the shoulders of Garuḍa.

"I will incarnate as your son and instruct your wife, Devahūti," Lord Viṣṇu had said.

Kardama Muni looked compassionately at his wife and said, "Please don't be disappointed in yourself. You are praiseworthy. Very soon, the Supreme Personality of Godhead will enter your womb as your son. He will remove the knot in your heart that binds you to this material world by giving you spiritual knowledge. You should worship Him with great faith and control your senses. You must follow the rules and regulations of religious principles, perform austerity, and give charity. Thus, you will no longer be fearful in this world."

Hearing this and accepting Kardama Muni as her spiritual master, Devahūti began to worship the Supreme Lord with faith and devotion. For many years she continued to faithfully and respectfully follow the order of her husband – to serve the Supreme Personality of Godhead.

Then the time came. There was no mistaking it. Rain clouds mysteriously played musical instruments. These had to be the demigods. Demigods even flew around showering flowers. The Gandharvas, the celestial musicians, sang the glories of the Lord while the Apsarās danced. An atmosphere of celebration. All the directions, the waters of the world, and everyone's minds were satisfied.

Devahūti looked up at the sky joyfully, radiant with a divine child in her womb. Suddenly, she saw something else in the sky coming toward her. It was someone magnificent seated on a majestic flying swan. She called her husband and they both gazed at the splendid arrival.

"It's my father, Lord Brahmā," explained Kardama Muni. "Can you see? He is accompanied by Marīci and other sages."

Devahūti brought her palms respectfully together.

Brahmā's swan landed gracefully at Devahūti's feet. Lord Brahmā alighted and bowed down to the Lord in Devahūti's womb and then worshiped Him joyfully with a pure heart.

Brahmā then beamed proudly at Kardama Muni and exclaimed, "You have followed my instructions perfectly, my son! You have certainly honored me.

"You have nine beautiful, chaste daughters who will increase this creation by their own descendants. Therefore, I would like you to wed them to the nine principal sages according to their individual temperaments and likings."

"Yes, father," replied Kardama.

"And now, my dear Kardama, the Lord has come as Kapila Muni by His own internal energy. He will have dazzling golden hair, lotus-like eyes, and lotus feet bearing the marks of the lotus flower. He will use mystic *yoga* and knowledge from the scriptures to help uproot people's deep-rooted material desires."

Kardama nodded.

Brahmā then turned to Devahūti and smiled. "The Supreme Personality of Godhead is now in your womb," he explained. "He will cut all your ignorance and doubts, and thereafter He will travel all over the world. He will be the head of all perfected souls, expert in giving real knowledge, and He will increase your fame."

Devahūti beamed, trying hard not to blink lest a tear should fall.

"Thank you," she whispered.

Lord Brahmā then boarded his swan

carrier and flew back to his planet, Brahmaloka, along with the four Kumāras and Nārada Muni.

As instructed by his father, Kardama handed his nine daughters to the nine progenitor sages: Kalā to Sage Marīci; Anasūyā to Sage Atri; Śraddhā to Sage Aṅgirā; Havirbhū to Sage Pulastya; Gati to Sage Pulaha; Kriyā to Sage Kratu; Khyāti to Sage Bhṛgu; Arundhatī to Sage Vasiṣṭha; and Śānti to Sage Atharva.

After marriage, the sages and their wives happily left for their own hermitages.

One day, after Lord Kapila was born, Kardama Muni approached Him in a secluded place and offered obeisances to his son.

"You have finally come," said Kardama. "After ages and ages, the demigods are pleased with the suffering souls in the material world because their suffering has caused You to descend. *Yogīs* try birth after birth to see You, but You have appeared in the home of ordinary householders. You have come to fulfill Your word and give us true knowledge.

"My dear Lord, You have no material form but innumerable transcendental forms, which are pleasing to Your devotees. You are full in all six opulences. You are the richest of the rich; You are the most detached – no one is more renounced than You; You are the

most famous; You have the most knowledge – no one knows more than You; You are the strongest of the strong; and the most beautiful – nobody's beauty exceeds Yours."

Kardama gazed in loving appreciation at the Supreme Lord. "I surrender to You, Lord Kapila," he said. Tears welled in his eyes as he brought his palms together. "You are the Lord of this material world. You maintain all the universes and absorb them back into You when the material world dissolves."

Kardama Muni sighed and closed his eyes, preparing to reveal to his son what was on his mind.

"I am now liberated from any debts to my father. All my desires have been fulfilled…"

Kardama opened his eyes and looked into his son's beautiful lotus-like eyes and swallowed hard. Kardama had been a strict follower of the scriptures. According to the Vedic injunctions, he had been an exceptional celibate monk, then an exemplary householder with children, and now, the Vedas were advising to renounce householder life and become a mendicant. Even though the Supreme Personality of Godhead had appeared as his son, he felt duty-bound to follow the instructions of the Vedas.

"Do I have your permission to leave household life and live as a mendicant,

thinking of You always in my heart?" Kardama finally said.

Lord Kapila smiled. "Whatever I say – whether directly or in the scriptures – is instructive to all people of the world."

Kardama Muni nodded. The Lord was confirming that following the instructions of the scriptures were the same as listening to Him directly.

"I've come as promised," continued the Lord. "I've come to explain the Sāṅkhya philosophy to those who want to be free from material desires. This difficult path of self-realization has been lost, so I've come to introduce and explain it again.

"Now, with My permission, go as you desire and surrender all your activities to Me. Worship Me throughout your life. In this way, you will see Me in your heart and within the hearts of all living entities. Thus, you will be liberated and be free from lamentation and fear.

"I shall also describe this divine knowledge to My mother, so she can also attain perfection and self-realization and become fearless."

Maitreya Ṛṣi continued to relate the story to Vidura, who was intrigued by the Lord's kindness and mercy. Maitreya described how Kardama at once left for the forest, accepted a vow of silence, and took complete shelter of the Lord. He traveled the world as a *sannyāsī* and fixed his mind upon the Supreme Lord.

Kardama eventually became unaffected by the false ego and free from material affection. His mind was turned inward and calm like an ocean undisturbed by waves. He began to see that the Supreme Personality of Godhead is seated in everyone's heart and that everyone is existing on Him. Becoming free from hatred and material desire, Kardama Muni performed pure devotional service and went back to Godhead.

Themes and Key Messages

Please go through this table of themes and key messages, with corresponding verses, and discuss each topic further.

Theme	Reference	Key Messages
The Lord comes to the material world to give spiritual knowledge that will cut the knot in people's hearts.	3.24.4, 5, 18	The Lord descends to cut the knot in the heart – this knot is of material attachments and the hankering for material possessions, society, friendship, and love. The Lord or His pure representative, such as Kardama Muni or the bona fide spiritual master, can cut the knot to pieces through spiritual instruction. This knowledge should be received with great faith just as Devahūti did.
The Supreme Lord becomes the son of devotees because of their loving devotion.	3.24.4, 5, 29	To please His devotees, the Lord appears as their child. The Lord agrees to appear in a householder's home where devotees engage in devotional service even though they do not practice other types of *yoga*. *Bhakti-yoga*, devotional service, is so easy that even householders can see the Supreme Personality of Godhead as their son. Devotional service therefore surpasses all other methods of spiritual realization.
The Lord appeared as Kapiladeva to explain the Sāṅkhya philosophy.	3.24.10, 16, 17, 30, 36–38	Lord Kapiladeva is an expansion of Kṛṣṇa and an incarnation of His internal energy. He appeared to explicitly explain the Sāṅkhya philosophy to his mother for the benefit of all people. Sāṅkhya is the analytical study of the Lord's material and spiritual energies. Its purpose is to establish devotional service, which can liberate the conditioned souls from the miseries of birth and death. Since the Sāṅkhya philosophy had been lost, the Lord appeared to reintroduce it. He delivered *jñāna*, knowledge received through disciplic succession free from the four human defects, and *vijñāna*, practical application of knowledge.
The instructions of the spiritual master should be carried out without hesitation.	3.24.12, 13, 15	Lord Brahmā praised Kardama Muni for following his instructions completely without duplicity. By following Brahmā's instructions, Kardama Muni had shown him proper respect and honor. As a result, Kardama Muni got the Lord as his son.
The Lord has no material form, but according to the different preferences of His devotees, He exists in multiforms.	3.24.31–33	According to the liking of different devotees, the Lord simultaneously exists in innumerable forms, like Rāma, Nṛṣimha, Varāha, Nārāyaṇa, etc. They are all *Viṣṇu-tattva*, in the category of Kṛṣṇa, and possess all six opulences in full: renunciation, fame, knowledge, wealth, strength, and beauty.
Exclusive devotional service can free anyone from fear and lamentation and is the real purpose of *sannyāsa*.	3.24.39–44	The Vedas encourage that after household life, the husband should renounce family life and all material attachments and exclusively take shelter of the Lord. Therefore, Kardama Muni wanted to follow the Vedic injunction and travel the world, engaging in devotional service and thinking of the Lord within his heart. Similarly, the Lord explained that devotional service would help Devahūti get rid of all fear and lamentation. In this way, both Kardama Muni and Devahūti would attain spiritual perfection and go back to Godhead.

Understanding the Story

Now it's time for you to check how well you understood the story by answering these multiple-choice questions.

1. What did Kardama Muni tell Devahūti to console her when she lamented about her lack of advancement in spiritual life?
   a) In her next life she will take birth in a family of advanced devotees.
   b) The Supreme Lord would shortly enter her womb as her son.
   c) She will soon return to the heavenly planets where she will advance steadily in her spiritual life.
2. What did Kardama Muni advise Devahūti to do after his departure?
   a) To return to her father's palace and stay under the care of Svāyambhuva Manu.
   b) To continue to live in the great mansion he had built with his mystic powers.
   c) To continue her worship of the Supreme Lord with great faith and sense control, give in charity, and observe religion and austerity.
3. What did Kardama Muni foretell would happen in Devahūti's life after her son, the Supreme Lord, was born?

a) She would worship her son, and He would teach her the knowledge of Brahman that would vanquish the knot of attachment in her heart.
b) She would continue with her life as normal, taking care of her son.
c) Out of fear she would leave her body and return to Godhead.

4. What was the name of the incarnation of the Supreme Lord who appeared in the womb of Devahūti?
   a) Lord Kapiladeva
   b) Lord Ṛṣabhadeva
   c) Lord Brahmā
5. What was Lord Brahmā's advice to Kardama Muni?
   a) To remain at his hermitage and serve Lord Kapila until He finished speaking His teachings.
   b) To leave his hermitage so that Devahūti could listen to Lord Kapila's teachings without any distractions.
   c) To marry his nine chaste daughters to the great sages so they can increase the creation in various ways.
6. What did Kardama Muni ask of the Lord?
   a) He asked to remain with his wife and continue with a life of sense enjoyment.
   b) He sought permission from the Lord to become a *sannyāsī* and wander about free from lamentation, always thinking of the Supreme Lord in his heart.
   c) He asked that his wife be protected.
7. What was Lord Kapila's response?
   a) He gave permission to Kardama Muni to take *sannyāsa* and gave the benediction that he will realize the Supersoul in his heart.
   b) He was upset that Kardama Muni was making demands of Him, instead of simply worshiping Him.
   c) He told Kardama Muni to stay at home and protect his wife.
8. What was the purpose of Lord Kapila's appearance?
   a) To reestablish Sāṅkhya philosophy, the science of self-realization, which was lost over the course of time.
   b) To please His loving devotees by becoming their son.
   c) Both of the above.

Higher-Thinking Questions

Now try to deepen your understanding of this chapter by delving into Śrīla Prabhupāda's purports and reflecting on the following questions:

1. Verse 3 and purport mention certain activities that would please the Lord and attract His mercy. What are those activities and why do you think they are important?
2. Kardama Muni states that the Lord would vanquish the knot in Devahūti's heart. What is this "knot" that Kardama Muni refers to in verse 4. Read the purport for further details.
3. Verse 6 describes how Lord Kapila "appeared in Devahūti just as fire comes from wood in sacrifice." How does Śrīla Prabhupāda explain this analogy in the purport?
   Think of other examples that brings out the same point, such as energy comes from coal, or ghee/fat comes from milk, etc.
4. What is the difference between the two Sāṅkhya philosophies and the different Kapilas mentioned in verses 10, 17, and 19 purports? Which process is bona fide?
5. What is the difference between the living entity and God who comes in many (human) forms mentioned in verse 16 purport?

6. As Lord Brahmā glorified the Lord, he told Devahūti that by receiving the Lord as her son, her fame would increase. Do you think fame in this respect is good? When do you think fame gets in the way of genuine devotional service?
7. Kardama Muni was granted the fortune of having the Supreme Personality of Godhead as his son. Why then do you think he took *sannyāsa* (the renounced order of life) in spite of having the Lord as his son? Refer to verse 35 purport.
8. In verse 35 Lord Kapila tells his father Kardama Muni, "Whatever I speak, whether directly or in the scriptures, is authoritative in all respects for the people of the world." In other words, His instructions in the Vedas and His personal instructions are equally important. How do we know that Kardama Muni understood this well? Give some examples of receiving direct instruction and scriptural instruction from the Lord.
9. Verse 15 purport explains that before a couple is matched, their character and taste should be considered. Why do you think it is important that they are compatible with each other?
10. How does Śrīla Prabhupāda explain verse 46, which says that "everyone is existing on Him [the Lord]"? Explain the misconception he mentions and compare this to the true meaning.

ACTIVITIES

In this section you will find many exciting things to do. These activities will get you thinking, moving, drawing, and having loads of fun.

Action Activity . . . to get you moving!

THE FOUR HUMAN DEFECTS

In the purports to verses 12 and 17 Śrīla Prabhupāda explains that knowledge should be received from the spiritual master through *paramparā*, or disciplic succession, so that the knowledge remains intact without anything being changed or distorted. He describes four human defects that could alter the knowledge that we receive: we have imperfect senses, we are sure to commit mistakes, to be illusioned, and to cheat others.

Now let us practically try to understand some of these defects and how they can influence an outcome.

Exercise 1: "Broken Telephone"
With a group of friends, play a game called "Broken Telephone."

Sit in a line with your friends; then the first person can whisper a message into the ear of the person sitting next to him. (It is better if this message is a bit long and complicated.) This person will whisper the message to the person next to him or her, until it reaches the last person. The last person will reveal the message. Often, if the original message was long and complicated, the message may come out differently at the end. Which human defect/s does this relate to?

Exercise 2: Optical Illusions

Now, look carefully at the optical illusions below:

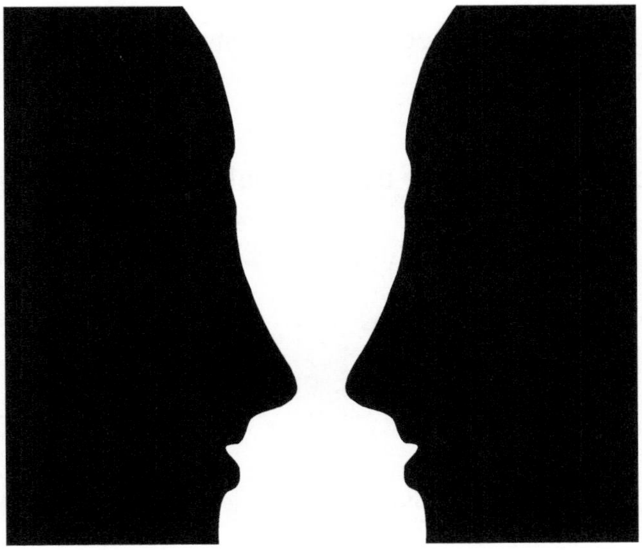

Do you see two heads, or a vase, or both?

Do you see a young woman, or an old woman, or both?

What does this tell you about what we can see? Do you think these illusions can influence the way we perceive things and relate them to others?

Can you see how these human defects can influence the message of God that was given many thousands of years ago?

Now explain how each of these four defects could change the original message of the Lord in the scriptures.

....

....

....

....

....

....

....

....

....

....

However, the pure devotee who perceives God directly, is not prone to these human defects, but passes the message of God intact to another pure devotee, who then passes it to another, until it reaches us without being changed in any way. Thus, the *paramparā* system of receiving knowledge from spiritual master to disciple is most reliable.

Analogy Activity . . . to bring out the scholar in you!

THE ORDER OF THE SPIRITUAL MASTER

"As a man cannot separate his life from his body, a disciple cannot separate the order of the spiritual master from his life." (*SB* 3.24.13, purport)

This analogy illustrates the importance of following the order of the spiritual master. Just as Kardama Muni was successful by following the instructions of Lord Brahmā perfectly, any disciple can achieve success in spiritual life by making the instructions of the spiritual master one with his life.

In the space below, write down what you understand from the analogy.

____

____

____

Śrīla Prabhupāda showed by his perfect example how one should follow the order of the spiritual master strictly. In 1922 and later again in 1936, he received an order from Śrīla Bhaktisiddhānta Sarasvatī to preach in English in the Western countries. Śrīla Prabhupāda dedicated himself to this instruction and spent his entire life trying to execute it.

Read Śrīla Prabhupāda's biography and answer the following:
- The order Śrīla Prabhupāda received from his spiritual master.
- What he did to execute it.

From the information you gathered, make a small skit to present how Śrīla Prabhupāda received the order and how he executed it, and then present it to your study group.

Introspective Activities
. . . to bring out the reflective devotee in you!

THE SECRET OF SUCCESS

"Lord Brahmā said: My dear son Kardama, since you have completely accepted my instructions without duplicity, showing them proper respect, you have worshiped me properly. Whatever instructions you took from me you have carried out, and thereby you have honored me." (*SB* 3.24.12)

Just as Kardama followed Lord Brahmā's instructions perfectly, Devahūti faithfully followed the instructions of her husband, and after many years the Lord appeared as her son.

Let us meditate on this topic:

- What do you understand by the word "instruction"?
- What do you think is the purpose of an instruction?
- How should we discriminate between instructions we must obey and those we must reject?
- Make a list of daily instructions you receive from different sources.
- Why is it important to obey instructions of elders? What is the result of executing the instructions?
- Discuss the consequences of not following the instructions.
- Can you think of ways to train yourself to follow good instructions without rejecting them?
- How would you deal with a junior who does not follow your instruction?
- According to the scriptures, what is the highest instruction? Explain why.
- Discuss why the secret of success in spiritual life depends on following instructions of the spiritual master.

THE PROCESS FOR PLEASING THE LORD

In this chapter Kardama Muni instructed his wife, Devahūti, to take up the process of faith in the Lord, sensory control, religious observations, austerities and gifts of her money or charity to the Lord, to please the Lord.

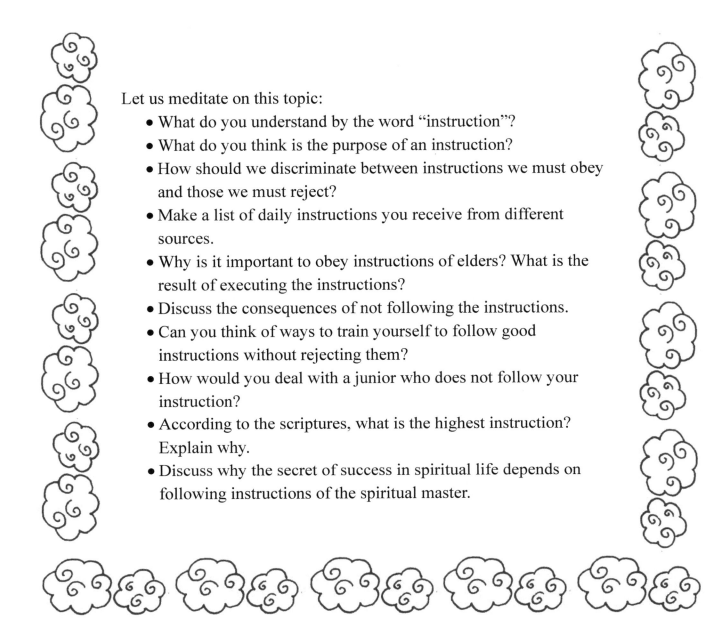

What do these processes consist of? In the box below, think of ways you can practice 1) faith in the Lord, 2) sensory control, 3) religious observations, 4) austerities, and 5) giving gifts of charity. List at least three examples for each process.

Process	Examples
Faith in the Lord	
Sensory Control	
Religious Observations	
Austerities	
Gifts of Money or Charity	

Critical-Thinking Activities
. . . to bring out the spiritual investigator in you!

REAL RENUNCIATION

This chapter describes how Kardama Muni gave up family ties to focus completely on Kṛṣṇa consciousness. Does this mean that we also should give up family, home, and everything that is dear to absorb ourselves in the Lord?

Renunciation does not always mean to leave everything and go away. Śrīla Rūpa Gosvāmī taught us the real idea of renunciation, and Śrīla Prabhupāda showed how to renounce things by his example. Let us focus on the word "renunciation" and understand it more deeply.

Below are some words and phrases that relate to Śrīla Prabhupāda's teachings about renunciation. Guess how each is related to renunciation. Ask your teacher for help where needed.

- Giving up the idea of "mine"
- sannyāsī
- Phalgu-vairāgya
- Use everything in the Lord's service
- Only the Lord should enjoy everything
- Everything belongs to God
- We are part of God
- Yukta-vairāgya
- ātmānandī
- Goṣṭhī ānandī

- Which of the above terms related to renunciation indicate that one need not leave one's home and go to the forest to practice renunciation?

- What do you understand about real renunciation from this?

- Which terms relate to giving up everything and dedicating oneself completely to the service of the Lord?

- Who do you think would do this? How can everyone else follow in their footsteps?

JÑĀNA VERSUS VIJÑĀNA

In verse 17 Śrīla Prabhupāda describes *jñāna* as "receiving knowledge from the scriptures through the spiritual master by disciplic succession" and *vijñāna* as "practical application of such knowledge."

Directions: Read the following sentences and state whether they are examples of *jñāna* or *vijñāna*.

1. Sukṛti Dāsī reads the Nectar of Devotion written by Śrīla Rūpa Gosvāmī.
2. Bhakta Joe listens to senior Vaiṣṇava Gaura Prema Dāsa who teaches him the art of book distribution.
3. After hearing how Kṛṣṇa has a form within the heart, Hari Gaura Dāsa begins to meditate on Nārāyaṇa, the form of God within his heart.
4. Bhakta Joe goes out on book distribution and starts to preach Kṛṣṇa Consciousness.
5. After hearing about how significant proper pronunciation is while chanting the holy name, Bhaktin Lisa sits and listens to her pronunciation.
6. Saṅkīrtana Dāsī takes a course in *Bhagavad-gītā* led by her spiritual master.

7. Draviḍa Prabhu reads the *Caitanya-caritāmṛta*.
8. Bhaktin Sammy hears how every living entity is part and parcel of Kṛṣṇa in *Śrīmad-Bhāgavatam* class one day and begins to treat others, regardless of their designation, with respect and reverence.
9. You transcribe a lecture because your spiritual master asks you to.

Now, try to come up with three examples each of *jñāna* and *vijñāna*.

KṚṢṆA IS ALWAYS KṚṢṆA

In the purport to verse 6, Śrīla Prabhupāda explains that although the Lord appears in different ways in the material world, from different sources or from His devotees, this does not mean that they are the source of His appearance. The Lord is always the Lord and is independent to appear in any way He wishes.

In this activity let us see if this is true. In the table below, list how, where, or from whom Kṛṣṇa appeared in each incarnation. Then give a percentage of Kṛṣṇa's original potency (0–100%) in that incarnation in the right column.

Incarnation of the Lord	Appearance from?	What percentage of Kṛṣṇa is He?
Lord Varāha		
Lord Nṛsiṁha		
Lord Kapila		
Lord Vāmana		
Lord Kṛṣṇa		
Lord Matsya		
Lord Rāma		
Lord Caitanya		

1. After completing this activity, what can you conclude about Kṛṣṇa's potency in different incarnations?

2. Now think of some extraordinary features of each incarnation, e.g., Lord Rāma performed superhuman feats in his youth; Lord Nṛsiṁha appeared as a half-man half-lion form; Lord Vāmana covered the universe with one step, etc. What does this tell you about the Lord? Is His birth ordinary? Explain.
3. Why do you think in different incarnations Kṛṣṇa chooses to be born from certain parents?

THREE PAIRS OF KṚṢṆA'S OPULENCES

Śrīla Prabhupāda describes in verse 26 purport that Kṛṣṇa is called *tri-yuga,* which means that he comes in only three *yugas* – Satya, Tretā, and Dvāpara. In Kali-yuga, Kṛṣṇa comes in the garb of a devotee, Lord Caitanya. Kṛṣṇa is also called *tri-yuga* because he has three pairs of divine attributes.

Below, name the three pairs of divine attributes. (Hint: Use Kṛṣṇa's six opulences and put them into pairs: *beauty, knowledge, strength, renunciation, fame, wealth.*)

Pair 1:

Pair 2:

Pair 3:

Explain how Kṛṣṇa's opulences are unlike anything in this material world.

Writing Activities . . . to bring out the writer in you!

ESSAY: CHARITY

In this chapter Devahūti was instructed to worship the Lord by performing charity – by giving money and gifts. Write an essay about your understanding of charity based on the questions below. Refer to *Bhagavad-gītā* 17.20–25 and other *śāstric* references.

- What is charity?
- When do you give charity?
- In what *āśrama* is charity a regular duty?
- Who gives charity?
- Are there different types of charity?

Now, think about the different ways you could give charity by writing a list for yourself:

Then, execute! Try to practice charity once a week for a month. Make sure you do this with the assistance and permission of your parents! After these four weeks, write a short essay on how it made you feel:

- How did you perform charity?
- To whom did you give?
- How did they respond?
- How did it make you feel?
- Will you continue giving charity?

Language Activities

. . . to make you understand better!

FILL IN THE BLANKS: MATTER OF FACT

1. Lord Brahmā is called *svayambhū* because he is______________________________.
2. *Parabrahman* means ________________________.
3. Honoring the spiritual master means to carry out his _______________________ word for word.
4. As devotees, our second mother and father are the _________________(mother) and the___________________________ (father).
5. The Lord is always approached by the __________________ with various complaints before He descends to the earth.
6. Complete practice of *yoga* means ________________ *yoga*.
7. In *Bhagavad-gītā*, Kṛṣṇa says: "One can only understand Me through ____________________________."
8. Lord Kapiladeva descended as Kardama Muni and Devahūti's son, not to annihilate the miscreants or to protect His devotees as much as to _______________ ________________________________.

ANSWERS

Understanding the Story: 1) b, 2) c, 3) a, 4) a, 5) c, 6) b, 7) a, 8) c

The Process for Pleasing the Lord *(Potential Answers)*

Process	Examples
Faith in the Lord	• Hearing the Vedic literature submissively. • Chanting the holy names in a humble state of mind. • Performing devotional service with love and conviction. • Serving the Vaiṣṇavas. • Taking on challenging devotional activities that you know only Kṛṣṇa can make possible. • Listening to spiritual authority by inquiring and seeking spiritual master's instructions.
Sensory Control	• Following the four regulative principles of freedom. • Learning to control the mind by thinking of Kṛṣṇa (reading, taking *prasādam*). • Chanting 16 rounds daily. • Cooking *prasādam*.
Religious Observations	• Coming to temple programs. • Attending *Bhagavad-gītā* classes. • Observing Ekādaśī and the appearance days of the *ācāryas*. • Chanting Hare Kṛṣṇa. • Having an altar in the home and worshiping the Deities.
Austerities	• Chanting 16 rounds daily. • Observing Ekādaśī and other special day fasts. • Getting up early in the morning at 4–5am.

Process	Examples
Gifts of Money or Charity	• Donating things to the temple or devotees. • Donating money to the temple. • Sponsoring feasts or specific items for events. • Sponsoring cows to protect them. • Providing personal needs of devotees fully dedicated to Kṛṣṇa. • Sponsoring specific temple/devotional projects.

Real Renunciation *(Potential Answers)*

- Giving up the idea of "mine"; *yukta-vairāgya*; using everything in the service of the Lord; we are part of God; everything belongs to the Lord; God should enjoy everything. These terms indicate that real renunciation is to use everything in the Lord's service, understanding everything to be His.
- Real renunciation does not mean giving up everything and going to the forest or solitary place; it means that we should use whatever we have in the Lord's service and not for our own enjoyment.
- *Sannyāsī* (renunciant); *ātmānandī* (self-satisfied renunciant, usually engaged in solitary *bhajana*); *goṣṭhī ānandī* (renunciant preacher who engages everyone in the Lord's service)
- One who is able to give up material obligations under the guidance of the spiritual master; everyone can follow in their footsteps by dedicating everything they have in the Lord's service.

Jñāna Versus Vijñāna

1. Jñāna; 2. Jñāna; 3. Vijñāna; 4. Vijñāna; 5. Vijñāna; 6. Jñāna; 7. Jñāna; 8. Vijñāna; 9. Jñāna

Kṛṣṇa is Always Kṛṣṇa

Lord Varāha – Lord Brahmā's nostril; Lord Nṛsiṁha – a pillar; Lord Kapila – Devahūti and Kardama Muni; Lord Vāmana – Aditi and Kaśyapa Muni; Lord Kṛṣṇa – Devakī and Vasudeva; Lord Matsya – river; Lord Rāma – Kauśalyā and Daśaratha; Lord Caitanya – Śacīdevī and Jagannātha Miśrā.

All incarnations are 100 percent Kṛṣṇa.

1. His potency does not change from one incarnation to the next. He is always 100 percent Kṛṣṇa!
2. His birth is not ordinary because in various incarnations He exhibited extraordinary activities and superhuman feats that are not possible for ordinary living beings. He appears in a spiritual form, not born from material elements, even though externally it may appear so.
3. He has loving relationships with his parents, who are His pure devotees.

Three Pairs of Kṛṣṇa's Opulence

Pair 1: Beauty and Fame; **Pair 2:** Knowledge and Renunciation; **Pair 3:** Strength and Wealth Kṛṣṇa has all six opulences in full; this means that no one has any of these opulences greater than Him.

Fill in the Blanks

1. self-born;
2. Ultimate Godhead;
3. instructions/order;
4. Vedas; spiritual master;
5. demigods;
6. *bhakti*;
7. devotional service;
8. increase the honor of His devotees.

25
The Glories of Devotional Service

Story Summary

"Can he tell us about Kapila?"

"We want to hear about Kapila…"

"What did Devahūti and Kapila do?"

The murmurs of "Kapila" drifted through the sea of sages at Naimiṣāraṇya.

Śaunaka Ṛṣi, the head of the sages, held up his right hand and silenced them. He was aware of their burning questions, and he would now ask the esteemed Sūta Gosvāmī to answer them. All eyes were on Śaunaka Ṛṣi as he began to speak to Sūta Gosvāmī.

"Dear Sūta," he began, "Lord Kapila came to give divine knowledge to help the human race.

We understand Him to be the Supreme Personality of Godhead, so hearing about Him gives pleasure to the senses. Please tell us about Him and His activities."

Sūta smiled. He was happy and grateful to speak of Lord Kapila. Indeed, Vidura too had asked Maitreya about transcendental knowledge. He would simply repeat Maitreya's answer.

When Kardama Muni left for the forest, Kapila stayed with His mother, Maitreya had explained to Vidura. Now, one day, as Lord Kapila and Devahūti sat on the banks of Bindu-sarovara, Kapila leaned onto a moss-covered rock and gazed at the sun-kissed sky. Smiling, He closed His eyes and rested His head on His arms.

Devahūti watched her son and smiled lovingly.

Instantly, Lord Brahmā's face flashed before her mind as she remembered his words:

"The Supreme Personality of Godhead is now in your womb…He will dispel all your ignorance and doubts…"

She had regretted not taking advantage of her husband's association. She didn't want to make the same mistake again. Here was her son, the Supreme Personality of Godhead, sitting right before her, and this time she was determined to receive real knowledge.

"Oh, my son," Devahūti muttered.

Kapila opened His eyes and sat up, "Yes, mother?"

Remembering the painful reality of this world, she said with tears in her eyes, "I'm sick of being disturbed by my senses. Because of this, I'm in utter ignorance. You're the only one who can remove this ignorance. You are my transcendental eye with which I can see the light of knowledge. Please dispel my false ego, which makes me think I am this body with all these bodily relationships. You are my only shelter – the ax that can cut the tree of material existence."

Her eyes glowed in eagerness. "O my Lord, what is the relationship between man and woman and between spirit and matter?"

Kapila sat upright, His face grave. Within His mind He thanked her for her sincere questions, and then smiled.

"There is a system of *yoga* that talks of the Lord and the individual soul," he began.

It is the highest *yoga*, which benefits all living entities and makes them detached from happiness and distress. Let me explain to you this ancient *yoga* system, which I've previously explained to the great sages and which is practical in every way."

Devahūti nodded.

"What is your consciousness attracted to?" Kapila rhetorically asked. "When it's attracted to the material world, it causes conditional life, a life of happiness and distress, but if it's attracted to the Supreme Personality of Godhead, then it is liberated from such a life. You see, when you think 'I am this' or 'this

is mine,' impure qualities like lust and greed develop in you.

"Once these impurities are cleansed, your mind becomes clean and you no longer get entangled in happiness and distress. The soul can finally see itself for what it is – small, yet self-effulgent and transcendental to material existence.

"In this position of self-realization, of knowing you are the soul and becoming detached from material attractions while performing devotional service, you are able to

see the material world for what it is, and it has less power over you.

"Therefore mother, *bhakti* is the only way for all *yogīs*. They cannot become perfect in self-realization without devotional service to the Supreme Lord."

"In addition, my dear mother, every learned man knows that attachment to the material is the greatest entanglement, but attachment to the Lord's self-realized devotees opens the door to liberation. If you associate with a *sādhu,* he will not give you instructions on how to improve your material condition, but he will give you instructions on how to cut the knot of material attachment and elevate yourself in devotional service."

"How will I know who the self-realized devotees are?" Devahūti asked.

"Well, they have distinct symptoms. They are tolerant, merciful, friendly to all living entities, have no enemies, peaceful, abide by the scriptures, and all their characteristics are sublime. They engage in staunch devotional service, renounce all material connections, and constantly chant and hear about Me. They never suffer material miseries as they are always thinking of My pastimes and activities."

"What do I do if I meet such a *sādhu*?"

"You must discuss the pastimes and activities of the Lord. In this way you will gradually advance on the path of liberation and your attraction will be fixed. Only then will real devotion begin for you.

"And as you continue with your devotional service in the association of devotees, your taste for sense gratification will melt away. In fact, you will experience an utter distaste for material enjoyment. Therefore, this process of Kṛṣṇa consciousness is the easiest process of *yoga*. Through this path of *bhakti-yoga*, anyone can control the mind. By fixing the mind on Me, one can achieve My association in this very life."

"But how?" Devahūti asked. "What devotional service can I do? This *yoga* system that you've explained aims at the Supreme Personality of Godhead that ends material existence. In how many ways can one understand this type of *yoga*? As my spiritual master, I'm sure you'll be able to instruct me. I'm a simple woman and not very intelligent, but I'm sure if you explain, I will understand and become happy."

Kapila was patient and compassionate towards His mother. He began to describe the Sāṅkhya system of philosophy, which is a combination of devotional service and mystic *yoga*.

"The senses are representatives of the demigods, and the mind is the representative of the Supreme Lord. The senses act under the influence of the demigods, who are servants of Kṛṣṇa. Therefore the natural inclination of the senses is to serve the mind, the leader of the senses. The mind's natural duty is to also serve. So when that service spirit is used to serve the Lord, without any motive or want of anything in return, that is better than liberation. In other words, devotional service is higher than liberation from this material world. Actually, a pure devotee is automatically liberated without separate effort.

"Furthermore, pure devotees never want to merge into the Lord. They simply want to glorify and serve Me. My devotees like to see Me and talk to Me. Seeing and hearing Me, they don't think of anything else. In this way their senses are freed from other engagements, and they are liberated even though they don't want liberation.

"Being completely absorbed in Me, My devotee doesn't want anything. He doesn't desire the benedictions of the highest planets in the universe, mystic powers, or even to go back to Godhead. Nevertheless, he gets all of this just by serving Me. And because I am everything to My devotees, they are never bereft of these opulences.

"Thus My devotee gives up all desire to be promoted to the heavenly planets or to become happy in this material world with material possessions and relationships. I take this devotee to the other side of birth and death – to My spiritual abode.

"If you take shelter of Me, you will also be freed from the fear of birth and death. No other shelter will allow you to escape this fear, for I am the Supreme Personality of Godhead, the original source of creation, and the Supreme Soul of all souls.

"The wind blows out of fear of Me
The sun shines out of fear of Me.
Indra showers rains out of fear of Me
Fire burns out of fear of Me and
Death takes its toll out of fear of Me.

"Therefore, fix your mind on Me and engage in intensive devotional service. This is the only way to perfect life."

Themes and Key Messages

Please go through this table of themes and key messages, with corresponding verses, and discuss each topic further.

Theme	Reference	Key Messages
One has to become frustrated with material sense gratification to hear divine knowledge from a pure devotee.	3.25.7	Beyond the temporary material senses are the permanent senses (the spiritual senses of our spiritual body), which are covered by the material body. When we become tired and frustrated of enjoying the material senses, we can properly hear of the Supreme Lord and engage in His devotional service and thus purify our material senses.
The spiritual master delivers the disciple from ignorance with the light of knowledge.	3.25.8–9	We are suffering because of ignorance. The spiritual master removes the darkness of ignorance by instructing the disciple about devotional service. He takes the disciple to the other side – to the spiritual world – by opening his eyes with spiritual knowledge.
The highest *yoga* system is that which relates to the Lord and the individual soul and is meant for our ultimate benefit.	3.25.13–14	Even though Lord Kapila is the Supreme Lord, He did not manufacture a new *yoga* system for his mother; He simply explained the highest *yoga* system already present in the Vedic scriptures. The best *yoga* system, called *bhakti-yoga*, is the science of the spirit, of devotion to God, and is meant to end all material happiness and distress. It is easy to perform and very practical.
We can transcend happiness and distress when our consciousness is fixed on the Supreme Personality of Godhead.	3.25.15–17	When our mind and consciousness become absorbed in Kṛṣṇa, they become purified. In this state we become cleansed of lust and greed and the false ego and are not attracted by the modes of material nature. We realize our true position as a minute spirit soul, which is self-effulgent and transcendental to material existence. Thus, in this purified condition, we become free from anxiety and unaffected by happiness and distress.
Attachment to material things causes bondage whereas attachment to Kṛṣṇa or His pure devotee gives liberation. 	3.25.20–26	Attachment cannot be killed. We will always be attached to someone or something. However, when we are attached to material things or material relations, we are bound to the material world. But when we transfer that attachment to Kṛṣṇa or His pure devotee (*sādhu*), we become liberated from the material world – we end the cycle of birth and death. This is because a *sādhu* instructs us how to elevate ourselves in devotional service, which gives liberation. Such *sādhus* possess divine qualities, and by associating with them, we develop a distaste for material sense gratification and we are able to control the mind.
Pure devotees are always attracted to the personal form of the Lord, which is the highest form and awards liberation.	3.25.33–40	Devotees do not aspire for any kind of liberation, especially to become one with the Lord. They find greater pleasure in serving the Lord personally. They do not want to go to the heavenly planets or even to the kingdom of God, but they automatically get all these benedictions. By performing *bhakti-yoga*, devotional service, they are naturally liberated from the cycle of birth and death without separate effort.

Higher-Thinking Questions

This chapter is important because it describes devotional service in detail. Therefore, there are extra questions in this section to deepen your understanding. Please delve into Śrīla Prabhupāda's purports and reflect on the following:

1. By constant association with the Lord, devotees become as good as the Lord Himself (See verse 2 purport). Can you give some examples from the scriptures of devotees becoming as good as the Lord Himself?
2. Explain why Devahūti was "very sick of the disturbances caused by the material senses" in verse 6. What was her solution? Can you remember any time when you felt disturbed because of some material desire? How did you deal with it?
3. What does it mean to be "captured by *māyā*"? When does the Supreme Lord free one from the entanglement of *māyā*? (Read verse 10 purport) Can you identify times when you were in *māyā*?
4. Why do you think Devahūti was inquiring about the relationship between spirit and matter? Do you think these topics are important to know in your life? Why?
5. What is the purpose of Sāṅkhya philosophy mentioned in verse 11 purport? How is it any different from *bhakti-yoga* as we practice it in our lives?
6. In verse 14 Lord Kapila explained "the ancient *yoga* system, which [He] explained formerly to the great sages." Do you think anyone could practice this system today? Explain.
7. If you were a *yogī*, what transcendental path would you take? Do you find the devotional (*bhakti*) path easy or difficult? Give some examples. How is the *bhakti* path less difficult than other spiritual paths, such as *aṣṭāṅga* or mystic *yoga*?
8. What are some of your material attachments? If you wanted to stop or get rid of these attachments, is it possible? Why or why not? How could you transfer or purify these material desires or attachments? (See verse 20 purport)
9. What are some symptoms of a *sādhu* mentioned in verse 21? Elaborate on two of these symptoms as described in the purport. In which verse of the *Bhagavad-gītā* are these symptoms also mentioned? Which symptoms would you want to have first?
10. Lord Kapila explains that each sense represents a demigod and it is naturally inclined to work under the direction of Vedic injunctions. According to verse 32, what is the mind's natural duty? Do you feel that sometimes it is hard to control the mind? What is the best way to control the mind?

11. In verse 29 purport Śrīla Prabhupāda mentions the nine processes of devotional service. To revise, note the nine processes of devotional service. Which one is your favorite?
12. Describe why devotional service is better than liberation (See verse 32 purport).
13. Why do pure devotees avoid becoming "one with the Lord"? (See verse 34 purport) Would you prefer to merge into the Lord's effulgence or play with Him? What is it that you like about serving Kṛṣṇa personally? Now think if Kṛṣṇa did not have a form, how would you feel?
14. Why doesn't a devotee desire any of the opulences offered by *māyā* even though he can easily achieve them? (See verse 37 purport) Why does the devotee get these opulences anyway? What is the real opulence that Kṛṣṇa has given you for which you are grateful?
15. Verse 27 states that we can attain the Lord's direct association even in this life. How is this possible? How is devotional service superior to humanitarian or philanthropic work (charity) as described in the purport.
16. Who did Śrīla Prabhupāda use as an example whose mind was constantly fixed on the Lord and who engaged in intensive devotional service? See verse 44 purport. Can you think of another example from the scriptures?
17. Are you afraid of God? Why or why not? Do you think people should be afraid of Him?
18. Verse 33 compares *bhakti* to the fire in the stomach that digests all we eat. Explain this analogy (See purport). How does it relate to a devotee who does not have to try separately to attain liberation? How is *bhakti* more glorious than liberation?

ACTIVITIES

In this section you will find many exciting things to do. These activities will get you thinking, moving, drawing, and having loads of fun.

Analogy Activity . . . to bring out the scholar in you!

THE MATERIAL TREE AND THE AX

> "Devahūti continued: I have taken shelter of Your lotus feet because You are the only person of whom to take shelter. You are the ax which can cut the tree of material existence. I therefore offer my obeisances unto You, who are the greatest of all transcendentalists, and I inquire from You as to the relationship between man and woman and between spirit and matter". (*SB* 3.25.11)

Here, Devahūti refers to material existence as a tree and refers to the Lord as an ax that can cut the tree of material attachments. Similarly, in *Bhagavad-gītā* Lord Kṛṣṇa asks Arjuna to cut the tree of material existence with the weapon of detachment.

This material world, or material existence, is compared to a tree with its roots upwards, which is a reflection of the real tree, the spiritual world. Kapiladeva explains to his mother that she should cut the material tree by purifying her mind and consciousness.

Below is a thematic representation of the tree, along with an ax. The ax represents activities that purify our mind and consciousness, which cuts material attachments and desires, and allows us to go closer to Kṛṣṇa.

The tree (as an upside-down reflection) represents our material attachments, desires, and undesirable qualities. Around the tree, write down some of these qualities that the mind needs to become purified of (refer to the chapter).

On the ax, write down the methods to purify these qualities. Then, cut out both the inverted tree and the ax and stick each on pieces of stiff cardboard. In this way make a model of the tree, hanging it upside down from an elevated platform. Use your ax to cut down the tree and purify the mind.

Artistic Activities

. . . to reveal your creativity!

KAPILADEVA'S TEACHINGS

Draw pictures to illustrate Lord Kapiladeva's instructions below:

- Attachment for material life is the greatest entanglement, but attachment to the *sādhus* opens the door to liberation.
- Seek attachment for such holy men – hear, chant, perform devotional service, and associate with them; then you will lose the taste for sense gratification.
- The mind's natural position is to serve; when we serve the Lord in devotion, it is better than liberation (*mukti*) or salvation (*siddhi*) because we get the personal association of the Lord.
- Devotional service automatically gives liberation from material existence without separate endeavor. Devotees never desire to become one with the Lord but glorify the personal form of the Lord and His transcendental pastimes. Thus, absorbed in devotional service, they become free from material activities and attain the final perfection of life – pure love for Kṛṣṇa.

THE KNOT IN THE HEART

The purpose of this activity is to learn two important points of this chapter:

1. Spiritual knowledge cuts the knot of material existence within the heart.
2. Just as fire in the stomach digests everything we eat, performance of devotional service automatically gives liberation even though a devotee does not desire or strive for it.

What you will need: Paper, pens, glue, string, collage material/paper, any other materials of red, orange, or yellow.

Description: (Refer to illustrations below)

- Draw two silhouettes of a body.
- In the head of the first body draw things in material life that one may be attached to. Draw a heart in the body and make a knot from string and stick it to the heart.
- In the head of the second body draw *sādhus* and various services to Kṛṣṇa.
- Look up a picture of the organs in the body; draw the stomach.
- In the stomach draw a flame, add glue on the flame shape, and stick your colored material/paper/color sting onto it, starting in the center with red, then orange and yellow. Around the outside of your flame write false ego.

As you can see from your drawings, the knot of material attachments in the heart gets cut when we receive transcendental knowledge of Kṛṣṇa and devotional service. Such knowledge, which is like a flame, purifies the mind, senses, and false ego, the false identification with the material body. In this purified state, one automatically becomes liberated just as the stomach digests everything we eat.

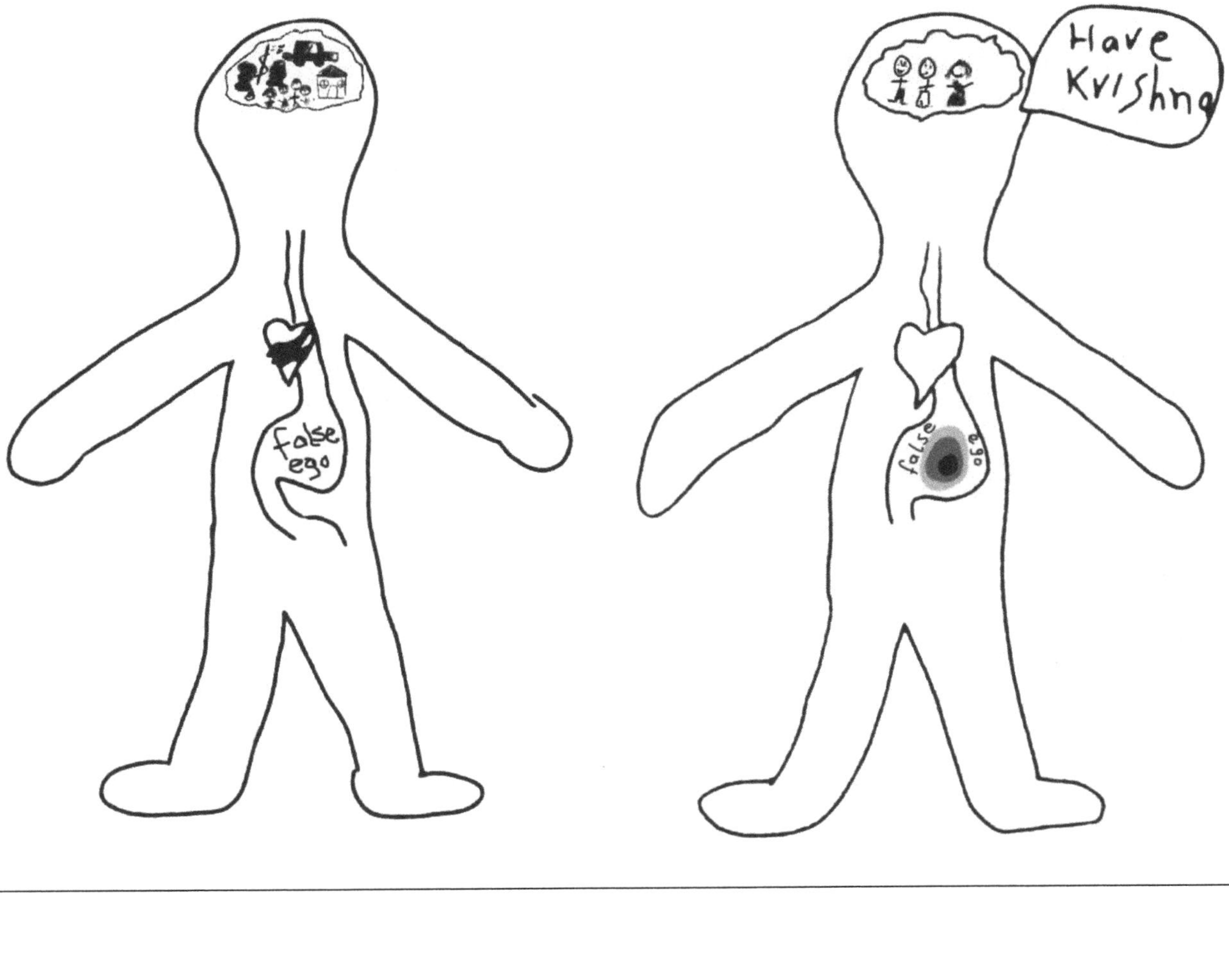

Introspective Activities

. . . to bring out the reflective devotee in you!

TRANSCENDENTAL KNOWLEDGE PURIFIES FALSE EGO

"Now be pleased, my Lord, to dispel my great delusion. Due to my feeling of false ego, I have been engaged by Your *māyā* and have identified myself with the body and consequent bodily relations." (*SB* 3.25.10)

Devahūti tells Lord Kapila that she is sick of the disturbance caused by her material senses. Because of the false ego, of thinking that she is the body, she has become attached to the body and everything related to it. She pleads to Kapiladeva to remove her ignorance by giving her transcendental knowledge.

Let us meditate on this topic:

- What is the meaning of "transcendental knowledge"?
- Discuss how and from where/whom you can get transcendental knowledge.
- What is meant by "ignorance" as mentioned by Devahūti?
- What is your understanding of "*māyā*" and "false ego"?
- How can transcendental knowledge purify the false ego?
- What is the great delusion that Devahūti is talking about?
- Who puts one into delusion? Discuss how you can overcome such delusion in your life.
- Make a list of some material desires of common people.
- What is the root cause of these material desires?
- What is your practical plan to reduce material desires and increase your spiritual desires?

FIVE IMPORTANT PROCESSES OF DEVOTIONAL SERVICE

In verse 36 purport, Śrīla Prabhupāda describes the five important processes of devotional service recommended by Sri Caitanya Mahāprabhu:

1. Chanting the holy names of the Lord
2. Associating with and rendering service to devotees
3. Hearing *Śrīmad-Bhāgavatam*
4. Worshiping the Deity, seeing the decorated temple and the Deity
5. Living in a place like Vṛndāvana, Mathurā, or Māyāpur (a holy place)

Directions: Contemplate these five auspicious activities and share how they are related to your life by answering the following questions:

Chanting the holy names of the Lord

Do you chant the *mahā-mantra* every day?

____

How many rounds do you chant?

____

Where do you chant?

____

Do you sit or walk while chanting?

____

Do you chant with others or by yourself?

____

Observe your chanting. Are you hearing each name with attention?

____

How do you plan to improve your chanting?

____

Associating with and rendering service to devotees

Do you associate with devotees every day? Which devotees?

____

Do you serve these devotees? How and where?

____

What is your favorite service to devotees?

____

Hearing *Śrīmad-Bhāgavatam*

How often do you hear or read *Śrīmad-Bhāgavatam*?

____

If you don't read every day, is there a way you could? How?

____

What do you like about *Bhāgavatam*?

____

Worshiping the Deity, seeing the decorated temple and the Deity

If you are near a temple, what temple do you visit regularly?

____

What are the names of the Deities?

____

What is your favorite part about going to the temple and about the Deities?

____

If you have Deities at home, how do you worship them?

____

Living in a holy place

Do you live in a holy place? If so, which holy place?

____

If not, which holy place do you like to be in?

____

What do you like best about this holy place?

____

How can you make your home a holy place?

____

Critical-Thinking Activities

. . . to bring out the spiritual investigator in you!

PURPOSE OF YOGA

Lord Kapila, the Supreme Personality of Godhead who came to teach Sāṅkhya, begins His instructions in this chapter. In verse 13, He says that He approves the process of *ādhyātmika yoga*, or *yoga* relating to the soul. Clearly, the term "*yoga*" is used by the Lord here, as well as in the *Bhagavad-gītā*, to refer to the science of the relationship between the soul and the body.

In modern times, however, the word "*yoga*" has come to mean other things that have little connection to the real meaning and purpose of *yoga*.

List some of these false meanings of *yoga* you may have come across?

Now, imagine you have been invited to a modern-day *yoga* studio to give a talk about *yoga*. Prepare a small talk about *yoga* for them using Kapiladeva's teachings in this chapter. Use the following chart to make your notes for the talk.

Purpose of the talk: To help listeners understand the real meaning of *yoga* as linking themselves to the Supreme Person.

Start with a 'hook'!

- Who is the audience? What do they think *yoga* is meant for?
- Can you think of something to say about real *yoga* that will interest them?
- How will you transition from your point to the real meaning of *yoga*?

Establish Authenticity

- Why is the system of *yoga* given by Kapiladeva and also by Lord Kṛṣṇa in *Bhagavad-gītā* authentic?
- How will you explain that *yoga* should be practiced only as taught by the Lord without sounding critical of the system your audience follow?

Explain your point

- How and why should real *yoga* be practiced in this age?
- What objections or doubts could your audience have (list them down)? How will you counter them and sound convincing?
- Conclude appropriately.

THREEFOLD MISERIES

Directions: List the threefold miseries of material life below. Then give at least one to three examples of each.

1.
Examples:____

2.
Examples:____

3.
Examples:____

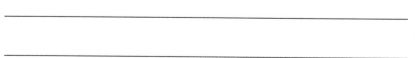

Writing Activities . . . to bring out the writer in you!

ESSAY: WHO'S A SĀDHU?

According to this chapter (3.25.20–23 and purports), a *sādhu* is explained as the following:

- Unflinchingly engaged in devotional service
- A strict follower of devotional service
- A devotee of the Lord
- Preaches Kṛṣṇa consciousness
- Always thinks of others
- Most compassionate toward the fallen souls
- Very tolerant and merciful
- Friendly
- Follows the principles of the scriptures
- Renounced and gives up all material responsibilities for the service of the Lord

Write your own story about a *sādhu*, someone you have read about in the scriptures or someone who has personally inspired you and include at least four of these qualities within your story. Then show how your character possesses these qualities. For instance, you may give examples of how your character *preached Kṛṣṇa consciousness or how they were compassionate towards the fallen souls.*

If your character is from the scriptures, describe who takes shelter of that *sādhu* and why he/she is taking shelter of the *sādhu* (refer to verses 20–23). Then draw a picture of your *sādhu* in pencil or color. As an option, present your story and a poster of your *sādhu* to your peers and family.

Language Activities

. . . to make you understand better!

WHAT DO YOU THINK?

Set 1 – Tick those statements that you think are correct. If false, write the true sentence by providing the correct information.

1. Devahūti said, "O Dear Lord, I am very sick of the disturbances caused by my ego."
2. She said, "Please dispel my great delusion and describe to me the difference between the ego and the soul."
3. After hearing His mother's contaminated desire for transcendental realization, Lord Kapila thanked her from within His heart.
4. Lord Kapila said, "Dear mother, the *yoga* system which relates to the Lord and the individual soul and causes detachment from all happiness and distress, is the *haṭha-yoga* system."
5. Just by engaging in devotional service in the association of devotees and hearing about the Lord, a person loses his/her attraction to sense gratification.
6. Lord Kapila said, "My devotee worships Me with unflinching devotional service and gives up all aspirations to be happy in a world with wealth, family, and children."
7. In order to identify the Lord, one can look for His symptoms, which include

tolerance, mercy, friendliness, adherence to the scriptures, and other sublime characteristics.
8. Lord Kapila knew His mother's bodily weakness and grew compassionate for her.
9. Lord Kapila said, "Because of My supremacy and out of love for Me, the wind blows, the sun shines, fire burns, Lord Indra sends showers, and death takes its toll!"
10. "O mother, the mind's natural duty is to serve."

Set 2 – INFERRING QUESTIONS

Which questions do you agree with and disagree with, using what the author says and what you know? Back up your argument with reasons.

1. As explained in this chapter summary, Lord Kapila says, "Without desiring the eight perfections of *yoga* nor being elevated to the kingdom of God, the devotee enjoys them all!" We can infer from this statement that one must not desire the eight perfections and one's elevation to the kingdom of God. By not desiring these things, one can attain them.
2. When Lord Kapila says, "My devotee worships Me in unflinching devotional service and gives up all aspirations to be happy in a world with wealth, family, and children," we can infer that Śrīla Prabhupāda is not necessarily discouraging devotees to have wealth or have a family, but rather he is discouraging them from putting excessive time and effort into a temporary situation, such as household life and social life, and encouraging them to put more effort in devotional service.

ANSWERS

Purpose of Yoga

False meanings of *yoga*: body poses and fitness, breathing technique, silent meditation, connection of mind-body-soul, inner connection, stress relief

Threefold Miseries

1. *Miseries arising from one's own mind and body*

Examples: Anger, attachment, pain

2. *Miseries inflicted by other living beings*
Examples: Someone physically hurts you or is mean to you; someone is smoking next to you; mosquito bites you.

3. *Miseries arising from natural catastrophes over which one has no control*
Examples: Earthquakes, tornadoes, hurricanes

What do you think?

1. **False:** Devahūti said, "O Dear Lord, I am very sick of the disturbances caused by my **material senses**."
2. **False:** She said, "Please, dispel my great delusion and describe to me the difference between **spirit and matter**."
3. **False:** After hearing His mother's **uncontaminated/pure** desire for transcendental realization, Lord Kapila thanked her from within His heart.
4. **False:** Lord Kapila said, "Dear mother, the *yoga* system which relates to the Lord and the individual soul and causes detachment from all happiness and distress is the highest *yoga* system."
5. **True.**
6. **True.**
7. **False:** In order to identify the ***sādhu (self-realized devotee)***, one can look for **his/her** symptoms, which include tolerance, mercy, friendliness, adherence to the scriptures, and other sublime characteristics.
8. **True.**
9. **False:** Lord Kapila said, "Because of My Supremacy and out of **fear of** Me, the wind blows, the sun shines, fire burns, Lord Indra sends showers, and death takes its toll!"
10. **True.**

Inferring Questions

1. **False.** It is not simply by denying the desire for these types of liberation that one will be given them. A person will give up taste for these desires for liberation only through devotional service and by seeking love of God; as a result, he will attain liberation and everything else.
2. **True.** (Refer to 3.25.39–40)

26
Fundamental Principles of Material Nature

STORY SUMMARY

"Now, mother," continued Kapila, "let me tell you about the different categories of the Lord, the Absolute Truth. This secret is like a sword that cuts the knots of attachment to this world. Any person who knows this secret will no longer be controlled by the modes of goodness, passion, and ignorance, for the sword would have freed you."

Devahūti sat up attentively. This is exactly what she desired. She needed this knowledge. She didn't want to miss a thing.

"The Supreme Personality of Godhead is spiritual," said Kapila. "He isn't bound to the material world, yet you can perceive Him everywhere. You see, this whole material world is maintained by the light that radiates from Him."

Devahūti wondered why we can't then directly see the Lord if the material world is His energy.

Kapila smiled and explained, "The Lord accepted something, which covered His spiritual energy. This made it hard for us to see Him."

"What did He accept?"

"The subtle material energy. Even though He can see through the material energy and can see us as spirit souls, the material energy is like a cloud for us. She masks our view of the Lord, just as a cloud blocks our view from the sun. She covers our knowledge and perception of the Lord but can never cover the Lord. She creates our bodies and senses and makes us forget who we are and who Kṛṣṇa is. She is very good at her job. Not only do we forget but we act under her control like puppets while we foolishly think we are the controllers. This is material consciousness – not Kṛṣṇa consciousness."

"So are we not in control of anything?"

"We are," replied Kapila. "We have the choice to try and enjoy this material world or to serve Kṛṣṇa. When we simply serve the senses, we get a material body, and when we serve Kṛṣṇa, we get a spiritual body. Therefore, we are the cause of our own happiness and distress."

"Oh," replied Devahūti, understanding the dire situation of the conditioned souls. "And what of the Lord's different energies? Does the material world come from them?"

"Yes. At the beginning of creation, the material energy is asleep. She's invisible. Her three modes are peacefully balanced and at rest. At that moment, she is called *pradhāna*. When she wakes up, she becomes visible. At that point, she is called *prakṛti*.

"Now the invisible, sleeping *pradhāna* carries the five gross elements – earth; water; fire; air; and ether – and the five subtle elements – smell; taste; color; touch; and sound.

"The *pradhāna* also consists of the four internal senses – mind; intelligence; false ego; and material consciousness – and the five senses for gathering knowledge – the senses of hearing; taste; touch; sight; and smell. Also present are the five organs of actions – for speaking; working; traveling; generating; and excreting. In total there are 24 elements.

"These 24 elements are mixed with time, which is the 25th element. This element of time is Kṛṣṇa. The Lord is in every element as the Supersoul and outside of every atom as time. As a woman cannot produce children unless impregnated by a man, material nature cannot produce anything unless impregnated by the Supreme Personality of Godhead in the form of the time factor.

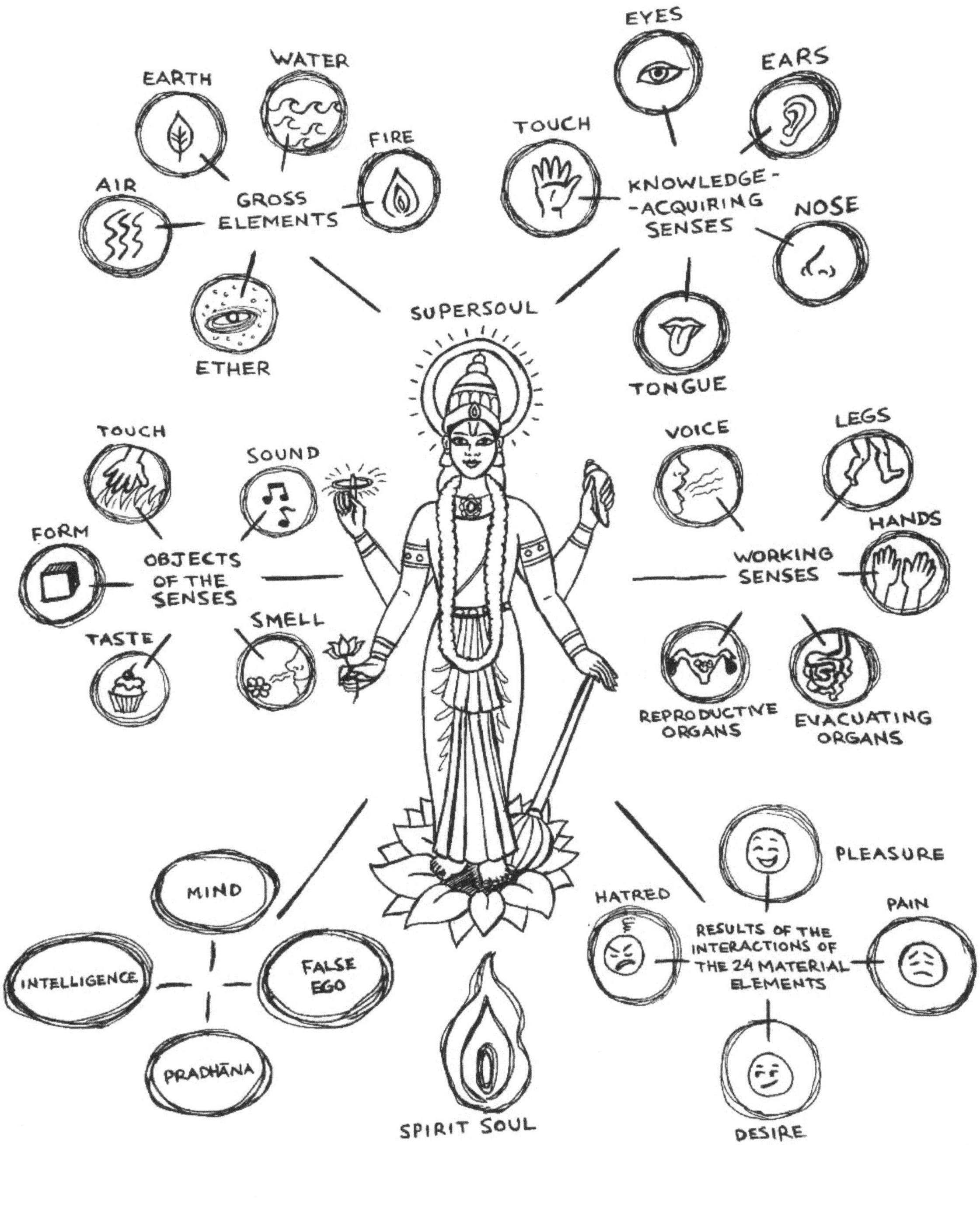

"So He glances at *pradhāna* as she sleeps. Merely by the Lord's glance, His children – the living entities – enter her womb. She stirs slightly, almost waking up, but then continues to sleep while her children become impatient with increasing desires. As she stirs, she is no longer *pradhāna*; she is *mahat-tattva* – the seed from which the whole material world comes. Now, this *mahat-tattva*, which is brilliant, swallows all the darkness from the time of annihilation. So it is bright everywhere. Kṛṣṇa consciousness is seen in the *mahat-tattva* in the form of Vāsudeva who is pure goodness. You can spot the Kṛṣṇa consciousness by its symptoms of complete serenity, clarity, and freedom from distraction.

"Now, from this Kṛṣṇa consciousness, the first material contamination appears – the false ego."

"False ego comes from pure Kṛṣṇa consciousness?"

"Yes, mother," Kapila replied, "this is because the living entities are marginal by nature – they are pure spiritual beings but have a choice. With this independence they may choose to remember Kṛṣṇa…or forget Kṛṣṇa."

Devahūti looked at her son in amazement. Kapila nodded and continued, "This false ego, thinking that we are this body and that we are the controllers, is influenced by the modes of goodness, passion, and ignorance. From the combination of these modes, the mind, the senses, the organs, and the elements of the *mahat-tattva* grow. This threefold false ego is known as Saṅkarṣaṇa, who is Ananta with a thousand hoods.

"Now let's look at this a little closer. The false ego in goodness is seen as serene. The mind grows from here and produces desires. This mind is known as Aniruddha. By meditating on the beautiful bluish-black form of Lord Aniruddha, one can become free from the mind's agitation, of accepting and rejecting.

"Then, false ego in passion is seen as active. The intelligence comes from this. The intelligence helps the senses to understand visible objects. You can notice intelligence when there is doubt, misunderstandings, correct understandings, memory, and sleep. It is not only the intelligence that comes from false ego in passion but also our life force. This life force ensures that we can act in the world.

"Now, false ego in ignorance is dull. Sound comes from this. Sound conveys an idea of an object and indicates the presence of a speaker. Sound is the cause of the creation but can also liberate us from material existence. From sound comes ether and the sense of hearing. Then from the ether comes touch; from touch comes air and the sense of touch. Over time, form is produced from touch. From form comes fire, and the eyes begin to see different forms in color. Again over time, taste is produced from form. From taste comes water and the tongue starts to work. Over time, smell is produced from taste. From smells come earth and the sense of smell. In other words, sound is the cause of the sky (ether); sky is the cause of air; air is the cause of fire; fire is the cause of water; and water is the cause of the earth. Earth is the sum total of all the elements.

"However, nothing else happened. It was all well that these elements and qualities were created, but they weren't moving; they weren't interacting with each other. So the Lord entered each of them as Garbhodakaśāyī Viṣṇu.

"Suddenly, they all began to move. They came together. They worked together. They were alive! And together they formed what looked like a large egg…or was it a bubble? A universal bubble.

"The universe, in the shape of an egg, is covered in layers of water, air, fire, ether, false ego, and *mahat-tattva*, increasing in thickness one after another, each layer ten times thicker than the previous. The final outer layer is *pradhāna*.

"The Supreme Personality of Godhead, in His universal form, the *virāṭ-puruṣa*, entered the universal egg where the 14 planetary systems formed part of His body. The Lord divided the universal bubble that lay on the water into many departments.

"First a mouth appeared in Him with the ability to speak, and the god of fire entered His mouth. Then a pair of nostrils appeared with the sense of smell and life air. The wind-

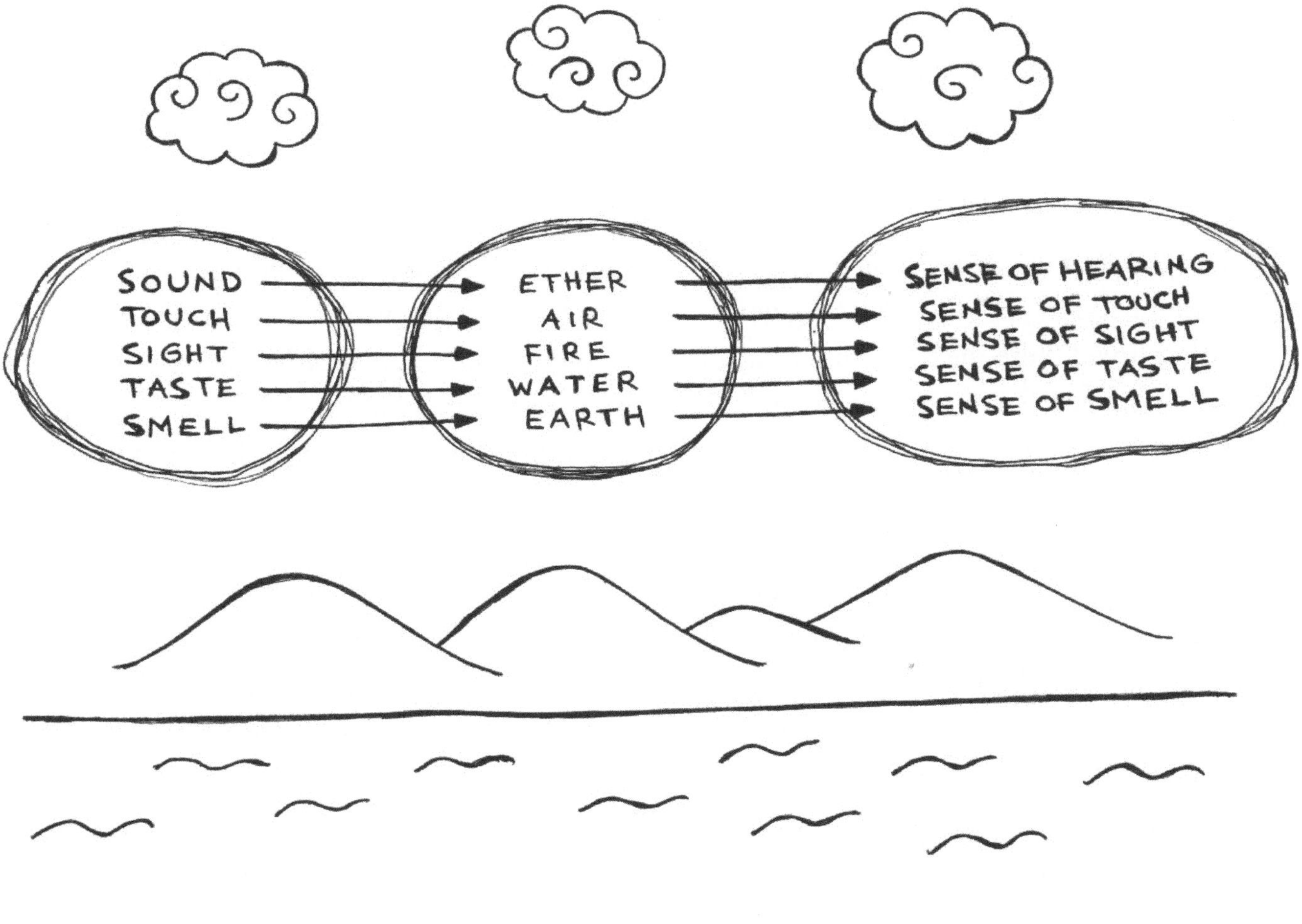

god entered that sense of smell.

"Soon after, a pair of eyes appeared in the universal form with the sense of sight. The sun-god entered that sense. Then a pair of ears appeared in Him with the sense of hearing. The gods of the directions entered this sense.

"Then the *virāṭ-puruṣa* manifested His skin with hair, mustache, and beard. After this, herbs and drugs appeared and then His genitals where the god of the waters appeared. Next appeared the anus and the organs used for excretion. The god of death appeared there.

"Then the two hands of the universal form appeared, and Lord Indra resided there. Then legs with their ability to move appeared, and Lord Viṣṇu came there. Thereafter, the universal form's veins appeared along with the red blood cells. Rivers came to live in the veins of the Lord. Then appeared the abdomen with feelings of hunger and thirst. The oceans came to live there.

"Then a heart manifested along with the mind, and the moon god, the presiding deity of the mind, lived there; next, the intelligence appeared in the heart, and Lord Brahmā moved there. The false ego also appeared in the heart wherein Lord Śiva decided to reside.

"Finally, the presiding deities of the various senses wanted to wake their origin – the *virāṭ-puruṣa*, the universal form of the Lord – but they failed. So they each re-entered the universal form to try to awaken Him.

"First, the god of fire went back into the Lord's mouth, but the Lord didn't awake. Then the wind-god entered His nostrils, but the Lord still refused to awake. The sun-god entered His eyes, the gods of directions entered His ears, the deities of skin, herbs and seasoning entered His skin, the god of water entered His genitals, the god of death entered His anus, Lord Indra entered His hands, Lord Viṣṇu entered His feet, the rivers entered His blood vessels, the oceans entered His abdomen, the moon-god entered His heart with the mind, Lord Brahmā entered His heart with the intelligence, and Lord Śiva entered His heart with the false ego… but nothing. Not even a stir.

However, when the deity presiding over consciousness entered His heart, the Lord arose from the causal waters."

"What does this mean for us?" wondered Devahūti.

Kapila, sensing His mother's thoughts, explained, "When a man is sleeping, only the Supersoul can help arouse him. Not his life air, his senses, his mind, his intelligence – only the Supersoul in the heart."

Devahūti furrowed her eyebrows. Was this all to explain that only the Supersoul can wake us up in the morning?

Kapila smiled before explaining further.

"In a similar way, mother, as sleeping souls who are forgetful of our reality, we have forgotten our true identity, and when we engage in devotional service, the Supersoul will arouse us, helping us understand who we are. In this way, you will automatically become detached from the world, and by His mercy you will receive transcendental knowledge and be able to see Him."

Themes and Key Messages

The following table summarizes some of the key messages and themes of this chapter. Use it as a quick reference guide to the verses listed and discuss each theme and message further with your teacher or friends.

Theme	Reference	Key Messages
Sāṅkhya philosophy in devotional service can free us from the three modes of material nature.	3.26.1–2	There are many paths to understand the Lord and our relationship with Him. The Sāṅkhya system of philosophy as explained by Lord Kapila analytically studies devotional service and is especially meant for persons conditioned in this material world. Sāṅkhya philosophy culminates in devotional service, which can free us from the three modes of material nature and make us qualified to enter God's kingdom.
The Supreme Lord is all-pervading but transcendental to the modes of material nature.	3.26.3–6	The Lord exists everywhere by His material and spiritual energies. Even though He is in His own abode, His light pervades the material and spiritual worlds. Although the modes of goodness, passion, and ignorance come from the Lord, they do not act upon Him; they only act on the conditioned souls, making them appear in different bodies and forget their spiritual nature.
The conditioned soul suffers because of his attachment to material nature; he creates his own happiness and distress.	3.26.7–8	A conditioned soul has to accept a body according to his desires and *karma*, so he is the cause of his own happiness and distress. By choosing to serve Kṛṣṇa, the soul can be liberated from conditional life and ultimately get a spiritual body, and by choosing to serve the senses, the soul again receives a material body and therefore has to enjoy or suffer. His suffering is because he is attached to material nature. When he becomes attached to Kṛṣṇa, he can experience true happiness.
The 24 elements are the source of the birth and subsistence of all living entities; however, only in contact with the Lord can they produce anything.	3.26.10–15, 17	*Pradhāna*, the unmanifest (invisible) material nature, consisting of five gross elements, five subtle elements, four internal senses, and five organs of action becomes manifest (visible) only when the Lord glances upon it. It is then called *prakṛti*. These 24 elements together with the time factor (the 25th element) brings about the creation of the living beings in the material world. However, only when the Lord glances at material nature does it manifest in various ways. Thus, the Lord is the ultimate cause of material nature.
Time represents the Lord and reminds us to surrender to Him.	3.26.16,18	With the influence of time, which is under Kṛṣṇa's control, we have to die and accept another body. We only fear death when we think we are the body. When we realize that we are a spirit soul that does not die, we are not afraid of the death of the material body. If we surrender to Kṛṣṇa and serve Him with love, we no longer have to accept material bodies. We become free from the influence of time and therefore do not fear death.
Sound can either bind us to the material world or liberate us.	3.26.32–33	The material creation began by sound, and sound can also end our material entanglement. When sound is purified, we can get immense benefit from hearing it. The Vedic knowledge is called *śruti*, knowledge received by hearing. By hearing spiritual sound, either the message of the Vedic literatures, knowledge from pure devotees, we can become liberated from material nature – especially hearing the *mahā-mantra* has the potency to end material entanglement.
Only by devotional service, detachment, and spiritual knowledge can we perceive the Lord in the heart.	3.26.71–72	The Lord as the Supersoul is present within the heart. Just as the sense organs and their presiding deities could not arouse the *virāṭ-puruṣa*, which was their original source, we cannot link with the Lord in the heart by material activities. Only through devotion, detachment, and divine knowledge we can understand the Supersoul and connect with Him. This is the essence of Sāṅkhya philosophy.

Understanding the Story

Now it's time for you to check how well you understood the story by answering these multiple-choice questions.

1. What is the state of material nature called in its original form before it manifests different varieties?
   a) *pradhāna*
   b) *prakṛti*
   c) *māyā*
2. What is *pradhāna* made of?
   a) It consists of time, the false ego, and the *mahat-tattva.*
   b) It consists of the manifested false ego and three modes of material nature.
   c) It comprises of 24 elements, which include the five gross elements, the five subtle elements, the five knowledge-acquiring senses, five action organs, and the four internal senses, and the 25th element of time.
3. What does the Lord do to the *pradhāna*?
   a) He destroys it with His glance, which is the Lord's manifestation as fire.
   b) He leaves it untouched and waits for it to transform with its own energy.
   c) He impregnates it with His glance, which is the Lord's manifestation as time, to agitate the *pradhāna.*
4. Why is it important for the Lord to impregnate *pradhāna* with His glance?
   a) He needs to do this as a matter of duty, not for a specific reason.
   b) Without the Supreme Lord's contact, the material nature cannot produce anything, just as a woman cannot produce children unless impregnated by a man.
   c) The Lord's glance carries the three modes of material nature into the *pradhāna.*
5. What happens when the Lord impregnates the *pradhāna* with time?
   a) The material nature becomes manifest with different varieties, which are produced from the interaction of the three modes of material nature.
   b) The modes of material nature are destroyed, and only the mode of goodness remains to produce varieties in material nature.
   c) The *pradhāna* continues to be invisible.

6. In what forms does the Lord remain in the material nature?
   a) As the three modes of material nature.
   b) In the form of time He enters every atom, and as the Supersoul He enters the heart of every living being.
   c) As the 24 elements such as fire, air, water, etc.
7. What is the source of the 24 material elements?
   a) The mind
   b) The intelligence
   c) The false ego
8. What is the material nature called after it manifests different varieties?
   a) *prakṛti*
   b) *pradhāna*
   c) *virāṭ-puruṣa*
9. How did Devahūti understand such a complex process of creation?
   a) By her own intelligence
   b) By the mercy of her son, Lord Kapiladeva
   c) By the explanations of her husband
10. What is the order in which the the five gross material elements evolve?
    a) air, ether, earth, fire, water
    b) ether, fire, water, air, earth
    c) ether, air, fire, water, earth

Higher-Thinking Questions

Now try to deepen your understanding of this chapter by delving into Śrīla Prabhupāda's purports and reflecting on the following questions:

1. Why do you think that time, which is the impersonal feature of the Lord, makes us fear death? (See verse 16 purport) What steps can we take to become fearless?
2. Describe the false ego when influenced by each of the modes: goodness, passion, and ignorance as described in this chapter.
3. How is a conditioned soul the cause of his/her own material happiness or distress? (See verse 8 purport) Can you think of a time when you were unhappy and realized you were the cause? How could you have changed the outcome?
4. Both the material and spiritual sky are covered by Brahman and therefore everything comes from Brahman. Explain the different types of Brahman. How can we get out of material Brahman existence and enter the spiritual sky to be with Kṛṣṇa? See verse 15 purport.
5. Verse 3 describes how the Lord is all-pervasive, that we can perceive Him in the material world. How can we see His illumination in this universe? Give examples from verse 3 purport.
6. If the Lord is all merciful and is a loving father who does not like to see us suffer, why does He create this material world in the first place? See verse 5 purport. What analogy does Śrīla Prabhupāda use to explain how the Lord corrects His parts and parcels, the living entities?
7. What is conditioned life or a conditioned soul? What is the cause of conditional life as described in verse 7? How can we transform this conditioned consciousness to Kṛṣṇa consciousness?
8. Describe how each of the material elements, ether, sky, fire, water, and earth, transform into the next.
9. Describe what Śrīla Prabhupāda says is the sum and substance of the Sāṅkhya philosophy mentioned in verse 72 purport. What is the perfection of this *yoga*? How can you personally apply the teachings of *Sāṅkhya-yoga* in your life?

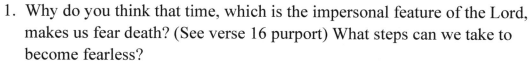

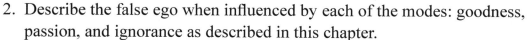

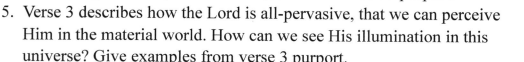

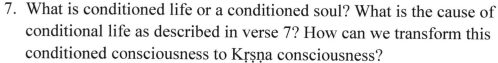

ACTIVITIES

In this section you will find many exciting things to do. These activities will get you thinking, moving, drawing, and having loads of fun.

Artistic Activities

. . . to reveal your creativity!

THE UNIVERSAL EGG

"This universal egg, or the universe in the shape of an egg, is called the manifestation of material energy. Its layers of water, fire, air, sky, ego and *mahat-tattva* increase in thickness one after another. Each layer is ten times bigger than the previous one, and the final outside layer is covered by *pradhāna*. Within this egg is the universal form of Lord Hari, of whose body the fourteen planetary systems are parts." *SB* 3.26.52

Make the universal egg!

What you will need:
Paper or cardboard; pencils/color pens/paints; scissors; ruler; paper glue

Directions:

- Draw and cut out a small egg shape from a sheet of card or paper. Draw a picture of the Lord's universal form in the center of this small egg.
- Make another egg shape by placing the small egg shape on top of the unused sheet of paper. Measure 10mm away from the small egg shape on the paper and

draw a guiding line around it so that your next egg will be 10mm larger all around (representing each layer as 10 times larger than the previous one). Cut out this shape.

- Next, use this second egg shape to make another egg shape 10mm larger* all around. Then use this larger egg shape as the next stencil to draw around, increasing 10mm in size each time until you have eight egg shapes of paper.
- Label each egg shape with the parts that make up the universal egg; for example, the layers, after the smallest one with the universal form, would be air, fire, sky, false ego, *mahat-tattva*, and *pradhāna* consecutively.
- Color, paint, or decorate each layer corresponding to the color of the element; for example, the water layer would be blue or have a water effect.
- Now place and glue all your eggs on top of each other, one layer at a time, from the largest to the smallest, so you can finally see the layers of the universal egg (see example below).

*The measurement of 10mm larger for each layer is only for the purpose of the creative exercise. If each layer is 10 times larger than the previous, then each of the layers would be much larger, e.g., for example, if the first layer of the egg diagram is 1cm (10mm), the next would be 1x10=10cm, then the next 10x10=100cm (1 meter), etc.

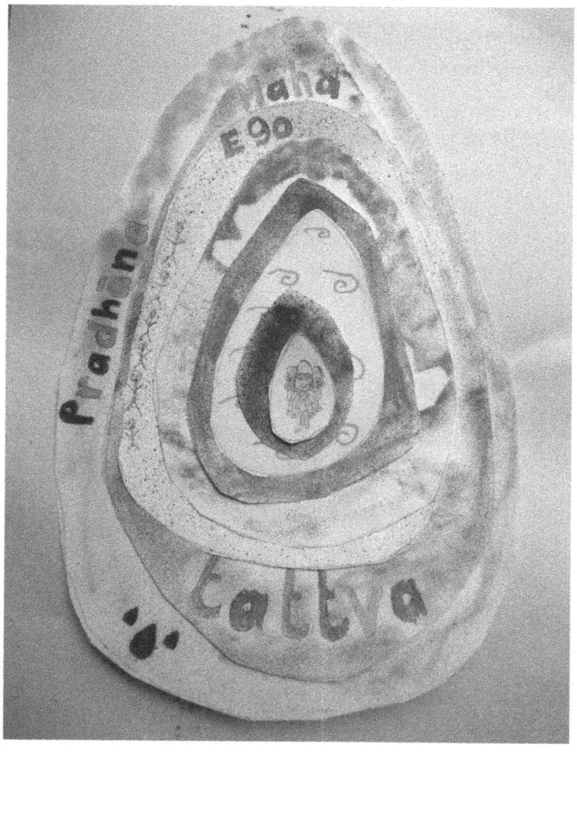

KṚṢṆA IS THE LIGHT OF ALL CREATION

Śrīla Prabhupāda describes in the purport to verse 3 that Kṛṣṇa is behind the creative energy of this material world, and the moonlight, sunlight, and *brahmajyoti* (Brahman effulgence) come from Kṛṣṇa. Since His light is spread everywhere, Kṛṣṇa is present all over the creation.

Directions: Illustrate what Prabhupāda is saying in this purport. In your illustration show where the moonlight comes from. Where does the sunlight come from? Try and show where the original light is coming from.

Use these four in your illustration below. Have fun illustrating!

Kṛṣṇa

Brahmajyoti

Sun

Moon

Analogy Activity . . . to bring out the scholar in you!

THE FATHER AND MOTHER OF CREATION

> "Prakṛti is connected with both the Supreme Lord and the living entities, just as a woman is connected with her husband as a wife and with her children as a mother." *SB* 3.26.9, purport

Devahūti wanted to understand the relationship between material nature, the Supreme Lord, and the living entities in the material world. Śrīla Prabhupāda explains that the Lord impregnates mother nature with children, living entities, so she is related to Him as a wife. And her relationship with the living entities is like that of a mother. Kṛṣṇa is the source of them both, as a husband to material nature and a father to the living beings.

"An analogy may be made with the father and mother: the mother and the father exist, but sometimes the mother begets children. Similarly, this cosmic manifestation, which comes from the unmanifest material nature of the Supreme Lord, sometimes appears and again disappears." *SB* 3.26.9

Śrīla Prabhupāda uses a similar analogy in the same purport to illustrate a similar point. Material nature is sometimes manifest and sometimes unmanifest, but she is always existing. When she has children – the *jīvas* – the cosmic manifestation, which is temporary, comes into being. So just as a mother sometimes has children by the seed of the father, the cosmic manifestation sometimes exists and sometimes disappears. Material nature (the mother) always exists even before the creation, while the cosmic manifestation is temporary. Kṛṣṇa, the seed-giving father of the living beings, is the source of material nature (the mother) and the cosmic manifestation.

In this chapter Kapiladeva discusses the relationship between the Lord, material nature, and the *jīva*. Let us understand this relationship between the three of them.

a. As described above, how are the Supreme Lord, material nature, and the living entity related?
   In the space below, draw a small tree diagram to illustrate this relationship.
b. Of the three, who do you understand to be the original? Support your answer with proper evidence.
c. Interestingly, although the Supreme Lord is related closely to both the living entity and material nature, He is not visible in the material world. Why do you think he keeps Himself hidden? And how can we begin to see Him?
d. Is it easy for us to connect to the Supreme Lord even though He is not visible to us? Explain in the context of the father-child analogy. (Hint: think of another father-son analogy Śrīla Prabhupāda gives.)

Critical-Thinking Activities

. . . to bring out the spiritual investigator in you!

ELEMENTS OF MATERIAL NATURE

Modern chemistry describes a Periodic Table of the elements. These elements are considered the simplest blocks of matter that build the material world and are the basis for all chemical interactions and varieties. The *Bhāgavatam* also has its own list of elements of matter from which the material world comes. We have already studied these elements in Canto 2 and at the beginning of Canto 3, Volume 1. In this chapter Kapiladeva describes in detail these elements to His mother in relation to the Sāṅkhya philosophy.

We will now refresh our memory of the elements by building our own Elements of Material Nature Table. By organizing the elements in this manner, we can easily understand and remember them.

Given in next page is the Elements of Material Nature Table, an ordered arrangement of the elements that are described in the *Śrīmad-Bhāgavatam* and that come from the original *puruṣa* form of the Supreme Lord.

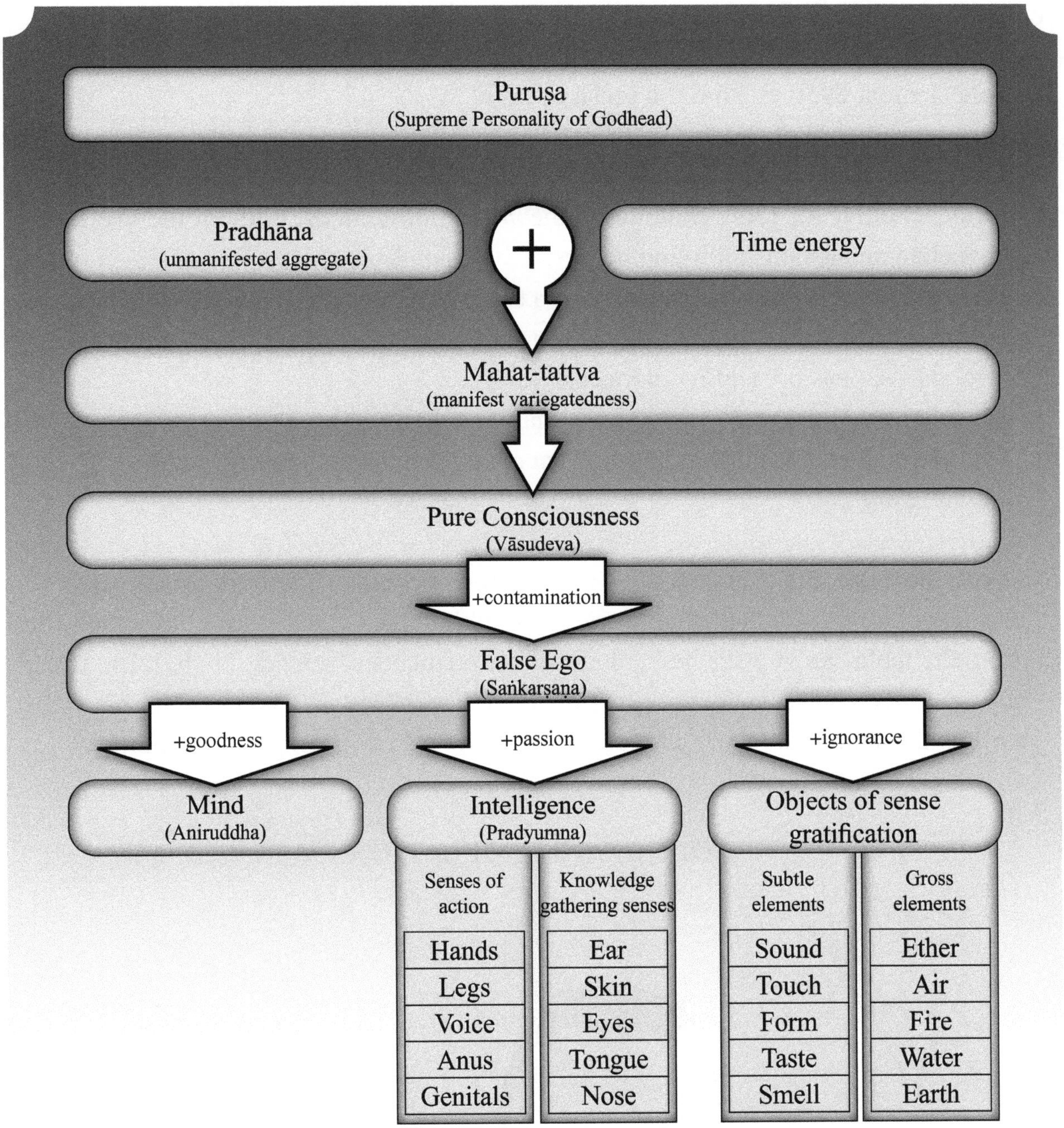

Elements of Material Nature Table

Given below are characteristics of ten different elements on this Elements of Material Nature Table. Can you guess the elements that they are referring to? (Refer to the chapter summary and above table for help.)

1. This element is called the 25th element and is responsible for transforming the modes of nature, which leads to creation.
2. This element evolves from the sense of taste.
3. The controlling deity of this element is Aniruddha.
4. This element provides proper functioning to all other senses.
5. This element is the representation of the *mahat-tattva* in the body of the *jīva*.
6. This element sustains all living beings.
7. This element indicates the presence of a speaker hidden from our view.
8. This element springs up from the *mahat-tattva* and has active power of three types – goodness, passion, and ignorance.
9. This element is the root of all cosmic manifestation.
10. This element lets us understand the concept of dimension, quality, and individuality.

a. Now write down the characteristics of five more elements. Then ask your study partners to guess which elements you are thinking of.
b. From the table can you see how all the subtle elements of sound, touch, form, taste, and smell are all present in the gross element earth? Now can you explain how the earth is the sum total of all other elements as described in verse 49 and purport.

SOUND CONTEMPLATION

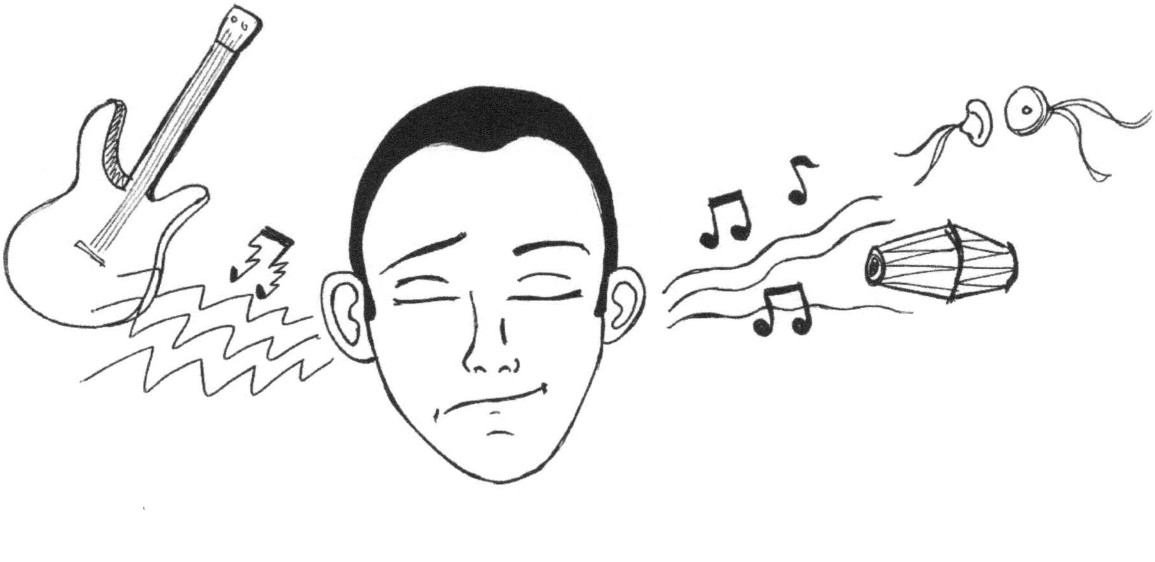

Śrīla Prabhupāda describes in the purport to verse 32 that hearing is most important because the ear is the first sense for receiving knowledge, whether material or spiritual. However, everything in this world is contaminated due to material sound. At the same time, pure sound can be the vehicle for liberation.

Directions: Contemplate sounds heard in this material world. In the table below write them down and describe why a sound is contaminated. Then suggest how the same sound could be used in Kṛṣṇa's service, making it the cause of liberation! Also include some spiritual sounds and explain why they are spiritual. (An example is done for you.)

Sounds	Why Contaminated? How could they be the source of liberation?
TV	1. Contaminated because it is mundane sound about how to enjoy material life and of material world problems. 2. TV can be used to hear spiritual sound in the form of Kṛṣṇa movies or documentaries or watching videos of Śrīla Prabhupāda.

Language Activities

. . . to make you understand better!

FILL IN THE BLANKS

1. *Ātma-darśanam* in Sanskrit means to see oneself by __________.
2. The pursuit of the systematic philosophic process called __________ is called knowledge and self-revelation.
3. Each mode of material nature is represented by a color: passion is represented by __________; ignorance by __________; and goodness by __________.
4. The forgetful living entity can be compared to a man who is influenced by a __________ and has gone __________.
5. __________ people think that a cloud can cover the sun.
6. The living entity is the cause of his suffering but can easily become the cause of his __________.
7. If a living entity simply understands that his constitutional position is to serve Kṛṣṇa and he tries to act on this principle, then however conditioned he may be, the influence of __________ is removed.
8. The attachment of the conditioned souls to material nature should be transferred from matter to __________.
9. One who is actually a worshiper of Lord __________ as a devotee of Saṅkarṣaṇa can be released from false, material ego.
10. In the beginning, consciousness is __________.
11. The *Upaniṣads* state that the path of spiritual realization is just like the sharp edge of a __________.
12. The advancement of civilization is a manifestation of the __________.

EXPANSIONS OF THE PERSONALITY OF GODHEAD

The Vedic literature mentions the Lord's expansions in four Personalities of Godhead who preside over different elements – Vāsudeva, Saṅkarṣaṇa, Pradyumna, and Aniruddha.

Directions: Read the purports to verses 21 to 29 and describe each Personality of Godhead and what purpose He serves with regards to the elements. When might you call upon each one? You can add any additional note mentioned in the purports.

Vāsudeva –

Saṅkarṣaṇa –

Aniruddha –

Pradyumna –

SYMPTOMS OF THE MATERIAL ELEMENTS

In this chapter the symptoms of fire, water, taste, and odor are clearly given. Fill in the blanks with examples of their symptoms (the first one has been done for you).

Symptoms of Fire

Light: the sun; light bulb

Ability to cook: gas flame on the stove; an open wood fire

To digest: bile in stomach

Destroy cold: heat from fire

Evaporate: boiling of water

Give rise to hunger and thirst: going on a long walk

Symptoms of Water

Moistening and thickening other substances:

Causing satisfaction:

Maintaining life:

Softening things:

Driving away heat:

Quenching thirst:

Types of Tastes

Sweet:

Bitter:

Pungent:

Sour:

Salty:

Types of Odor

Mixed:

Offensive:

Fragrant:

Mild:

Strong:

Acidic:

CROSSWORD

Across:

4. The state of material nature right before the manifest stage.
6. Water and taste perception interact to evolve this element.
7. 25th element in material nature.
10. Acquiring knowledge depends on this element.

Down:

1. 26th element in material nature.
2. A place for sustenance for all the elements.
3. This subtle element evolves by the interaction of fire and visual sensation.
5. Manifested material nature. [answer spelled phonetically]
8. Element that is the origin of all material possessions.

ANSWERS

Understanding the Story: 1) a, 2) c, 3) c, 4) b, 5) a, 6) b, 7) c, 8) a, 9) b, 10) c

The Mother and Father of Creation

a. Kṛṣṇa is the father, material nature is the mother, and the *jīva* is the child.

b. The Supreme Lord is the original because the *jīva* and *prakṛti* are His energies. Verse 17 and purport describe how the Lord impregnates material nature by His glance, the time factor, which produces the living entities.

c. He doesn't manifest Himself to the conditioned souls because their vision is covered by the illusory energy (*māyā*) of the Lord, just as a cloud covers the sun. As we become purified by devotional service, the cloud of illusion fades away, and we will be able to see Him.

d. Yes, it is natural to connect to Kṛṣṇa because it is natural for a son to connect to a father. Śrīla Prabhupāda gives the analogy of the lost son of a rich man who is reunited with his father. The father is happy to receive the child, and the child is happy to be under the shelter of the father. Similarly, as children of the Supreme Lord, we are lost in the material world, separated from our Eternal Father, and only when we are reunited with Him in love can we be happy.

Elements of Material Nature

---

1. time; 2. water; 3. mind; 4. air; 5. consciousness; 6. earth; 7. sound; 8. false ego; 9. *mahat-tattva*; 10. form

b. In the sky there is only sound; in the air there are sound and touch; in the fire there are touch, sound, and form; in water there are touch, sound, form, and taste; and in the earth there are touch, sound, form, taste, and smell. The earth has all five qualities of the elements and therefore is considered the sum total of all.

Sound Contemplation *(Potential Answers)*

Sounds	Why Contaminated? How could they be the source of liberation?
Music	1. Contaminated because it is mundane vibrations of this material world. It is often for enjoyment and not for glorifying the Lord. 2. If the music is used to glorify the Lord and His pastimes, then it is the source of liberation.

Sounds	Why Contaminated? How could they be the source of liberation?
Bell or Musical Instruments	1. Contaminated because it is mundane sound of this material world and used for sense enjoyment. Bells are also used to dictate time or for musical purposes. 2. If the bell is used for worshiping Kṛṣṇa and to glorify Him and the musical instruments used in *kīrtana*, then this sound is the source of liberation.
Mahā-mantra	1. Completely spiritual and transcendental. 2. Kṛṣṇa is nondifferent from His name.

Fill in the Blanks

1. knowledge; 2. Sāṅkhya; 3. red; blue; white; 4. disease; mad; 5. unintelligent; 6. eternal happiness; 7. *māyā*; 8. Kṛṣṇa; 9. Śiva; 10. pure; 11. razor; 12. false ego

Expansions of the Personality of Godhead

Vāsudeva – This manifestation is called pure goodness, or *śuddha-sattva*. Vāsudeva represents Kṛṣṇa Consciousness and Kṛṣṇa as the Supersoul in the hearts of all living entities. Vāsudeva is also Kṛṣṇa alone, without His internal potency.

Saṅkarṣaṇa – Saṅkarṣaṇa lies on the bed of snakes (Ananta) and is the expansion of the Lord that Lord Śiva meditates upon. Those who would like to conquer the false ego are recommended to worship Lord Saṅkarṣaṇa.

Aniruddha – He is four-armed with Sudarśana *cakra*, conchshell, club, and lotus flower and has a bluish-blackish form resembling an autumn lotus flower. Aniruddha is the Lord of the mind. One who wants to get free from mental disturbances worships Aniruddha. While meditating on Aniruddha, one can become free from the agitation of acceptance and rejection, and gradually becomes God-realized.

Pradyumna – He is also the four-armed form of the Lord, which represents intelligence. To be fixed in one's intelligence, one must worship Pradyumna, who is reached through the worship of Brahmā.

Symptoms of the Material Elements *(Potential Answers)*

Symptoms of Water – Moistening and thickening other substances: adding water in *gopī-candana*; adding water to thick *sabjīs*; Causing satisfaction: taking a shower after a long day; Maintaining life: for drinking; Softening things: soaking nuts and dried fruit in water; soaking water in a sponge; Driving away heat: using cold water on cloth for a fever; Quenching Thirst: drinking water after a long walk.

Types of Tastes – Sweet: sugar candy; Bitter: bittermelon (*karelā*); Pungent: ginger; Sour: yogurt; Salty: soy sauce.

Types of Odor – Mixed: dal; Offensive: spoiled milk; Fragrant: jasmine flower; Mild: cucumber; Strong: orange; Acidic: vinegar.

Crossword

Across: 4. Pradhana; 6. Odor; 7. Time; 10. Intelligence

Down: 1. Supersoul; 2. Earth; 3. Taste; 5. Prakriti; 8. Sound; 9. Egg

27

Understanding Material Nature

STORY SUMMARY

It was a day like all others. The serene beauty of the forest was striking, the birds sang their melodious songs, and the warm gentle breeze carried the fragrance of the forest flowers to every part of the hermitage.

But for Devahūti the day was different. Today she had hope – not for the return of her husband or of children or grandchildren. It was a hope she hadn't felt before. A bigger hope. A hope that she could be free – free from fear and attachment.

"My son!" Devahūti exclaimed, beaming as she came before the Lord.

Kapila smiled. "Come, mother. Let us sit."

"We are all spirit souls," began the Lord.

"Yes," replied His mother. She knew that at least.

"Material nature controls the spirit souls in this world."

"Yes, I know," she said and sighed.

"But mother, there are some spirit souls in this world that are not affected by material nature at all. Their bodies may experience reactions in this world, but they stay aloof. They stay separate from the reactions."

"Even while in their bodies?"

"Yes."

Devahūti furrowed her brows and tilted her head. Was it possible to be free from the strong influence of material nature? She didn't ask though. Not yet anyway.

"And then there are the spirit souls who are controlled by material nature and deeply affected by its modes."

"How do the modes affect them?"

"Oh, the modes make them think that they are the body and that they own things around them. They think they are the proprietors of everything."

Devahūti thought, "Yes, I do think and feel that I am Devahūti. I feel I'm the mother of Kapila and He belongs to me. He is my son. I feel Kardama Muni is my husband and Svāyambhuva Manu my father. I feel these relations belong to me, and I consider this hermitage my home."

"Mother, are you okay?"

Devahūti nodded and urged her son to continue.

"Because of this," said Kapila, "the spirit soul moves into different species of life every time the body dies."

Devahūti nodded. Was this to be her fate? Was there anything she could do about this?

"The spirit soul is pure. It's only the mentality of wanting to be the owner and enjoyer of everything and the friend of everyone that binds us to material nature. A bit like being in a dream. We are fooled into thinking it's all real."

"This is me!" Devahūti panicked to herself. "So what can we do?" she asked.

Her attention was hooked onto Kapila's every word. She anticipated the movement of His sweet lips and the spiritually gratifying sound that would emanate from them.

"Use that material consciousness for Kṛṣṇa. Engage it in devotional service by chanting and hearing about Him with a mood of detachment. Practice self-control by controlling your mind and senses. This will control your consciousness, and your faith will develop.

"As you continue to hear and chant the glories of the Lord, your devotional service will become pure. It will become unmotivated and uninterrupted. Unmixed."

"So we must serve the Lord and control our senses at the same time?" asked Devahūti.

"Yes," confirmed Kapila. "While doing so, we must see every living entity equally. We mustn't be inimical towards anyone, but also, we must avoid intimate connections with anyone not engaged in the Lord's devotional service. Furthermore, observe celibacy and be grave. Offer the results of all your activities to the Lord.

"A devotee must be satisfied with what he earns without over endeavor. He should not eat more than necessary. He must live in a secluded place with devotees and always be thoughtful, peaceful, friendly, compassionate, and self-realized. He should understand the difference between matter and spirit and identify with the spirit, not the body. And he should definitely not be attracted to bodily

relationships."

Devahūti took in every word although it was a lot to digest.

"A liberated soul sees Kṛṣṇa everywhere, in His material energies and even within each atom. He is free from false ego and sees himself as the Lord's servant just as clearly as he sees the sun in the sky. Even in the dark material world he sees that the only light is Kṛṣṇa!"

Devahūti smiled. "How wonderful to see Kṛṣṇa everywhere!" she thought.

"So, dear mother, you can see the Lord just as you see the sun's reflection on water even though the sun is far away in the sky. Similarly, even though Kṛṣṇa is aloof from material nature, you can perceive Him in the material world through His energies…in the aroma of a flower, the taste of water, the light of the sun…When we see a beautiful rose, for example, we can see it belonging to the Lord, as a reflection of His energy, and we can offer it to Him."

Devahūti nodded. This was something she

could try to do.

"But this doesn't mean that the realized soul doesn't have ego. He does. When we say to give up the ego, this means to give up the false ego, but real ego is always present. The real ego is to see ourselves as loving servants of Kṛṣṇa. Even though a devotee seems to engage in activities in the three modes with the body, mind, and senses, he is free from the false ego – free from thinking he is this body and that everything belongs to him.

"The conditioned soul forgets his real ego, and because of the false ego he feels lost. For example, if a person loses all his money, he may feel distressed and lost, but actually he is not lost at all. His distress is just because he's so attached to the money. So a living being is never lost – we just forget our identity due to the false ego."

Devahūti was speechless. She felt enlightened yet troubled.

Finally, she asked, "Does material nature ever release the spirit soul? It's just that matter and spirit are so closely combined. Can they ever be separated?"

She thought of how the body could never exist or function without the soul and how the consciousness of the soul couldn't be seen or experienced without a body.

"How can there be freedom for the soul?" Devahūti continued. "I mean, even if we understand the difference between spirit and matter and are unafraid of material bondage – I believe we will always be bound to this material world if the cause of our bondage hasn't stopped. The cause is the false ego. If we still want to be the owner and enjoyer of everything and the best friend and rescuer of everyone, we still are envious of the Lord and want to take His position."

"Yes," Kapila agreed, "we can only get rid of the cause through devotional service of hearing about Me or from Me for a long time. Then when you execute your prescribed duties, there will be no reactions and you'll be free!

"However, your devotional service must be strong in full knowledge of Me; you must be austere and renounced – and only then will you be firmly fixed."

Devahūti nodded, satisfied with the answer.

"You see, the material energy has covered the living entity, and so it's as if the living entity has always been in the blazing fire of material energy.

"But there's a different fire inside the living entity. The spark of devotional service. So if the living entity hears and chants My glories, this spark of devotional service ignites and spreads voraciously, burning the fire of material energy. Even the cause of our being covered by material existence is burned away. The cause is our envy of the Supreme Lord and our desire to be the enjoyer like Him. Just as wooden sticks that start a fire are consumed by the fire, the cause of our material bondage is also consumed by the fire of devotional service.

"The living entity can then see that he was trying to be the owner, enjoyer, and savior of all. Immediately he gives up this mentality, and although still in his body, he is no longer under the control of material nature. He now stands independently.

"In a dream your consciousness is almost covered and you see bad things, but when you awake, you are not bewildered anymore. Similarly, when you awaken and understand your relationship with the Lord, you become fully satisfied and the three modes of material nature cannot affect you anymore.

"You see, the influence of material nature can't harm an enlightened soul. He knows the truth, and his mind is fixed on the Lord.

"When a person engages for many, many years and births in devotional service, he doesn't feel like enjoying the material world – even up to the highest planet of Brahmaloka. This is because his consciousness has developed into Kṛṣṇa consciousness.

"This happens by My mercy. My devotees become self-realized, then steadily progress to My abode under My protection. This is the goal. They go to My abode and never come back to this material world. Death cannot touch them."

Themes and Key Messages

Please go through this table of themes and key messages, with corresponding verses, and discuss each topic further.

Theme	Reference	Key messages
A devotee knows Kṛṣṇa to be the real enjoyer, controller, proprietor, and friend of all living beings.	3.27.1–2, 4–5	When a person is covered by the false ego, thinking that he is the body, he becomes absorbed in material activities and thinks that he is the enjoyer and proprietor of everything. When he becomes purified by devotional service, he does not claim ownership of anything nor wants to enjoy anything because he knows that Kṛṣṇa is the actual proprietor, enjoyer, and friend. (He's not attracted to welfare work, knowing that Kṛṣṇa is the real friend; a devotee rather directs a person to Kṛṣṇa, who will permanently end all suffering.)
We can control our mind and consciousness by devotional service.	3.27.6–9	By hearing and chanting about the Supreme Lord, we can elevate our minds and consciousness, seeing every living being equally and offering the results of our activities to the Lord.
When we are freed from the false ego, we realize our real position and see the Supreme Lord in everything.	3.27.10–14	When we see ourselves as servants of Kṛṣṇa, not the material body meant to enjoy the mind and senses, we can perceive Kṛṣṇa's presence everywhere and in everything. Just as we see the sun reflected in water, we can see Kṛṣṇa reflected through His energies.
When we falsely identify with matter, we think we are lost.	3.27.16–17	When we forget our identity, it is as if we are in a deep sleep. But the soul is never lost. As soon as we wake up and realize that we are eternal servants of the Lord, we are not affected by the false ego and will not feel lost or unhappy.
We have to get rid of the root cause of material bondage otherwise we will always be bound to this material world.	3.27.19–23	We are bound to this material world because of our desire to enjoy separately from the Lord or to be as great as the Lord. Our envy of Him is the root cause of our contamination. We can destroy this cause by devotional service.
A person becomes fully independent when he realizes that he is a servant of God.	3.27.24–25	A servant of the Lord has the greatest position because he is not dependent on the three modes of nature. He is also free from frustration of being the enjoyer and therefore has complete spiritual independence. When we try to simply enjoy the senses and material nature, we are in a dream state, and when we realize our true positions as servants of Kṛṣṇa, when we are Kṛṣṇa conscious, we are in an awakened state. When we realize that Kṛṣṇa is the proprietor of the three worlds and the true friend of everyone, we become peaceful and independent.
The influence of material nature cannot harm a devotee who is fixed on the Lord; he goes to the Lord's spiritual abode.	3.27.26, 28–30	A devotee whose mind is fixed on the Lord and who knows that the Lord is the supreme enjoyer and he is meant to serve and please the Lord is not influenced by the modes of material nature nor gets any material reactions to his activities. He does not desire to enjoy the material world, even the higher planets. As a result, he goes back to the spiritual world and never returns to the material world.

Understanding the Story

Now it's time for you to check how well you understood the story by answering these multiple-choice questions.

1. How can a soul become free from the modes of material nature?
   a) By doing difficult *yoga* postures
   b) By meditating on the impersonal Brahman
   c) By realizing that the Supreme Lord is the proprietor of everything
2. How can one get out of the repeated cycle of birth and death?
   a) Only by devotional service to The Supreme Lord
   b) Only by studying the Vedas for many years
   c) Only by doing severe penance in the Himālayas
3. How does one perform devotional service to the Lord?
   a) By eating a healthy diet and exercising regularly
   b) By controlling the mind and faithfully following the process of chanting and hearing about the Lord
   c) By performing severe austerities and penances
4. How should a person live so that he is able to follow the process of devotional service?
   a) He should earn a lot of money during his youth, so he does not have to work later in life and thus have time in his old age to focus on hearing and chanting.
   b) He should leave his family and live in the forest by begging, so he can focus on hearing and chanting.
   c) He must see every living entity equally, observe celibacy, be satisfied with what he earns, only eat as much as necessary, live in a secluded place, remain always thoughtful, peaceful, friendly, and compassionate, and not identify himself with his body.
5. Why does the soul suffer in the material world?
   a) Because of his desire to be the master of everything around him
   b) Because his original nature is to be sad and distressed
   c) Because the Supreme Lord does not provide everything he needs for his enjoyment
6. How does a self-realized person think?
   a) He sees everything as items provided by the Supreme Lord for his enjoyment.
   b) He sees everything as a reflection of the Lord and thinks how to use everything in His service.
   c) He becomes frustrated with the material world and rejects everything.

7. Why does the spirit soul feel lost in the material world?
   a) Because he identifies with matter and has forgotten his loving relationship with the Supreme Lord
   b) Because he has no one to turn to
   c) Because he has been wandering in the material world for many births
8. How can the spirit soul be separated from material nature when both have been eternally attracted to each another?
   a) Only by constantly thinking that "I am not this body," the spirit soul can cut its attraction to material nature.
   b) Simply by serving the Supreme Lord, the spirit soul can rise to the transcendental platform and separate itself from material nature.
   c) It is not possible to separate them.
9. How can we take up the process of chanting and hearing about the Lord?
   a) We have to force ourselves to take up this process because it is not natural for us to chant and hear about God.
   b) We have to give up the desire to be God and realize that we are His servants.
   c) It is only a matter of luck that one can take up this process.
10. What happens when the living entity realizes that he does not belong in the material world but in the spiritual world?
    a) This material world is like a dream. Just as when we wake up, we are not disturbed or even care for the dream, when we engage in devotional service, we realize our true identity and can let go of this material world easily.
    b) The living entity gets fearful because he doesn't want to leave the material world.
    c) Regardless of the desire of the living entity, the forces in the material world keep him in the material world for eternity.

Higher-Thinking Questions

Now try to deepen your understanding of this chapter by delving into Śrīla Prabhupāda's purports and reflecting on the following questions:

1. Verse 20 describes that the cause of our material bondage – envy of Kṛṣṇa and our desire to become God – needs to be removed otherwise we will always be bound to this material world. Why does Śrīla Prabhupāda say that the living being is envious of God (see purport)? In the world today there are indications that men and women desire to be God. Can you think of examples? What do you think are the negative effects of wanting to be God? For example, animal slaughter, social oppression, etc.
2. What does Devahūti mean in verse 20 when she says that "even if the great fear of bondage is avoided by mental speculation and inquiry into the fundamental principles," it will not end material bondage? Why can't theoretical knowledge free one from material bondage? (Refer to purport.)
3. In verse 5 Lord Kapila states that it is the soul's duty to engage the consciousness in serious devotional service with detachment. What do you think the Lord means by "detachment" here (see purport)? Can you think of ways you can engage yourself in Kṛṣṇa's service in detachment and fulfill Lord Kapila's instructions?
4. In verse 15 purport Śrīla Prabhupāda uses the analogy of a man who has lost his fortune and feels distressed. To what is he referring? Have you lost something valuable and felt so distressed that it made you feel lost? Describe and relate the incident to the analogy in the purport.
5. Devahūti is asking how the soul becomes freed from material nature. How does Lord Kapila respond? When is the living entity freed from the covering of material nature?
6. Analyze verse 24: Why is the Lord telling His mother that the living entity becomes independent and stands in his own glory? Does this contradict our Vaiṣṇava philosophy regarding our dependence on Kṛṣṇa? Make up your own definition of the word "independence" based on verse 24 purport.
7. Why is material life compared to a dream? What is Kṛṣṇa consciousness compared to in this context in verse 25 purport?
8. Describe Śrīla Prabhupāda's definition of self-realization as mentioned in verses 28–29 purport?

9. What is the difference between the conditional and liberated state of consciousness as described in the purport to verse 13? What is the actual liberated stage, and why is it superior to impersonalism?
10. Śrīla Prabhupāda also describes in verse 13 purport how the liberated soul or Kṛṣṇa conscious person sees everything in material nature as a reflection of Kṛṣṇa. Give some examples from material nature that can remind you of Kṛṣṇa.

ACTIVITIES

In this section you will find many exciting things to do. These activities will get you thinking, moving, drawing, and having loads of fun.

Analogy Activities . . . to bring out the scholar in you!

IMPORTANT CHAPTER ANALOGIES

This chapter is full of analogies that help us understand important philosophical concepts or themes.

To see how well you understand these analogies, explain in your own words what each of the following analogies mean – what each thing in the analogy is being compared to, and what principle it explains (see verse references).

1. The sun reflected in water (This analogy is used twice in verse 1 and in verse 12 – explain both instances.)
2. Different mental conditions in dreams (verse 4)
3. Seeing the sun in the sky (verse 10)
4. A person who has lost his money (verse 15)
5. The earth and its aroma; the water and its taste (verse 18)
6. Wooden sticks causing the fire are consumed by the fire (verse 23)
7. Dreaming and awakening states (verse 25)

THE EMPTY PADDY HUSK

"There is no benefit in husking the skin of an empty *paddy; the rice is already gone. Similarly, simply by the speculative process one cannot be freed from material bondage, for the cause still exists." (*SB.* 3.27.20, purport)

* raw rice grains in the husk

This analogy explains that to become free from material existence, we have to serve the Lord and thus become happy – not by any other process. A *jñānī* may think that just by gaining knowledge, he is freed, but as long as he speculates about spiritual matters, he will not achieve any results.

The analogy compares the *jñānī* to a person who beats the empty paddy after the grain has been taken away—there is no benefit in husking the skin of an empty paddy. He ends up empty-handed despite doing so much hard work. Similarly, a *jñānī* ends up with nothing even after studying so much because the cause of his bondage still exists. He still has material desires to enjoy and to be as great as God. Only by devotional service can this cause be destroyed. Therefore, the devotee is like the farmer who gets the paddy full of grain.

To understand this analogy better, do the following exercise:

In the picture below is a lost *jñānī*, who has come to two mysterious doors on his spiritual journey. One of the doors has a picture of empty paddy husk on it, and the other door has a picture of paddy grains on it. The following signboard is hung at the entrance of the doors: ONE DOOR LEADS TO EXHAUSTION, THE OTHER TO HAPPINESS. PICK THE RIGHT KEY. YOU HAVE ONLY ONE CHANCE. There are two keys from which he can choose: one with a picture of a *tilaka* on it that opens the door to happiness, and the other with nothing on it that opens the door to exhaustion.

Write a note to the *jñānī* to help him decide which key to match to the door that leads to happiness? Use the analogy above to explain your point.

Complete the table below to help you write an accurate message:

	Is compared to…
Paddy grain	
Paddy husk	
Beating the paddy	

Message:..

....

....

....

....

....

....

Artistic Activity

. . . to reveal your creativity!

THE CYCLE OF BIRTH AND DEATH

Just thinking of the process of birth and death and the soul's transmigration from higher and lower species made Devahūti cringe!

Let's make an image of the cycle of birth and death. Refer to the directions and picture below.

What you will need: Cardboard; stiff paper; paint; sequins, beads, or fancy buttons; scissors; glue

Directions:

- On a big piece of cardboard, paint a background of the universe, planets, moon, and stars, and leave to dry.
- On a sheet of stiff paper draw different species of life that the soul travels through and paint them.
- Also draw and paint a picture of Kṛṣṇa.
- Once the pictures are dry, cut them out, and stick a sequin on each to represent the soul.
- Place your cut-out images in a circular pattern on your dry universe background. Place Kṛṣṇa in the center and the living entities around Him, showing that He is the source of the living beings and the destroyer of the cycle of birth and death.
- Cut out strips of card and glue them to the back of your living entities so they are slightly raised.
- Now glue the living entities and Kṛṣṇa to the background. Connect them with dots of paint as in the image on the previous page.

Action Activity . . . to get you moving!

STEPPING-STONES AND STUMBLING BLOCKS GAME

Description: In this chapter Lord Kapila talks about things favorable to Kṛṣṇa consciousness and things unfavorable for our progress. Design a board game based on these concepts.

Steps:

- Read the story summary and the verse translations.
- Pick a board game that you would like to use for your design, or create an entirely new design.
- For example, if you chose the game "Snakes and Ladders," then design your board with a hundred numbered squares, placing the snakes and ladders (or stepping-stones) at appropriate places.
- Here the snakes would correspond to unfavorable qualities or attitudes, and ladders (or stepping-stones) would be favorable attitudes in Kṛṣṇa's service.
- Now create labels for each snake on your board with a negative behavior, e.g., envious of Kṛṣṇa; desire to be master of everything; uncontrolled mind, etc. Positive behaviors corresponding to ladders could be self-controlled; sees with equal vision; detached; chants the holy names, etc.
- Instead of a label you could draw an image of the behavior, e.g., for chanting, you may draw a bead bag, or a person doing *kīrtana* with *karatālas*. (The artwork can be simple but self-explanatory.)
- Once you label all the snakes, which are the stumbling blocks, and the ladders, which are the stepping-stones in your devotional service, play the game with a friend using a dice and tokens as you would in "Snakes and Ladders."

Introspective Activity

. . . to bring out the reflective devotee in you!

JOURNAL OF WAKING AND DREAMING ACTIVITIES

"Consciousness acts in three stages under the material conception of life. When we are awake, consciousness acts in a particular way, when we are asleep it acts in a different way, and when we are in deep sleep, consciousness acts in still another way. To become Kṛṣṇa conscious, one has to become transcendental to these three stages of consciousness." (*SB*.3.27.10, purport)

The stages of being awake, being asleep (with dreams), and being in deep sleep (with no dreams) are the three stages of consciousness that we all experience. But we are different from these three states – we are the spirit soul who causes these different states of consciousness to appear real, just like the sun causes all activities on earth to continue.

- To understand this better, keep a journal, not just of your waking activities in the day but also of your activities in your dreams at night. And if you don't have any dreams, make a note of your deep, dreamless sleep. Make a note of all your different feelings, desires, and fears in your waking state and dream state.
- Fill in the journal for a week, and then look back through it. Imagine yourself like the sun, which witnesses all activities on Earth but doesn't get involved in any of them. Similarly, you (the soul) are a witness to all the activities of the mind and body, but you are not actually involved in them. Because of attachment you think you are involved. As Śrīla Prabhupāda points out in the purport to verse 4: "The spirit soul has nothing to do with this material nature, but because of his mentality of lording it over, he is put into the position of conditional existence."
- So, as you read through your journal, try to think about how you are different to the mind and body. Try to capture a feeling of what you really are, the soul, which never changes even through all the changes of the body and mind. This is called *ātmavān*, realising the self. "The word *ātmavān* especially means that one should be self-possessed. He should always remain in the pure consciousness that he is spirit soul and not the material body or the mind. That will make him progress confidently in Kṛṣṇa consciousness." (*SB*.3.27.8, purport)

Critical-Thinking Activity
. . . to bring out the spiritual investigator in you!

KṚṢṆA: THE PROPRIETOR, ENJOYER, AND DEAREST FRIEND

Śrīla Prabhupāda describes how one must be firmly convinced of these three principles: 1) Kṛṣṇa is the proprietor, 2) Kṛṣṇa is the enjoyer, and 3) Kṛṣṇa is the friend of all living beings.

Directions: First explain how Kṛṣṇa is three of these principles. Then describe how humanity tends to act like Kṛṣṇa in these three ways, give an example of each, and explain the results of acting in these ways. Then write your conclusion from this exercise.

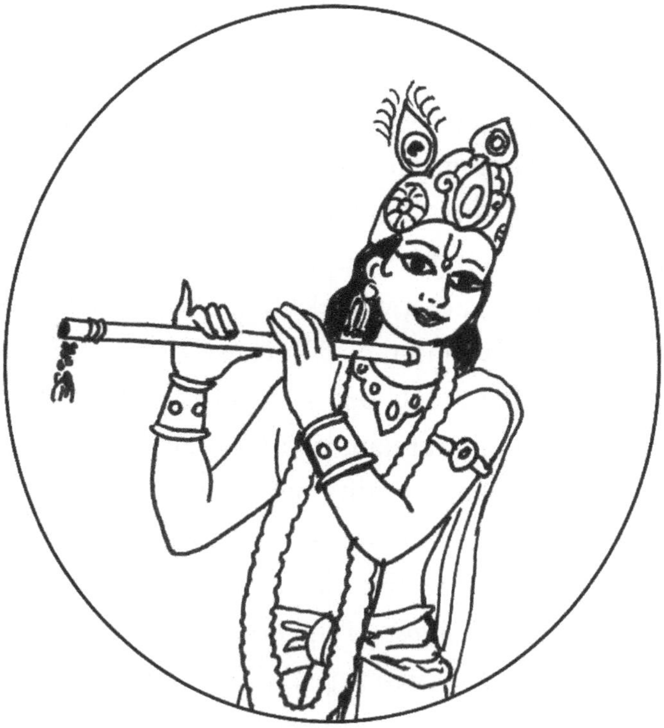

1. How is Kṛṣṇa the ultimate proprietor?

____

____

How do humans think they are the proprietors? What is the disadvantage of acting like this?

____

____

2. How is Kṛṣṇa the enjoyer?

____

____

How do humans think they are the enjoyers? What is the result of acting like this?

____

____

3. How is Kṛṣṇa the friend of all living beings?

____

____

How do humans think they are the great friends of everyone? What is the result of acting like this?

____

____

Conclusion: ____

____

____

Writing and Language Activities

. . . to make you understand better!

ESSAY: LORD KAPILA'S LESSONS

As a quick review and an in-depth study, read and discuss with your teacher or friends some of the main lessons in this chapter that were taught by Lord Kapila. In a short essay, summarize some of the lessons Lord Kapila is teaching his mother, Devahūti.

Follow the guidelines below:

- Choose at least three main points/topics of Lord Kapila's discussion. Refer to the themes of this chapter for ideas or choose topics that appeal to you.

- Elaborate on them, using the explanations from Śrīla Prabhupāda's purports. You may use some of the analogies to illustrate the points.
- Describe or give examples how we can practice Lord Kapiladeva's teachings in our everyday lives.

WHAT DO YOU THINK?

Set 1 - Tick the statements that you think are correct. If they are incorrect, write the sentence with the correct information.

1. Unless and until a person begins offering rituals to the Lord, he will never be freed from the cycle of birth and death.
2. The soul suffers so many misfortunes only due to his desire to be the master of everything around him.
3. "O mother, by controlling the mind, becoming faithful, and following the process of chanting and hearing about Me, a devotee can attain pure devotional service."
4. The self-realized person sees everything the same as the Lord, always thinking how everything can be engaged in His service.
5. It is only due to forgetfulness of his relationship with God for so long that the soul thinks he is lost.
6. How can the human being be separated from material nature when they have been eternally attracted to each another?
7. "A person can liberate himself from matter simply by continuous service to Me, and hearing about Me or from Me."
8. The secret to freedom from material nature is giving up the desire to be a demigod!

Set 2 – INFERRING QUESTIONS

Using the story summary and what you know, do you agree or disagree with the following questions? Back up your argument with reasons.

1. When Lord Kapila says "Therefore, he should engage his mind in devotional service to Me and offer everything to Me, without desiring to enjoy himself," we can infer that the Lord means that the soul should not enjoy anything.

2. Lord Kapila said that the process of awakening from material life is like a dream: When we wake up, we are not disturbed or even care for the dream. Here we can infer that when we awaken our relationship with God, we will let go of any attachment which binds us to the material world because it is simply not appealing to us anymore.

EXECUTING DEVOTIONAL SERVICE

In this activity, contemplate the qualities one needs to develop while executing devotional service as stated in this chapter. Then in your notebooks describe in your own words what you understand of the qualities or characteristics below. Give a reason why you think they are necessary or conducive to devotional service as Śrīla Prabhupāda mentions in the purports to these verses:

1. Seeing every living entity equally
2. Having no enmity towards anyone
3. Observing celibacy
4. Being grave and executing eternal activities
5. Offering the results of work to the Supreme Personality of Godhead
6. Being satisfied with what you earn
7. Not eating more than necessary
8. Living in a secluded place
9. Being thoughtful, peaceful, friendly, compassionate, and self-realized
10. Not unnecessarily identifying with the body and thus becoming attracted to bodily relationships

FILL IN THE BLANKS

Fill in the blanks by choosing the appropriate answer from the box below:

faulty	purified	sun	proprietorship
detachment	welfare	individuality	
devotional service	*vairāgya*	mental	matter
peace	ignorance	spirit	

1. Simply by beginning the discharge of devotional service one can attain ____________________ and transcendental knowledge for understanding the science of God.
2. One who is free from the modes of nature becomes like the ____________________ reflected on water, unaffected by the wavering of the water.
3. Liberation means reinstatement in one's ____________________________ position.
4. The false sense of ______________________ can be avoided simply by engaging in devotional service under the direction of the Supreme Lord or His representative.

5. A conditioned soul cannot understand that any action he performs in sense gratification is ________________.
6. One who desires liberation has to turn his activities into ______________________.
7. Due to different _________________________ conditions, in dreams we are put into different positions.
8. We perform _____________________________ work, thinking we are the friends of human society.
9. True detachment is called ______________________ in Sanskrit.
10. ______________________ of mind is necessary for executing Kṛṣṇa consciousness.
11. A person should learn how to distinguish between the nature of _______________ and the nature of ___________________.
12. Real service to the Lord begins when the senses are _________________________.
13. A green bird enters a green tree and appears to merge into the tree but does not lose its ___________________________. Similarly, the living entity, merged either in the material or spiritual nature, does not lose his individuality.
14. Only in _______________________________ does the living entity think he is lost.

ANSWERS

Understanding the Story: 1) c, 2) a, 3) b, 4) c, 5) a, 6) b, 7) a, 8) b, 9) b, 10) a

Important Chapter Analogies

1. In verse 1: A liberated soul is compared to the sun. The material world is compared to water. Just as the sun is millions of miles away from the water, is not affected by the water but is reflected on it, the liberated soul is detached from and unaffected by material nature. He is always in the spiritual world even though in the material world.
2. Material existence is compared to a dream. And a conditioned soul's mentality is compared to experiences in a dream. A living entity is transcendental to material nature but because he desires to enjoy the material world, he is put into material existence just as a person who experiences different mentalities in a dream.
3. A person who has lost his money may feel lost even though it's only the money he has lost. Similarly, as soon as he realizes that he is an eternal servant of the Lord and not the body, which makes him distressed, he will no longer feel lost or unhappy.
4. The person freed from false ego is compared to the sun. When a person is free from false ego, he regains his vision and sees himself as a servant of God just as he sees the sun in the sky.
5. Just as the earth and its aroma or the water and its taste cannot be separated, the intelligence and consciousness cannot be separated. When there is consciousness (the earth), there is intelligence (aroma).
6. Wooden sticks are compared to the cause of material existence, and the fire is compared to devotional service. Just as wooden sticks that light a fire are consumed by the fire, so the cause of our bondage (the fire of material existence) can be consumed by the fire of devotional service.
7. Dreaming state is compared to covered consciousness and awakened state is compared to awakened consciousness. Just as in a dream, one is covered and sees unfavorable, disturbing things that give him anxiety, in material consciousness one is covered by the false ego and is affected by many disturbances. And just as when one who awakens from a dream is unaffected by the dream, one who is awakened in Kṛṣṇa consciousness is unaffected by material nature.

The Empty Paddy Husk

Paddy grain – devotional service; paddy husk – thinking oneself as God and acting out of envy and desire; beating the paddy – attempts to fulfill the desire by *jñāna* (knowledge).

Sample answer: Dear Jñānī, remember that paddy is beaten to get the rice grain inside it out, for that is the valuable thing. The husk is useless on its own. Similarly, according to *Śrīmad-Bhāgavatam*, we should act to get real happiness through serving the Supreme Lord, not by just acquiring knowledge. No matter how much you study, you will not be free of material desire.

Kṛṣṇa: The Proprietor, Enjoyer, and Dearest Friend *(Potential Answers)*

1. *Kṛṣṇa is the proprietor:* Kṛṣṇa is the cause of all causes and the original creator. Everything is part of His energies, so He owns everything.

   Humans think they are the proprietors: Humans claim plots of land, people, material things, and ideas as their own, dismissing that everything comes from God. *Example:* Wars fought between indigenous people and colonists. *Disadvantage:* There is misery and bloodshed from wars and oppression.

2. *Kṛṣṇa is the enjoyer:* Kṛṣṇa creates everything for His enjoyment. He is the original *puruṣa* (male) and material nature is *prakṛti* (female), which is meant to be enjoyed by Him. No one can enjoy like Kṛṣṇa; unlike us, He can enjoy unlimitedly.

   Humans think they are the enjoyer: People think that the mind, body, and senses are simply meant to enjoy. *Examples:* They enjoy rich foods, recreation, intoxication, sex, and even philosophical speculation. *Result:* By simply gratifying the mind and senses, people are left unsatisfied and unfulfilled because they have neglected the soul, which can only get real happiness and enjoyment from serving Kṛṣṇa. There is only a limit to what we can enjoy.

3. *Kṛṣṇa is the friend of all living beings:* Kṛṣṇa is accompanying the living being as the Supersoul through lifetimes, so he is the closest friend. He truly knows every living being, their sufferings, needs and wants, and only He can completely help and satisfy them. He loves us unconditionally even though we have turned away from Him and tries to remind us to return to Him.

   Humans think they are the great friends of everyone: Humans practice charity, altruism, and philanthropic work to relieve others from suffering. *Examples:* The opening of hospitals and old age homes and feeding the poor. *Result:* Although this is in the mode of goodness and give temporary results, material welfare work cannot help people permanently end their suffering – from the cycle of birth, sickness, old age, and death. It's best to give people a permanent solution to their suffering by directing them to their best friend Kṛṣṇa, who will free them from material existence and give them lasting happiness.

Conclusion: Real enjoyment or happiness can only be experienced through connecting with Kṛṣṇa. Our attempts to be the controllers, enjoyers, and so-called friends end up in frustration and suffering. When we understand that Kṛṣṇa is the ultimate proprietor, enjoyer, and friend, we can take shelter of Him. This will give us true happiness and satisfaction.

What do you think?

1. False: Unless and until a person **begins devotional service to the Lord**, he will never be freed from the cycle of birth and death.
2. True
3. True
4. False: The self-realized person sees everything **as a reflection of the Lord**, always thinking how everything can be engaged in His service.
5. True
6. False: How can the **spirit soul** be separated from material nature when they have been eternally attracted to each another?
7. True
8. False: The secret to freedom from material nature is giving up the desire to be **God**!

Inferring Questions

1. False: Kṛṣṇa is referring to material enjoyment or enjoying separately from Him. Because we are part of Kṛṣṇa and the soul's nature is to be blissful, when we connect with Kṛṣṇa, the supreme enjoyer, we will feel true happiness and enjoyment.
2. True

Fill in the Blanks

1. detachment; 2. sun; 3. original; 4. proprietorship; 5. faulty; 6. devotional service; 7. mental; 8. welfare/philanthropic; 9. *vairāgya*; 10. peace; 11. matter; spirit; 12. purified; 13. individuality; 14. ignorance

28
Kapila's Instructions on the Execution of Devotional Service

Story Summary

"Mother," called Kapila.

"Yes, my son?"

"Shall we begin?"

Devahūti was ready. She was always ready. Every day she anticipated her son's discourse. So far she had learned everything about material nature: how material nature came into being, the principles of material nature, how Kṛṣṇa is the proprietor and controller of material nature yet is reflected in it, and how the influence of material nature cannot touch a devotee. Now she would learn about devotional service – the topmost *yoga* system.

"I'd like to describe the *yoga* system that has eight limbs, or parts," Kapila began. "It's called *aṣṭāṅga-yoga*. If you practice this *yoga*, you will be able to concentrate your mind. You will become joyful and get closer to the Lord."

"This seems practical and promising," thought Devahūti.

"There are eight parts to this form of *yoga*," said Kapila, "*yama, niyama, āsana, prāṇāyāma, dhyāna, dhāraṇā, pratyāhāra, and samādhi*."

Devahūti nodded.

"The first two, *yama* and *niyama*, basically means all the things you should do (*yama*) and the things you should not do (*niyama*) to be good and come closer to God. For instance, one should perform his duties to the best of his ability and avoid duties not meant for him. One should not steal and should be satisfied with what he gains by the grace of the Lord. One should eat only a little and live in a secluded place to practice spiritual life. One must be nonviolent, truthful, celibate and austere, and clean and silent. Silence means not to speak about nonsensical topics but only on topics of the Lord. Most importantly, one should study the Vedas and worship the spiritual master and the supreme form of the Lord.

"The third limb is called *āsana* – the practice of different *yogic* postures; by sitting in one place without becoming distracted, you'll become steady in mind.

"The fourth of the eight limbs of *aṣṭāṅga-yoga* is *prāṇāyāma* – controlling your breathing; the fifth is *pratyāhāra* – withdrawing the senses from sense objects; the sixth is *dhāraṇā* – concentrating the mind on the heart. In this stage you can fix your *prāṇa*, or life air, and mind on one of the six *cakras*, the six circles of air circulation within the body.

"This helps one to achieve *dhyāna* – meditation on Kṛṣṇa's pastimes. By meditating on the Lord, you will eventually reach the eighth limb, known as *samādhi* – total absorption in Lord Kṛṣṇa.

"By this process, or any other true process, one can control the contaminated mind and always think of Kṛṣṇa."

This all sounded wonderful to Devahūti.

She wanted to know more.

"Tell me more about the fourth part – *prāṇāyāma*. How shall I control my breathing?"

"After controlling the mind and practicing the *āsanas*, sit in a clean, quiet place with your body erect and practice breath control," replied Kapila. "You can breathe in very deeply, hold the breath in, and then exhale, or do it the other way around – first exhale, hold your breath, and then inhale. This steadies the mind and clears all mental disturbances."

"Oh!" Devahūti exclaimed. "*Prāṇāyāma* alone steadies the mind. Do the other stages have their own effects?"

"Well, *prāṇāyāma* also frees one from diseases of the body and mind; *pratyāhāra* (controlling the senses) frees one from material association; *dhāraṇā* (concentrating the mind) frees one from sinful activities; and *dhyāna* (or meditating on Lord Kṛṣṇa) frees one from the modes of material nature."

Freedom from the modes of nature? Yes, this was what Devahūti so desperately wanted. "How does one meditate on Lord Kṛṣṇa in *dhyāna*?" she asked.

"Concentrate on the tip of your nose and see the Supreme Personality of Godhead within your mind.

"The Lord has a cheerful, lotuslike expression with reddish eyes like the inside of a lotus and a dark complexion like the petals of a blue lotus. He bears a conch, discus, and mace in three of His hands. His loins are covered by a shining cloth, yellowish like the filaments of a lotus. On His breast He bears the mark of Śrīvatsa, a curl of white hair. The brilliant Kaustubha gem is suspended from His neck. He also wears a garland of attractive sylvan flowers around His neck, and a swarm of bees, intoxicated by its delicious fragrance, hums about the garland. He also wears a pearl necklace, a crown, and pairs of armlets, bracelets, and anklets.

"His loins and hips are encircled by a girdle, and He stands on the lotus of His devotee's heart. He is most charming, and His serene disposition gladdens the eyes and souls of the devotees. The Lord is eternally very beautiful, and He is worshiped by all the inhabitants of every planet. He is ever youthful and always eager to bestow His blessing upon His devotees."

Devahūti's eyes widened in wonder. How she wished she could see the Lord like this!

"Meditate on the glories of Kṛṣṇa and His devotees and meditate on His form until the mind is fixed. In devotional service the *yogī* visualizes within himself the Lord standing, moving, lying, and sitting.

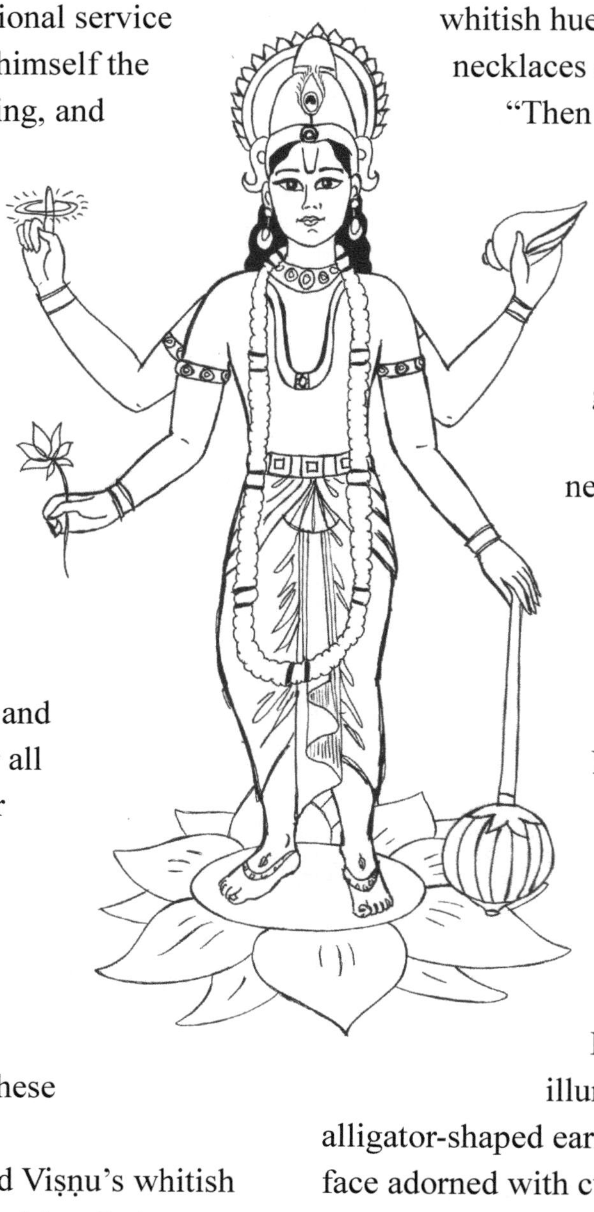

"But, my dear mother, it's better that you don't think of His whole body at once; rather, think of each of His different limbs, beginning with His feet. Meditate on His lotus feet for a long time, which are decorated with auspicious marks of the thunderbolt, goad, banner, and lotus. His lotus feet shatter all sin in the mind. Remember how Lord Śiva held the river Ganges on his head? The Ganges water had washed the Lord's lotus feet, and so Śiva became more blessed by carrying these waters on his head.

"Next, meditate on Lord Viṣṇu's whitish blue legs and thighs that Goddess Lakṣmī massages and that look graceful when the Lord sits on Garuḍa's shoulders.

"Focus next on the Lord's rounded hips, which are embraced with a girdle. His yellow silk cloth drapes majestically to His ankles.

"Move up to His navel, the origin of the lotus from where Lord Brahmā was born and from where the planetary systems manifest. His nipples look like emeralds with a whitish hue because of the white pearl necklaces on His chest.

"Then see His chest. Oh, it brings such pleasure and satisfaction to the eyes! Then His neck. His neck enhances the beauty of the Kaustubha gem.

"See His four arms next, which are the power of the demigods; then His ornaments, which came from the Mandara Mountain during the churning of the ocean. Next, look at His *cakra*, conch, and club. Admire His garland surrounded by bumblebees, His pearl necklace, His countenance, His nose, His crystal-clear cheeks illuminated by His glittering alligator-shaped earrings, and His exquisite face adorned with curly black hair, lotuslike eyes, and dancing eyebrows."

Devahūti already had her eyes closed in deep meditation with a smile on her lips.

"With devotion look at His compassionate glance, which soothes all agonies; His smiling glances full of grace; His benevolent smile, which drives away grief; and His arched eyebrows, which can charm even Cupid. See His captivating laughter, which reveal His small teeth. They are just like jasmine buds that appear rosy by the splendor of His lips.

"Seeing this form, the *yogī* no longer desires to see anything else. Gradually, pure love and joy develop, and the mind withdraws from material activities. The mind is now one with the Lord – it does not act separately but acts to fulfill the desire of the Lord. The *yogī* realizes His relationship with the Lord and discovers that pleasure and pain come from the false ego, which comes from ignorance. Because he has realized his true identity, he forgets his bodily demands.

"At this point, Lord Kṛṣṇa takes charge of the *yogī's* body until his activities are finished in this world. The liberated soul realizes he and his body are not the same just as his family and wealth are different from him. He sees Kṛṣṇa in everything and so sees all living entities equally. He sees that just as fire is in different forms of wood, the soul is in different bodies.

"So this, mother, is how the liberated *yogī* reaches the highest perfectional stage of *yoga*, *samādhi*. He becomes self-realized after conquering the spell of *māyā*."

Themes and Key Messages

Please go through this table of themes and key messages, with corresponding verses, and discuss each topic further.

Theme	Reference	Key Messages
The eight limbs of *aṣṭāṅga-yoga* are meant to realize the Supreme Lord Viṣṇu.	3.28.1–5	The eight limbs of *aṣṭāṅga-yoga* (see story summary) are meant to develop steadiness or discipline and to eventually concentrate the mind on the Lord's personal form. The different stages of *yoga*, including *yoga* postures and breathing techniques, are only meant to help us absorb our mind in Viṣṇu or Kṛṣṇa.
Kṛṣṇa consciousness is the topmost *yoga* system – we can control the mind and achieve concentration in *yoga* by hearing and chanting the glories of the Lord.	3.28.6–11	The easiest way to control the unbridled mind is to focus it on Kṛṣṇa's form or pastimes. The mind cannot be fixed on something void or impersonal. Lord Caitanya recommended that in this age one should chant Hare Kṛṣṇa to purify the mind and realize Kṛṣṇa. Devotional service, or *bhakti-yoga*, begins with hearing and chanting and is considered easier and more practical in this age, whereas *aṣṭāṅga-yoga* begins with concentration and restraining the mind and senses and is more difficult in this age.
We should focus our mind on the form of the Supreme Personality of Godhead.	3.28.12–14, 16–18, 29–30	Impersonal meditation is very difficult, so we should meditate on Kṛṣṇa's personal form. His form is not a concoction of imagination but described in detail in the authorized scriptures. His form and beauty are ever- existing; therefore, He is always youthful. When we focus the mind on this form of Kṛṣṇa, we can reach the perfection of *yoga*, which is *samādhi*, complete absorption in the Lord.
The process of hearing is easier than meditating on the Lord in the heart.	3.28.18–19	The process of thinking of the Lord within oneself and of chanting the holy names give the same results. However, visualizing the Lord in the heart is more difficult because the mind gets easily disturbed and interrupted. But when there is sound, we are forced to hear. When hearing enters the mind, we automatically perform *yoga*, because when we hear about the Lord our mind immediately thinks of Kṛṣṇa.
One should not meditate on the entire form of the Lord at once but start from His lotus feet.	3.28.20–30	Lord Kapila recommends that we meditate on the Lord's form one limb at a time, starting with the Lord's lotus feet. When we first meditate upon the auspicious markings on the Lord's lotus feet and the brilliance of His nails, we can be freed from the darkness of ignorance. His lotus feet shatter the mountain of sin within the heart. Even Lord Śiva becomes more blessed and important because he carries on his head the Ganges that has washed the Lord's lotus feet.
Meditating on different physical attributes of the Lord frees one from misery and grief.	3.28.31–34	One becomes free from all suffering and becomes fully happy and satisfied when he meditates on the Lord's face and compassionate glance, His smile, eyebrows, and laughter. In this way, a *yogī* develops pure love for the Supreme Personality of Godhead.
When one dovetails his mind with the mind of the Lord, he reaches the perfectional stage of *nirvāṇa*.	3.28.35–36	In the *Bhagavad-gītā* we see how Arjuna dovetailed his mind with Kṛṣṇa's mind. First Arjuna didn't want to fight in the war, but after Kṛṣṇa spoke to him the *Bhagavad-gītā* and convinced him about his duty, he agreed and followed Kṛṣṇa's wishes to fight. When the mind becomes purified with love for Kṛṣṇa, it acts to fulfill Kṛṣṇa's desires. This is called *nirvāṇa*, in which the mind becomes free from material desire. Just as when a flame of a lamp is extinguished but the energy of the flame is still conserved, the mind's material desires are extinguished but conserved or transformed to perform devotional service. In this stage the mind becomes unaffected by happiness and distress, knowing that this is caused by the false ego.
The individual living entity is one with and at the same time different from the Lord. This is Lord Caitanya's *acintya-bhedābheda-tattva* philosophy.	3.28.40–44	The liberated *yogī* sees that he is different from the body and that the Lord is also different from him, just as the blazing fire is different from the sparks and smoke. The fire is like the Supreme Lord, the sparks are like the living entity, and the smoke is like material nature. The sparks and smoke come from the fire and are small compared to the fire but have the same qualities as the fire. Similarly, the living entities and material nature that come from the Lord are small and insignificant compared to Him but are His energies.

Understanding the Story

Now it's time for you to check how well you understood the story by answering these multiple-choice questions.

1. What is the secret to controlling the mind?
   a) Following the eight limbs of the *aṣṭāṅga-yoga* system, which culminates in *bhakti-yoga*
   b) Focusing the mind on the impersonal Brahman effulgence of the Lord
   c) Following various religious practices and austerities
2. Who is a true *yogī*?
   a) One who practices the difficult *yoga* postures
   b) One who fixes the mind on the Supreme Lord and His pastimes
   c) One who meditates on something void or impersonal
3. What is the name of the *yoga* process which leads to devotional service, described by Lord Kapiladeva in this chapter?
   a) *haṭha-yoga*
   b) *dhyāna yoga*
   c) *aṣṭāṅga-yoga*
4. How should such a *yogī* live his life?
   a) He should live simply and peacefully, study the Vedas, and worship the Lord by concentrating the mind on the Supersoul within the heart.
   b) He should do penance in a secluded place and focus on the *brahmajyoti* of the Lord.
   c) He should give in charity and practice breath control.
5. What is the technique to fix the mind upon the Supersoul within the heart?
   a) Chanting oṁ with every breath
   b) Controlling the mind through *prāṇāyāma* and then visualizing the Lord's beautiful form within the heart, starting from His lotus feet
   c) Visualizing the Lord's entire form all at once
6. What part of the Lord should one focus on first?
   a) On his whole body, not each individual limb of the Lord
   b) On the Lord's lotus feet first, which purifies the mind and heart
   c) On his beautiful face since the Lord's face is the most attractive

7. What happens when one meditates on the form of the Lord?
   a) One becomes freed from material desires and develops pure love for the Lord.
   b) One is still not able to control the mind.
   c) One gets promoted to the heavenly planets after death.
8. What should be the attitude of a devotee towards hearing about the Lord as shown by Devahūti?
   a) He should force his mind to hear about the Lord.
   b) He should not make any special effort to hear about the Lord.
   c) As Kṛṣṇa wants our love and devotion, a devotee should have complete willingness to hear of the Lord and engage in devotional service.
9. What stage of *aṣṭāṅga-yoga* involves meditating on the Lord's form?
   a) *pratyāhāra*
   b) *samādhi*
   c) *dhyāna*
10. Which divine personality is always engaged in massaging the feet of the Lord?
    a) Lord Brahmā
    b) Lakṣmī Devī
    c) Lord Śiva

Higher-Thinking Questions

Now try to deepen your understanding of this chapter by delving into Śrīla Prabhupāda's purports and reflecting on the following questions:

1. Have you ever attended a *yoga* class or practiced *prāṇāyāma*? What was your experience? Do you think it is possible to develop love of Kṛṣṇa only through this process of *haṭha-yoga*? What would you prefer for developing your love for Kṛṣṇa – *haṭha-yoga* or *bhakti-yoga*? Give a reason for your answer.
2. According to verse 2, in order to concentrate the mind, one should perform his prescribed work and avoid another's work. What are the next steps to concentrate the mind mentioned in verse 2? Reflecting on the next step, are you grateful for what you have, or do you always want more? Explain.
3. Based on the descriptions of the Lord's form in this chapter, which part of the Lord's body do you find most attractive? What is the best way for us to meditate on the form of the

Lord?

4. Where are the six vital airs or *cakras* situated in the body?
5. Lord Kapila describes how the devotee comes to understand the difference between the soul and the body. What examples does Śrīla Prabhupāda use to describe how the soul is different from the body in the purports to verses 39 and 40?
6. How is the liberated soul protected by the Lord as mentioned in verse 38 purport?
7. In verse 18 Lord Kapila mentions how one should glorify and meditate upon the Lord and His devotees. Which devotees of the Lord are your favorites to glorify? Śrīla Prabhupāda explains in the purport that "as one becomes purified by chanting the holy name of the Lord, so one can be purified simply by chanting the name of a holy devotee." Why is this so?
8. Chanting the names of the Lord and meditating on the form of the Lord are the same. But what is the only difference between the two activities described by Śrīla Prabhupāda in verse 19 purport? Explain what the added advantage of hearing is.
9. How is Lord Śiva even more blessed with the Ganges water on his head as described in verse 22 and purport? Explain what this proves about Lord Śiva's position as well as the demigods' position compared to Lord Kṛṣṇa's.
10. The Lord is wearing a very beautiful garland with a swarm of bees around it. Why are these bees attracted to the garland? What does this say about the garland itself and how it represents the spiritual world? See verse 15 purport.
11. Lakṣmī is considered Brahmā's mother even though he was born from Lord Viṣṇu. How can a father give birth to a child? How does Śrīla Prabhupāda answer this question in verse 25 purport.

ACTIVITIES

In this section you will find many exciting things to do. These activities will get you thinking, moving, drawing, and having loads of fun.

Analogy Activity . . . to bring out the scholar in you!

ONENESS AND DIFFERENCE

> "The blazing fire is different from the flames, from the sparks and from the smoke, although all are intimately connected because they are born from the same blazing wood.
> The Supreme Personality of Godhead, who is known as Parambrahma, is the seer. He is different from the *jīva* soul, or individual living entity, who is combined with the senses, the five elements and consciousness." (*SB* 3.28.40–41)

In this analogy the fire is compared to the Supreme Lord, the flames and sparks are the living entities, and the smoke is material nature.

In the table below, draw two separate diagrams to show the following:

- Components of the fire (the fire, sparks, and smoke) and how they are separate yet appear as one unit.
- The Supreme Lord and His energies (*jīva* and material body), clearly bringing out how they are different yet appear as one unit; for example, you can draw a person's body with the soul and Supersoul within the heart.

If you look at the fire, you will notice that all the elements it's composed of (the flames, sparks, and smoke) appear to be different from one another and yet they are also one with the fire. In the same way, the body, the soul, and the Supersoul are different from one another, but at the same time the *jīva* and the material universe are also part and parcel of the Supreme Lord and therefore one with Him. Just as the sparks and smoke are the same as the fire in quality (they possess heat and light), they are still different from the fire. Similarly, just as the *jīva* and material nature are the same in quality as the Lord (as His parts and parcels and His energies), they are different from the Lord.

Answer the following questions to further understand the body-soul-Supersoul to the fire-flame-smoke analogy:

1. What philosophy of Caitanya Mahāprabhu is Śrīla Prabhupāda using this analogy to explain (see verse 41 purport)? Briefly describe this philosophy in your own words according to your understanding.
2. What should we do to recognize the existence of the separate energies of the Lord within the body?
3. After one realizes this principle of oneness and difference, what does he naturally do according to verse 42?

Artistic Activity

. . . to reveal your creativity!

BE A YOGĪ

What you will need: paper and tracing paper, pens or pencils

Directions:

- Use tracing paper to trace the *yogī* silhouette given here and reproduce it on a page, coloring it in with black felt pen.
- Alternatively print, cut out, and paste it on a sheet of paper.
- Read about the qualities a *yogī* should develop. How should he act, where should he live, what should he practice, etc.?
- Around the silhouette draw thought bubbles and write his thoughts in them. Also write the mood, attitudes, and desirable activities surrounding the *yogī*.

Introspective Activity

. . . to bring out the reflective devotee in you!

WILLINGNESS TO HEAR

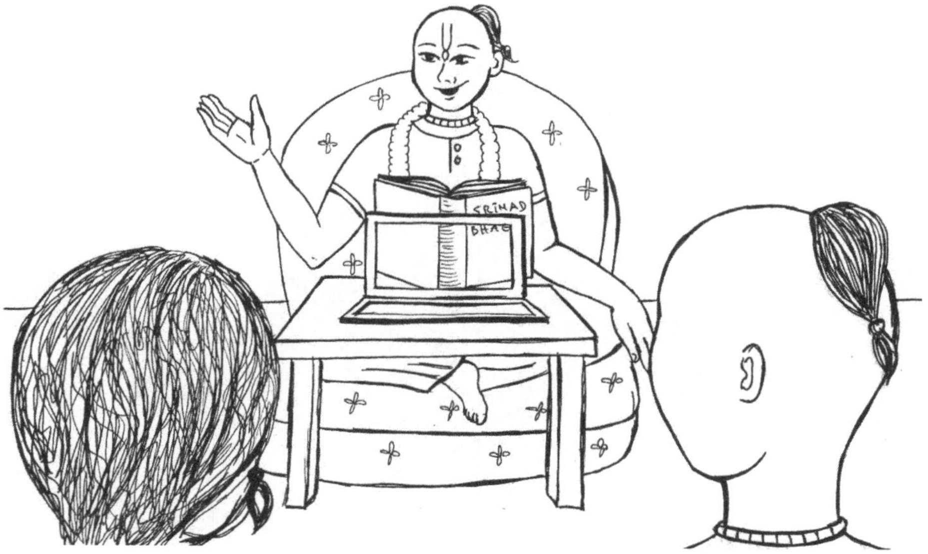

Devahūti is always eager to hear more about the Lord; thus, she demonstrates that hearing is the most effective method to meditate upon the Lord and engage in devotional service. The entire *Śrīmad-Bhāgavatam* is based on hearing: Mahārāja Parīkṣit heard from Śukadeva Gosvāmī; the sages of Naimiṣāraṇya heard from Sūta Gosvāmī; Vidura heard from Maitreya; Devahūti heard from Kapila, etc. How willing are you to hear of the Lord and engage in devotional service?

Instructions: Let's conduct an experiment. You will choose three hearing activities (doing *japa*; hearing *Śrīmad-Bhāgavatam* class; or performing *kīrtana*) or services to do every day for a week. Keep a journal and answer the following questions every day:

- Did you perform the three services today?
- Were you willing to do them or were you unwilling but did it anyway?
- Did the service inspire you to do more service or was it enough?
- Were you thinking of Kṛṣṇa? How?

Now, based on your journal entries and experience, write a paragraph on why willingness to hear and perform devotional service is the most necessary ingredient in *yoga* practice and how that translates in your life. For example, do you sometimes perform a chore or a service you do not want to do but are willing to do it because you said you would or it needs to be done? Do you think this willingness is an act of love? Does this service give a result anyway? Explain. Now write a conclusion as to why hearing is the secret ingredient to the *yoga* process.

Critical-Thinking Activities

. . . to bring out the spiritual investigator in you!

KṚṢṆA'S LOTUS FEET

Lord Kapila advises that we should meditate on the Lord, starting from His lotus feet. Verse 22 describes that "the lotus feet act like thunderbolts hurled to shatter the mountain of sin stored in the mind of the meditating devotee."

Here sin is compared to a mountain, which is difficult to destroy. But Kṛṣṇa's lotus feet are like thunderbolts that can easily smash a mountain. Therefore, gazing at the lotus feet, meditating on the lotus feet, touching the lotus feet, and worshiping the lotus feet of Kṛṣṇa, His expansions, or His pure devotees can remove the results of lifetimes of great sins. We become purified of the false ego, from material desires that make us commit sinful activities, and of various negative qualities.

To take shelter of the lotus feet also means to bow down in obedience to the teachings of Kṛṣṇa and His pure representatives.

In this research assignment you will be learning more about Kṛṣṇa's lotus feet and the importance of taking shelter of them. Answer the following questions based on your online research, help from your teacher, and the *Śrīmad-Bhāgavatam* and other texts.

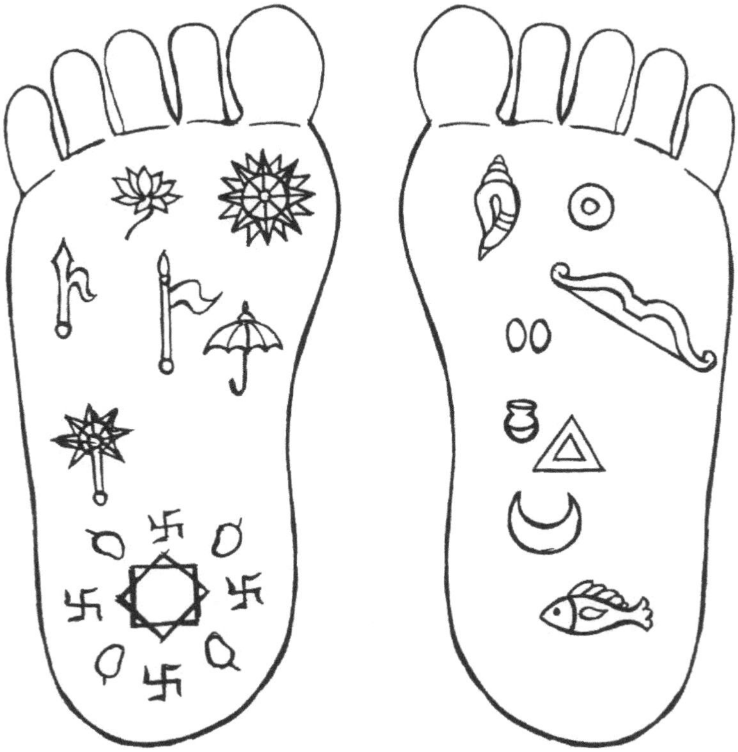

1. Why are Kṛṣṇa's feet referred to as "lotus feet"?
2. In the above illustration of Kṛṣṇa's lotus feet there are auspicious markings/ symbols on each of His feet. Research the names of each of the symbols and what they mean.
3. There are countless references to glorifying the "lotus feet" of Kṛṣṇa or His devotees in the scriptures. Quote a few verses or prayers from *Śrīmad-Bhāgavatam* or from songs that glorify the lotus feet of Kṛṣṇa or His pure devotee. For example, the *Śrī-Guru-Vandanā* that is sung during *guru-pūjā* wonderfully glorifies the lotus feet of the spiritual master.
4. Give three examples from the Lord's pastimes of His lotus feet being the shelter of His devotees; for example, the Kālīya-līlā.
5. Śrīla Prabhupāda explains in the purport to verse 21 that "one has to fix one's mind first on the lotus feet of the Lord if he wants to be freed from the darkness of ignorance in material existence." What specifically on the Lord's lotus feet is brilliant and can eradicate this darkness of ignorance?
6. Usually feet are considered unclean and something not deserving attention. Yet, the feet of Kṛṣṇa and great souls are considered most sacred? Why do you think this is so?

THE TOPMOST YOGA SYSTEM

Try the following experiments and then answer the questions that follow:

A. First practice some of the steps of *aṣṭāṅga-yoga*. Sit on the floor in an upright position with your legs folded (*āsana*). Now practice *prāṇāyāma* by inhaling deeply, holding the breath, and exhaling as described in this chapter. Then practice *pratyāhāra* by withdrawing the mind, not becoming distracted by anything. Now meditate on Lord Viṣṇu in the heart (*dhyāna*), starting from His lotus feet and then proceeding to the different parts of His body. Observe whether this is difficult or easy to do. How do you feel?

B. Now practice the same steps with the process of hearing involved. Follow the first two steps of *āsana* and *prāṇāyāma*. Next, instead of visualizing the Lord on your own, allow your teacher or a friend to read aloud some of the verses in this chapter that describe the Lord's beautiful form or alternately, read aloud your favorite pastime of Kṛṣṇa. Notice whether the mind is more attentive this time. Do you find it is easier or more difficult to concentrate on the Lord when sound is introduced? How do you feel?

1. To recap, list the eight limbs of the *aṣṭāṅga-yoga* process as described in the story summary and verse 1 purport. Describe each limb and what are the results of each.
2. Did you find it easier to meditate on the Lord on your own or when the descriptions or pastime were read to you? Why do you think this is so? (hint: see verse 19 purport)
3. Śrīla Prabhupāda also describes in verse 18 purport that seeing the Lord as the Deity in the temple is the same as meditating on His form in the mind? Why is this so? Do you find it easier to think of the Lord when you meditate on the Deity or even serve the Deity?
4. Why is chanting the holy name the most effective method in this age to control the mind and develop love for Kṛṣṇa?
5. What do you think should be the goal of all *yoga* practice? Do you think that the goal is just meditation as you experienced in your meditation activity? What does Śrīla Prabhupāda describe as the goal and topmost *yoga* system (see verse 34 purport).

Whether one meditates on the Lord's form within the mind, sees His form in the temple, or hears about Him, one should meditate on and worship the personal form of the Lord, not disregard the Lord's form. Even the impersonalists who deny the Lord's form meditate on the *oṁkāra*, the letter form of the Lord.

Writing and Language Activities
. . . to make you understand better!

B
A C

YOGA BROCHURE

Imagine you are a servant of Kapiladeva who has been asked to open an *aṣṭāṅga-yoga* studio in your town. You need to design a brochure to help visitors understand the process of *aṣṭāṅga-yoga*.

Directions:

- Given below are some notes from this chapter that list the purpose of *aṣṭāṅga-yoga*, its different steps, and the results one can achieve from its practice. Use the information provided to create a small booklet-style brochure for the studio.
- Each point in the first column can be the title of the page, and you can use the information in the second column to create details on the page. Write in full sentences with paragraphs. You may include your information under subheadings so it stands out clearly.
- Remember that you are trying to promote this style of *yoga*, so your brochure should look appealing. Add color, images, fun facts (from your memory of *Śrīmad-Bhāgavatam* study), and language and presentation techniques meant to convince and attract the reader.
- Don't forget to add details, such as your name, the name of your studio, its address, etc., to make the brochure look "real."
- After you plan your brochure on paper, you may design and lay out the brochure on a computer. Then print and hand it to your teacher or show it to your friends.

What is *yoga*?	• *yoga* = link (to the Supreme Person) • An ancient system of eight-step *yoga* taught by the mystic sage Kapila thousands of years ago in India • Guarantees inner peace, joy, and connection with God
Purpose	• Control the mind and focus it on the Supersoul (Lord Kṛṣṇa's form in our heart) • Progress in one's spiritual practice and achieve complete dependence on and surrender to the Lord • Become joyful and peaceful
Steps 1 and 2 – *yama* and *niyama*	• Pre-conditions to starting *yoga* practice – list of do's and don'ts that help purify the mind and prepare it to practice *yoga* • Helps one come to the mode of goodness, which makes *yoga* practice easy • Includes worship of *guru*, performing prescribed duties, practice of celibacy, nonviolence, truthfulness, etc.

Step 3 – *āsana*	• Practice of different body postures that make one steady • Brings harmony between body and mind, which makes it easy to focus the mind
Step 4 – *prāṇāyāma*	• Breathing exercises to help focus the mind and move the life air through the six bodily cakras or energy centers within the body • Makes the mind pure and peaceful
Steps 5, 6, 7 – *pratyāhāra, dhāraṇā, dhyāna*	• Withdrawing the peaceful mind from all disturbances of the senses • Increasing and intensifying meditation on the Supreme Lord
Step 8 – *samādhi*	• Complete absorption in meditation of the name, fame, qualities, pastimes, etc., of the Supreme Lord • Complete absence of desire to enjoy the material world
Experience/Result	• No more thinks oneself as the body • Develops pure love of God, which fills one with inner joy and satisfaction • Externally, experiences symptoms like hair standing on the end, tears of joy flowing from the eyes, etc. • Constantly in touch with and absorbed in thoughts of the Lord • Sees the Lord reflected in His energies; sees everyone equally

Note: If you are not familiar with creating a brochure, ask your teacher to show you samples and request help to create the brochure.

THE ORNAMENTS ON THE LORD'S BODY

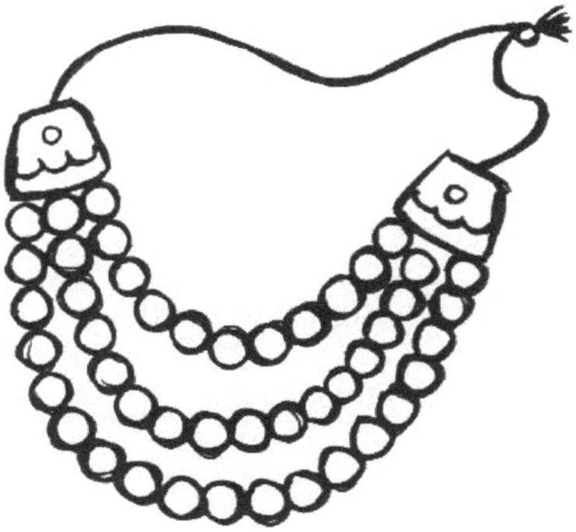

This chapter describes many of the beautiful ornaments decorating Lord Viṣṇu's body. Describe the following ornaments and decorations on His body and give one additional interesting point on each as mentioned in the verses and purports:

Shiny yellow cloth (verse 14): ....

....

Śrīvatsa (verse 14): ....

....

Kaustubha (verse 4): ....

....

Garland of sylvan flowers (verse 15): ....

....

Milk-white pearl necklaces on His chest (verse 25): ....

....

The Lord's polished ornaments (verse 27): ....

....

FILL IN THE BLANKS

1. One should not be attracted to get _______________ power through *yoga* practice.
2. The greatest *yogī* is he who constantly fixes his mind on __________________, the Supreme Personality of Godhead.
3. The execution of ____________________ is to be elevated to the spiritual platform and serve the Supreme Lord.
4. Practicing *yoga* without ___________________ the standard literatures is simply a waste of time.
5. ______________________ *yoga* is not an end in itself; it is a means to the end of attaining steadiness.
6. The power of the thunderbolt on Kṛṣṇa's feet can shatter the __________________ of dirt in the mind of a *yogī*.
7. ______________________ is Lord Brahmā's mother.
8. Generally, the lower part of the body of the Lord is dressed in _____________ silk.
9. Lord Brahmā was born from the abdomen of ______________________________.
10. The Lord's ____________ is the source of all transcendental pleasures of the mind.
11. The Lord's club is named _____________________.
12. The Lord descends to the material world out of His deep ____________________ for His devotees.

ANSWERS

Understanding the Story: 1) a, 2) b, 3) c, 4) a, 5) b, 6) b, 7) a, 8) c, 9) c, 10) b

Oneness and Difference

1. Lord Caitanya's philosophy of *acintya-bhedābheda-tattva* – the philosophy of simultaneous oneness and difference, which shows that the *jīva* and material nature are the same in quality as the Lord (as His parts and parcels and His energies), but they are different from the Lord because they are infinitesimal (very tiny).
2. The only way to realize this is by practicing *yoga* (in this age, *bhakti-yoga*); physically not seeing something should not be taken as proof of its non-existence.
3. A self-realized person understands the Lord's greatness and his position as His servant. He sees material nature as the Lord's energies, and he sees all living entities equally because he sees Kṛṣṇa in everyone's heart as the Supersoul.

The Topmost Yoga System *(Potential Answers)*

1. Refer to story summary for answers.
2. It is easier to meditate when sound is introduced because we are forced to hear. When we hear about the Lord, our mind immediately thinks of Kṛṣṇa.
3. All the limbs of devotional service, such as hearing, chanting, remembering, worshiping the Deity, etc., are on the absolute platform and give the same results.
4. It is the easiest method for self-realization in this age recommended by Caitanya Mahāprabhu. There are no strict rules to follow and one can chant in any place or at any time. Chanting attentively cleanses the heart of all dirt accumulated for lifetimes and immediately connects us with Kṛṣṇa.
5. The goal of *yoga* practice is to realize the Lord and our eternal relationship with Him and to connect with him in love (*bhakti-yoga*). Meditation is not the goal; it is the means to achieve the goal – when one realizes his relationship with the Lord, he wants to serve the Lord; service to the Supreme Lord is the goal. Since meditation in the lower stages is meant to come to the platform of devotional service, those already engaged in loving service to the Lord are above such meditation; therefore, Kṛṣṇa consciousness is the topmost *yoga* system.

Fill in the Blanks

1. mystic; 2. Kṛṣṇa; 3. *sva-dharma*; 4. reading/studying; 5. *haṭha-*; 6. mountain; 7. Lakṣmīdevī; 8. yellow; 9. Garbhodakaśāyī Viṣṇu; 10. chest; 11. Kaumodakī; 12. compassion

29
Explanation of Devotional Service by Lord Kapila

STORY SUMMARY

Devahūti was grateful. Her son had described the Sāṅkhya philosophy, the analytical study of all existence, which scientifically describes the symptoms of material nature and the characteristics of the spirit soul. But His description of devotional service captured her.

"Please explain devotional service now, my dear son," she said. "I understand that all types of *yoga* and philosophical systems end in devotional service."

Kapila smiled and nodded.

"Please tell me about the trials and tribulations of birth and death," Devahūti continued. "Hearing about such calamities will help us become more detached from this world. Please also describe eternal time, which represents You and which influences people to act piously when they know that their end is near.

"My Lord, people's eyes of knowledge are closed, so they are sleeping in darkness, falsely engaged in the actions and reactions of their activities in this world. They're tired. You're the light that can illumine their lives with knowledge."

Pleased with his mother's words and moved by compassion for the suffering conditioned souls, Lord Kapila explained, "There are different paths of devotional service depending on the person engaged in devotional service."

Devahūti's eyes widened in disbelief. She always thought devotional service to be of one kind. This would be interesting.

Kapila continued, "If a person is envious, proud, violent, angry, and a separatist and engages in devotional service, his devotional service is in the mode of ignorance."

"A separatist?" Devahūti raised her eyebrows.

"Yes, a separatist is a person who has separate interests from the Lord; he wants to get as much from the Lord as possible for enjoying his senses.

"If a person continues with this separatist mentality, serving the Lord in the temple just to get material enjoyment, fame, or opulence, his devotional service is in the mode of passion.

"And if he worships the Lord, offering the results of his activities to the Lord so he can be liberated from the material world, his devotional service is in the mode of goodness.

"However, there is a type of devotional service that is not influenced by the three modes of material nature – pure devotional service. This is when a person's mind is immediately attracted to the name and qualities of Lord Kṛṣṇa. Nothing can interrupt his service just as the Ganges flows naturally towards the ocean uninterrupted. Such a person doesn't even want the five types of liberation. In other words, he doesn't want anything material or spiritual from the Lord. He just wants to serve."

"This is a very exalted stage," thought Devahūti, and just as she wondered how one can progress from mixed devotional service to pure devotional service, Kapila explained, "A devotee must do his prescribed duties without expecting anything in return, and he must engage in devotional service without excess violence."

"Excess violence?" Devahūti pondered. "Ah yes. To live, we sometimes must take life from another – even from plants. But eating fruits and vegetables instead of animals reduces the amount of violence."

Kapila continued, "Devotees should regularly see My deity, touch My feet, worship Me, and pray to Me. From the mode of goodness, they should see everyone equally as spirit souls. They should offer great respect to the spiritual master, be compassionate to the poor, and be friends with equals. They must control their senses and live a regulated life. "In addition, devotees should always try to hear about spiritual matters and use their time to chant the names of the Lord. They should have simple, straightforward behavior. They should be friendly to everyone but avoid the company of persons not spiritually advanced.

"When a devotee develops these qualities, he'll be attracted to hearing about Me and hearing My names."

A gentle breeze suddenly carried a sweet fragrance of wild jasmine. Devahūti inhaled the scent, smiling. Kapila too inhaled the sweet scent.

"Mother, just see how the air carries the sweet aroma of jasmine. It caught our sense of smell. Devotional service is like this beautiful scent. One whose consciousness is filled with devotion for the Lord captures the existence of the Supersoul everywhere and in the hearts of all living entities. You see, mother, I'm in the hearts of all living entities as the Supersoul. If someone just worships the Deity in the temple but neglects or disrespects the Supersoul present in everyone's heart, this is simply imitation. In fact, these people are separatists. Envious. Their inimical behavior towards others, even if they worship Me with proper rituals and paraphernalia, will never bring them peace of mind. Neither would these persons please Me. Instead, they should offer all respect to others and engage them in the service of the Lord."

Devahūti was troubled. Surely there would be devotees with this mentality. Were they doomed? What could be done?

As if reading her mind, Kapila said, "The devotee must simply perform his duties and worship the Deity until he realises My presence in his and others' hearts. It's important to realize this, because at the time of death I cause fear in anyone who considers himself different to other living entities in any way."

Devahūti swallowed a lump in her throat.

"Therefore, through gifts, attention, friendly behavior, and seeing all alike, one will please Me.

"In fact, all classes of living entities should be respected because I am present in them. There are many classes of such living beings. For example, higher than inanimate objects, like stones and mountains, are living entities with life symptoms; even higher are animals with developed consciousness; then higher are entities with developed sense perception like trees. And then among the living entities who have developed sense perception, there is a certain hierarchy. First are those who have a developed sense of touch, higher than that are those with a developed sense of taste, then a developed sense of smell, then a developed sense of hearing. Higher than even that are living entities who can distinguish between one form and another, and higher are those with sets of teeth, then those with many legs. Higher than them are those with four legs, and higher are the human beings.

"Among the human beings, a society divided according to their qualities and work is best. Of these, the intelligent *brāhmaṇas* are best, and of these, the *brāhmaṇas* who study the Vedas are best. Of the *brāhmaṇas* who study the Vedas, those who know the purport of the Vedas are best, and of those, *brāhmaṇas* who can clear all doubts are the best. Of those, one who strictly follows principles are the best. Better than those is one who is liberated from material contamination. The best is the pure devotee who engages in devotional service with no expectation of reward.

"You see, mother, I do not find anyone greater than he who engages and dedicates all his activities to Me without interruption. Such a person respects all living entities, knowing that the Supreme Personality of Godhead is in their body as the Supersoul.

"My dear mother, follow this science of devotional service and you can achieve the abode of the Supreme Person."

Devahūti bowed her head with folded palms, ready to follow her son's instructions.

"I am also time," Kapila said. "Anyone who doesn't know this is afraid of time. Lord Viṣṇu is the time factor who enters everyone's hearts, supports everyone, and causes every being to be destroyed by another.

"In fact, no one is dear to the Lord, nor is anyone His enemy or friend. He simply inspires those who remember Him and destroys those who forget Him.

Out of fear the wind blows
Out of fear the sun shines
By fear only – rivers flow
And the rain pours

Heavenly bodies shed their luster
Plants, trees blossom. Fructify.
Fire burns all it can muster
Oceans are mortified
refusing to overflow
fear throughout is sown

Out of fear the earth doesn't sink
Even with its heavy, burdensome weight
Glorious demigods work in sync
As they create, maintain, and annihilate
Out of fear
Fear of the Supreme Personality of Godhead

"Therefore, dear mother, everything in the material world is controlled by me by the time factor, which has no beginning or end; it represents the Supreme Personality of Godhead and causes the creation and annihilation of the material world. It destroys even the Lord of death, Yamarāja."

Themes and Key Messages

Please go through this table of themes and key messages, with corresponding verses, and discuss each topic further.

Theme	Reference	Key Messages
The path of devotional service is the goal of all philosophy and *yoga* systems.	3.29.1–2, 35	All systems of *yoga* can only be successful when *bhakti-yoga*, or devotional service to the Lord, is applied. Any philosophy that does not aim toward devotional service is simply mental speculation and there is no result. It is like beating the husk when the grain is removed. Even Sāṅkhya philosophy is only meaningful when devotional service is applied. When one performs any authorized *yoga* process with *bhakti-yoga*, he achieves the Lord's abode.
Devotional service can be practiced in three modes: ignorance, passion, and goodness.	3.29.7–10	Different types of people take up to devotional service for various purposes. When devotional service is performed by someone who is envious, proud, violent, and angry, it is in the mode of ignorance; when a separatist performs devotional service, a person wanting material enjoyment, fame, and opulence, it is in the mode of passion; and when a devotee performs devotional service, offering the results to the Lord so he can be liberated, it is in the mode of goodness.
Pure devotional service is the transcendental stage and above the influence of the three modes of material nature. The Lord considers a devotee on this stage to be the topmost.	3.29.11–14, 33	Devotional service is pure and not influenced by the three modes when a devotee is only attracted to hearing the name and qualities of the Lord. He doesn't expect anything in return and thus serves the Lord unconditionally without any interruption. He does not even desire the five kinds of spiritual liberation and dedicates his life and activities to the Lord.
A devotee comes to the highest stage of devotional service by developing divine qualities and getting rid of negative qualities.	3.29.17–19	A devotee should greatly respect the spiritual master and *ācāryas*; be compassionate to the poor and make friendship with equals; control his senses; always hear about spiritual matters; and chant the Lord's holy names. He should be simple and straightforward, non-envious, friendly to everyone, and avoid the company of people who are not advanced. In this way he comes to the highest stage – simply attracted to hearing and chanting about the Lord.
A Kṛṣṇa conscious person can see and experience the Supersoul everywhere and in everyone's heart.	3.29.20–25, 34	A devotee understands that the Lord is present in everyone as the Supersoul, so he respects every living being and does not discriminate between anyone, although he treats them appropriately according to their positions. He is friendly to his equals and compassionate to the ignorant or lower forms of life. A devotee who simply worships the Deity in the temple and does not see the Lord, as Paramātmā, in everyone's heart is never peaceful and cannot please the Lord.
The time factor is the Supreme Lord, and anyone who doesn't know this is afraid of time, in the form of death.	3.29.37–38, 45	Everyone is fearful of death, which happens by the influence of time. No one can live in the material world forever – even Yamarāja, the lord of death dies. Everything is also changed and transformed by the time factor, but a devotee knows that the time factor is another manifestation of the Supreme Lord. He knows how it acts and is therefore not afraid.
Natural phenomena happen under the direction of the Lord.	3.29.40–45	Out of fear of the Supreme Lord, the natural phenomena in this world exists – the sun shines, the rain pours, the planets float, the plants and flowers blossom, etc. This is just to say that everything is working under the direction of the Lord's energies – His energies work so nicely that it seems that everything is working automatically. Since there are laws of nature, there must be a law maker. This is the Supreme Personality of Godhead.

Higher-Thinking Questions

Now try to deepen your understanding of this chapter by delving into Śrīla Prabhupāda's purports and reflecting on the following questions:

1. In verse 10 purport Śrīla Prabhupāda describes the nine devotional activities in three categories based on the three modes of material nature. Read the purport and describe how they are multiplied.
2. Lord Kapila mentions how the devotee in the mode of ignorance and passion sees himself as separate from the Supreme Lord. What is the result of such a "separatist" mentality, and in what ways can we prevent this in our lives? (hint: see verse 9 purport)
3. Although the pure devotee sees all living entities equally, he does not associate with those who are not spiritually advanced. He even avoids Vaiṣṇavas who are not of good character. Why is this so? (See verse 16 purport). How can we avoid this association without making people feel inferior?
4. As described in verse 28 purport, why is it important to understand and accept the difference in the consciousness of living entities although all spirit souls are created equally? Explain using the example of animals and how we should treat them.
5. Describe the three types of Vaiṣṇavas mentioned in verse 32 purport. Which Vaiṣṇava do you aspire to be and why?
6. What does it mean to dovetail one's enjoyment with the Supreme Lord as described in verse 35 purport? Think about your own experience as a devotee. How do you dovetail your desires and "cooperate with the Supreme Lord"? What analogy does Śrīla Prabhupāda use to describe this? Explain.
7. In verses 40–42 the Lord describes different natural phenomena in the universe occurring due to a fear of the Lord. Read the purports and try to describe what "fearing" the Lord truly means.
8. Text 4 describes that due to the fear of time, people commit pious activities to avoid suffering in this life and get a better life in the future. Is there anything wrong with this? How does a Vaiṣṇava see time and what does he do instead?
9. In the beginning of this chapter Devahūti describes how the conditioned souls neglect the Lord's supreme shelter and think they are their supreme shelter instead. How do people take shelter of their own activities? How do they take shelter of the Lord?

10. What does the Lord mean when he says, "the pure devotee does his best to commit the least amount of violence possible?" Is it possible to not commit violence at all? Why is it important to commit the least amount of violence (*nātihiṁsā*)? How can a devotee nullify the reactions even to *nātihiṁsā*? See purport to verse 15.
11. Text 1 purport describes that *bhakti-yoga* without philosophy is sentiment and philosophy without *bhakti-yoga* is mental speculation. What does this mean? Give examples from your knowledge to explain. Why do you think it's important to have both?
12. Why is the Lord displeased by someone who just worships the Deity in the temple but does not respect others? How did Śrīla Prabhupāda instruct devotees to treat people who come to the temple? See example in verse 24 purport.

ACTIVITIES

In this section you will find many exciting things to do. These activities will get you thinking, moving, drawing, and having loads of fun.

Action Activity . . . to get you moving!

ŚLOKA MEMORIZATION

Directions: To practice the mood of pure devotional service taught by Sri Caitanya Mahāprabhu and to understand these devotional principles explained in this chapter, read and memorize the third and fourth verses of the Śikṣāṣṭakam prayers.

Tips!

- Try memorizing each *śloka* line by line by finding the right meter. If it helps, read the Sanskrit word-for-word translation so you know what each word means. Then read the full translation.
- You can also make flash cards with the Sanskrit on one side and the translation on the other side of the card.
- Give yourself a reward once you've memorized each *śloka.*
- Have fun!

tṛṇād api sunīcena
taror api sahiṣṇunā
amāninā mānadena
kīrtanīyaḥ sadā hariḥ

One should chant the holy name of the Lord in a humble state of mind, thinking oneself lower than the straw in the street; one should be more tolerant than a tree, devoid of all sense of false prestige, and should be ready to offer all respect to others. In such a state of mind one can chant the holy name of the Lord constantly.

na dhanaṁ na janaṁ na sundarīṁ
kavitāṁ vā jagad-īśa kāmaye
mama janmani janmanīśvare
bhavatād bhaktir ahaitukī tvayi

O almighty Lord, I have no desire to accumulate wealth, nor do I desire beautiful women nor do I want any number of followers. I only want Your causeless devotional service, birth after birth.

Analogy Activity . . . to bring out the scholar in you!

CAPTURING THE EXISTENCE OF THE SUPERSOUL

"As a breeze carrying a pleasant fragrance from a garden of flowers at once captures the organ of smell, so one's consciousness, saturated with devotion, can at once capture the transcendental existence of the Supreme Personality of Godhead, who, in His Paramātmā feature, is present everywhere, even in the heart of every living being." (*SB*.3.29.20, purport)

1. What does each of the items below represent in the analogy?

Breeze	Fragrance	Sense of smell
		Paramātmā (Supersoul)

2. In your own words explain what principle is being discussed here.
3. How does a person who experiences the Supersoul act?
4. Write down three personal services you can engage in regularly with this vision.
5. A person who does not have this vision of the Paramātmā in everyone's heart but just serves the Deity in the temple is considered ignorant. He is compared to one who offers oblations into ashes. Explain what this analogy means.

Artistic Activity
. . . to reveal your creativity!

HAND-PRINT PICTURES

This chapter describes the different grades of living entities in a certain hierarchy: first those who have consciousness; then those who display symptoms of life; those who are animals, etc.

Directions:
Make hand-print pictures of the different grades of living entities described in this chapter summary.

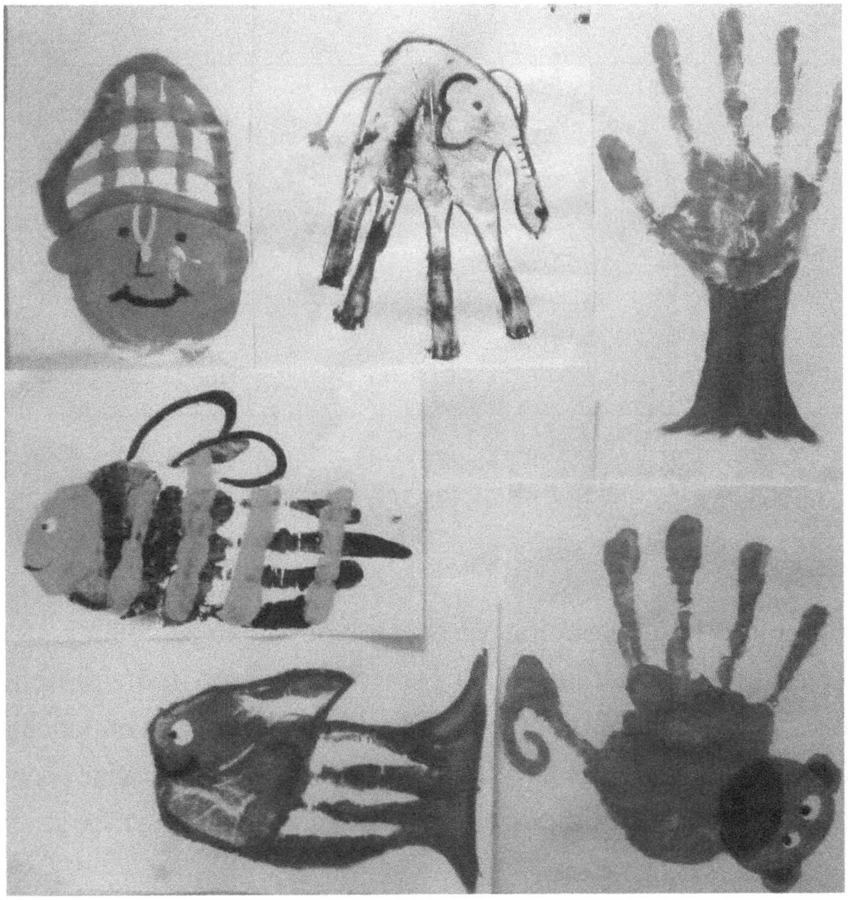

What you will need:
Paper; paints; hands that don't mind getting messy!

Instructions:
- Dip your hand in paint and place it steadily on a piece of large paper. Then make various handprints out of different colors of paint.
- Now adapt these into animals and other living entities as shown in the sample picture below. Choose your color and how you place your fingers, depending on the image you want to create. You can make stones, trees, fish, serpents, wasps, four-legged animals, humans, *brāhmaṇas*, and pure devotees.
- Paint details over the handprint to give it a body structure.

Introspective Activity

. . . to bring out the reflective devotee in you!

EVERY LIVING BEING IS SPIRITUAL

"The devotee should regularly see My statues in the temple, touch My lotus feet and offer worshipable paraphernalia and prayer. He should see in the spirit of renunciation, from the mode of goodness, and see every living entity as spiritual." (*SB*.3.29.16)

Discuss with your parents, teacher, or friends about what it means to see every living entity as spiritual.

There is a famous saying, *ātmavān manyate jagat*, which means "as I see so the whole world sees." This means that I see other people in the same way I see myself. If I see myself as a material body, then I will also see everyone else in terms of their material body; if I see myself as a human being with a particular type of body, then I will automatically see other living entities as cats, dogs, rabbits, fish, etc.

So to see other people as spiritual, we have to first see ourselves as spirit souls.

Use the technique described in Canto 3, Volume 1: think about each part of your body and ask, "Is this hand me, or is this hand mine?" When we begin to feel that we are something different from this body, we can project the same idea onto other living beings and also see them as spirit souls.

After you develop this mentality a bit more, look around at how some of Kṛṣṇa's parts and parcels are acting. Some are serving Him as the Deity in the temple while others engage in sense gratification. Still, Kṛṣṇa is present in every living being as the Supersoul, witnessing their activities.

With this spiritual vision, you are now seeing everyone and everything with detachment from the mode of goodness.

Critical-Thinking Activity

. . . to bring out the spiritual investigator in you!

THE CLASSES OF BHAKTI

Pure *bhakti* or devotional service to the Lord is beyond the three modes and can elevate the devotee beyond the three modes. Yet in this chapter Kapiladeva speaks of *bhakti within* the modes: goodness, passion, and ignorance. How do we understand this?

Do one of the following exercises based on the classes of *bhakti*:

Exercise 1:
Given below are three sets of circles, each representing one of the three modes. Color in the first set blue to indicate *tamo-guṇa* (mode of ignorance), the second set red to indicate *rajo-guṇa* (mode of passion), and the third set yellow to indicate *sattva-guṇa* (mode of goodness). The last column with flowers represents pure devotional service or *śuddha-sattva* (mode of pure goodness). Color them in different colors.

Bhakti in *tamo-guṇa*	Bhakti in *rajo-guṇa*	Bhakti in *sattva-guṇa*	Bhakti in *śuddha-sattva* (pure goodness)
◯	◯	◯	✿
◯	◯	◯	✿
◯	◯	◯	✿
◯	◯	◯	✿
◯	◯	◯	✿

On the next page are some desires and symptoms of people performing *bhakti*, belonging to the different classes of devotional service (verses 8–14).

Sort them into characteristics of *tāmasic*, *rājasic*, *sāttvik*, and transcendental devotional service based on the intention of the performer. Then write them on the appropriate colored circle or flower above.

• Has separate interests from the Lord's interests • Desires fame • Wants to serve the Lord • Becomes angry • Offers results of activities to the Lord	• Desires opulence • Wants to be free of karma • Is proud • Wants liberation • Feels automatic attraction to Kṛṣṇa	• Is envious • Desires sense enjoyment • Worships out of duty • Wants to only please the Lord • Is vengeful • Rejects liberation • Experiences uninterrupted devotion

Now cut out the circles of each group. Tie each of the groups of circles on separate strings, representing a rope. Cut out the flowers. Give a presentation to your study group, explaining how *bhakti* in each of the modes acts like a rope that keeps the performer from becoming free and going back to Godhead. Referring to the cut-out flowers, explain how pure devotional service brings one closer to the Lord. (Refer to verses 8–14 and purports.)

Exercise 2:
Define the four types of devotional service below, and then give one or two hypothetical or true examples of each:

Devotional service in the mode of ignorance:

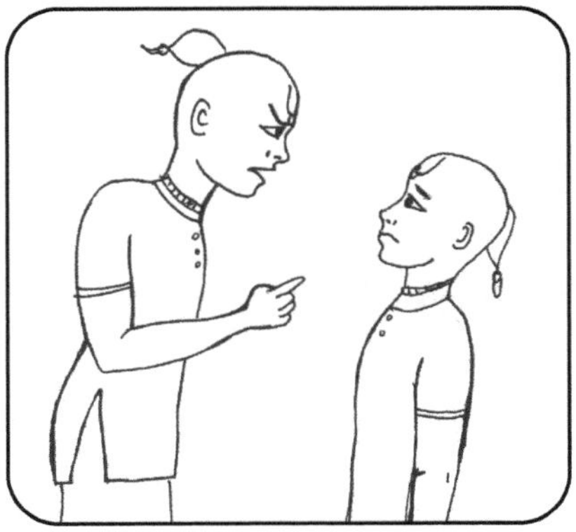

Example 1:

Example 2:

Devotional service in the mode of passion:

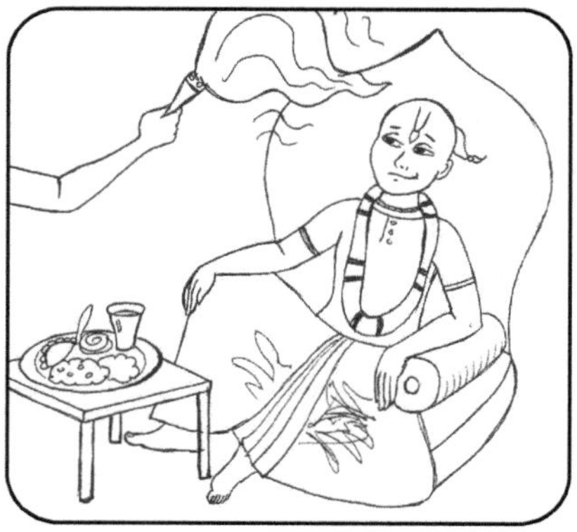

Example 1:

Example 2:

Devotional service in the mode of goodness:

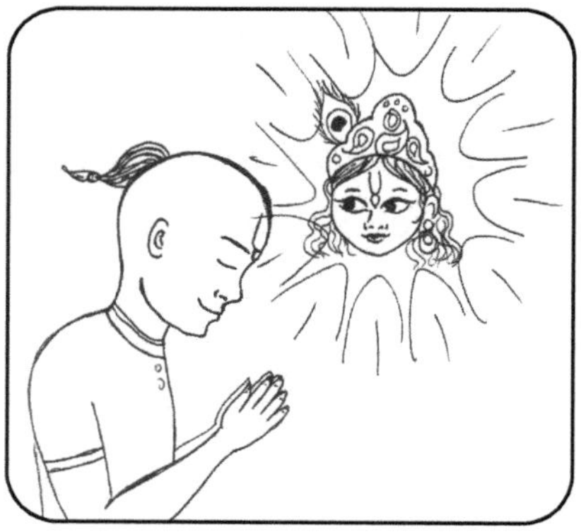

Example 1:

Example 2:

Pure devotional service:

Example 1:

Example 2:

Now try to see under which category you perform devotional service! Is it just in one mode or a mixture of them?

Writing Activities . . . to bring out the writer in you!

ESSAY ON LIBERATION

In the purport to verse 13 Śrīla Prabhupāda describes the five types of liberation pure devotees never aspire for. Write an essay on these types of liberation by answering the questions below:

1. What are the five types of liberation?
2. Why do the pure devotees not desire these kind of liberation?
3. Would you desire these qualities?

Remember to include an introduction to the topic as well as a conclusion.

Language Activities

. . . to make you understand better!

KṚṢṆA IS TIME

Directions: Complete the sentences below with the word or phrase that explains the time factor as Kṛṣṇa.

1. Time causes everything to change and ____________________ from one thing to another.
2. Anyone who does not know that time is the Supreme Personality of Godhead is ________________ of time.
3. Kṛṣṇa as time ______________________ every being through another being.
4. People are conscious of the last stage of life when they will meet the cruel hands of ________________; therefore, they engage in ________________activities.
5. The influence of time is present everywhere except in the ________________ world.

Fun Contemplation Questions!

Think about what you have learned so far, brainstorm, and explain the answers to these questions:

a. Would the material world exist without the time factor?
b. What would a world be like without time?
c. How would people exist/act?

INFERRING QUESTIONS

Which questions do you agree with and disagree with, using the chapter summary and what you know? Back up your argument with reasons.

1. When the Lord says that by achieving the ultimate goal of pure devotional service, His devotee is already liberated, we can infer that one does not need to become liberated first to achieve the ultimate goal; by achieving the ultimate goal, love of God, one is already liberated from material miseries.
2. Because devotional service can be enacted in the modes of material nature, it seems like material nature has more power than devotional service.

SUPERIORITY OF THE LIVING ENTITIES

List the different living entities in the order of superiority given in the chapter summary, starting from the least superior to the most superior.

1)	10)
2)	11)
3)	12)
4)	13)
5)	14)
6)	15)
7)	16)
8)	17)
9)	18)

APPROPRIATE RELATIONSHIPS

Directions: Fill in the blanks with the best word or phrase that completes the sentence.

The Supreme Lord advises us to relate with others in the following ways:

1. Giving ______________________________ to those more advanced than us.
2. Being ______________________________ to the poor or less advanced.
3. And making ______________________________ with persons who are our equals.

NĀTIHIṀSĀ: MINIMUM VIOLENCE

Directions: Read verse 15 purport and fill in the blanks with the correct words or phrases.

1. *nātihiṁsreṇa* means "______________________________."
2. Even eating __________________ is violence.
3. Every living entity has to live by killing another entity; that is the ______________.
4. But for a ________________________ that violence should be committed only as much as necessary.
5. A human being should eat ____________ that is offered to the Supreme Personality of Godhead. In this way he becomes freed from all __________________________.
6. When a devotee offers the Lord foodstuff from __________________________, with devotion, He eats that. Such food becomes __________________________.
7. If the Supreme Lord wanted foodstuff prepared from __________________________, the devotee could offer this, but He does not order to do that.
8. We cannot avoid violence, but we should commit minimum violence ____________________________. This is called __________________________.

Reflection Exercise:

Now write three thoughts, questions, or realizations that came to you while reading this purport and doing the exercise. Then answer the questions: What is violence considered in the passage? Can we avoid it? Why or why not? What can we do instead?

ANSWERS

Capturing the Existence of the Supersoul

1. Breeze: consciousness; Fragrance: saturated devotion; Sense of smell: Paramātmā in everyone's heart.
2. When a breeze blows over a flower garden, it carries the fragrance of the flowers and captures the sense of smell through the nose. In the same way, when the consciousness (breeze) becomes full with devotion to the Lord (aroma), we can immediately realize the Lord's presence as Paramātmā (sense of smell).
3. Because he sees the Lord in the heart of every being, he not only worships the Deity in the temple but tries to give every living being spiritual benefit by either chanting to them, helping them chant, or giving them *prasāda*, etc.
5. One offers sacrifice by offering ghee into a fire and chanting Vedic mantras, but if the ghee is poured into the ashes, the sacrifice is useless. Similarly, one should realize that in the heart of every living entity is the soul and the Supersoul and therefore every living being should be treated with respect. If he doesn't realize this and kills living entities in the name of religion, he cannot make any advancement either materially or spiritually.

The Classes of Bhakti

Exercise 1: Bhakti itself is not in the mode of goodness, passion, or ignorance, but is classified according to the mentality of the performer. Because the performer has motives within the modes, he uses the process to get results that are tainted by the modes.

Tamo-guṇa: Has separate interests from the Lord's interests; becomes angry; is proud; is envious; is vengeful
Rajo-guṇa: Desires fame; desires opulence; desires sense enjoyment
Sattva-guṇa: Wants to serve the Lord; offers results of activities to the Lord; wants to be free of *karma*; wants liberation; worships out of duty
Śuddha-sattva: Feels automatic attraction to Kṛṣṇa; wants to only please the Lord; rejects liberation; experiences uninterrupted devotion

Exercise 2: *(Potential Answers)*
Devotional service in the mode of ignorance: A person engaged in devotional service who is envious or proud, violent and angry, and considers himself separate from the Lord (a separatist).
Example 1: A *yogi* who comes to the temple just to argue with the devotees.
Example 2: A devotee who is envious of another and puts him down.

Devotional service in the mode of passion: One who also considers himself separate and worships the Deity in the temple with a motive for material enjoyment, fame, and opulence.
Example 1: A devotee who uses his position to increase his fame in the community and get wealthy so he can enjoy life in abundance.
Example 2: A person doing important service just to become popular in the devotee community.

Devotional service in the mode of goodness: One who worships the Lord and offers all the fruits of his work to the Lord to free himself from the results of this fruitive activity. The Lord dismisses any imperfections when his devotee simply offers the fruits of his work to Him.
Example 1: A devotee who works to support his family, has an altar at home, offers his home and his food to the Deity, and supports the temple or temple events.
Example 2: A college student pursuing a career strengthens the mind by Kṛṣṇa conscious practice, such as listening to *Kṛṣṇa-kathā*, chanting *japa*, doing *kirtana*, or reading and associating with devotees.

Pure devotional service: When a pure devotee is at once attracted to hearing the transcendental names of the Lord and will serve Him at every moment without any material motivation.
He does not accept any kind of liberation offered by the Lord, for he wants to serve Him unconditionally.
Example 1: Nārada Muni who is always chanting and broadcasting the glories of the Lord.
Example 2: Śrīla Prabhupāda who engaged unconditionally in the Lord's service by giving people Kṛṣṇa consciousness amidst all hardships.

Kṛṣṇa Is Time

1. transform; 2. afraid; 3. destroys/annihilates; 4. death; pious; 5. spiritual

Contemplative Questions (Potential Answers):

a. No. The material world is meant for living entities who want to be separate from the Lord and be independent from Him. The material is temporary by nature, which is dictated by time.
b. The world without time would be free from birth, death, old age, disease, and anxiety – like Vaikuṇṭhaloka, which is not influenced by time.
c. People would act like those in the spiritual world, in a spirit of pure devotional service. There would be no envy and negative traits. People would be aware of their spiritual identity, which is eternal, full of knowledge and bliss.

Inferring Questions

1. True. (Refer to 3.29.14)
2. False. The modes of material nature never have any advantage over pure devotional service. However, personal motives contaminate the performance of devotional service, which results in different categories of devotional service. Pure devotional service cannot be tainted.

1) Inanimate objects with consciousness e.g., certain stones or mountains
2) Living entities who display symptoms of life
3) Animals with developed consciousness
4) Those with developed sense perception
5) Those with taste perception
6) Those with touch perception
7) Those with a sense of smell and hearing
8) Those who can distinguish one form from another
9) Those with upper and lower sets of teeth
10) Those with many legs or quadriceps
11) Human beings
12) *Brāhmaṇas*
13) *Brāhmaṇas* who study the Vedas
14) *Brāhmaṇas* who understand the purpose of the Vedas
15) *Brāhmaṇas* who can dissipate all doubts
16) Those who follow brahminical principles
17) Those who are liberated from material contamination
18) The pure devotee of the Lord

Superiority of the Living Entities

Appropriate Relationships

1. respect; 2. compassionate; 3. friends

Nātihiṁsā: Minimum Violence

1. "with minimum violence or sacrifice of life"
2. vegetables
3. law of nature
4. human being
5. food sinful reactions
6. the vegetable kingdom *prasāda*
7. animal food
8. only as much as it is necessary by the order of the Lord; *nātihiṁsā*

Reflection Question *(Potential Answer):* Violence is defined as killing anything, even vegetables. We should avoid it as best we can, with the least amount of killing as possible. (Most vegetables can be used without even killing the plant). We cannot completely avoid killing because we are in conditioned life controlled by the laws of nature. Although we have to kill the plants or vegetables, we can offer them to Kṛṣṇa, and with His mercy and blessings it becomes *prasāda*, which when eaten frees us from sinful reactions.

30

Description by Lord Kapila of Adverse Fruitive Activities

STORY SUMMARY

The gentle Lord Kapila had spoken a lot about devotional service. And, oh, Devahūti relished this very much. But she had also asked about the distresses of birth and death. Now her son was ready to explain. It wasn't going to be pleasant though, but she was determined to hear, for it would help her become detached from this world.

"Mother, see the clouds above. Do you know what's moving them?"

"Why, it's the wind of course," she replied, knowing there was a lesson to come.

"Yes," said Kapila, "unknown to them, the mass of clouds is being pushed across the sky by the force of the wind. In the same way, materialists don't realize that they too are being pushed through life by the force of time."

Devahūti nodded, realizing that she also had been oblivious to the influence of time in her own life.

"Now, let me tell you about the life of such a materialist."

Devahūti took a deep breath. The story about the materialistic man or woman who only focuses on material wealth and progress could not be pleasant.

Kapila continued, "People of this world really try to be happy – even if it's hard work; even if it's painful. They'll do anything for so-called happiness. And then do you know what happens? The Lord in His form as time destroys all their hard work, and they are left lamenting.

"You see, mother, they are misguided. They think their body, home, wealth, and land are permanent. They are under the illusion that everything will last forever. And it's not just human beings who think like this. In any species of life, the living entity will find something about his body to be satisfied with. Even a hog, for example, finds pleasure in eating stool and doesn't feel inclined to cast off the body.

"After all, there is such a thing as hellish enjoyment. And do you know what makes this attachment so strong? It's the deep-rooted attraction for family and friends. Even though such a living entity thinks he is happy, he is in constant anxiety. He will go to any length, even performing deviant activities, to care for his family. He gives his heart to the woman in his life who carries the charm of *māyā* as she embraces him in a solitary place. And then there are the sweet… oh, so sweet…words of his small children that enchant him.

"He tries to counteract any miseries in his life, and if he successfully cancels out a misery, he thinks, 'Now I'm happy!' He tries desperately to make money even if it's by violent means and goes to hell for his acts. He doesn't even consider it. He just wants to serve his family. Then there are complications at work, reverses in his job. Now he must borrow money from others. He feels unsuccessful. He has failed to maintain his family, which makes him grieve deeply. His family sees this, and they don't treat him with respect anymore. It's like the way farmers treat their old and worn-out oxen who cannot work anymore.

"But can you believe he is *still* not averse to family life. He stays home like a pet dog. He must eat whatever little is given to him, and as he gets older, he suffers from many illnesses. His eyes start bulging, his glands become congested with mucus, and his breathing becomes difficult, producing a rattling sound in his throat. He becomes an invalid.

"As he lies on his death bed, his friends and family lament around him. He wants to speak to them, yet he can't – the control of time is too strong. So he tragically dies in great grief and pain as he watches everyone crying around him.

"Death.

"He sees some ghastly creatures coming toward him. They are the Yamadūtas, messengers of the lord of death. Their eyes are terrifying. The Yamadūtas come closer and closer. 'You are a criminal!' they snarl at him, 'Using your senses to enjoy yourself!' They cast a noose around his neck. They then cover his subtle body, preparing him for severe punishment.

"As they carry him along a 792,000 mile-long road, he trembles in their hands. Suddenly, vicious dogs on the road bite his flesh. And then he remembers all his sins and is thus terribly distressed! But nothing can be done now.

"Under the scorching sun the criminal walks through roads of burning hot sand. Can he escape? No! The road is surrounded by forest fires. It's too hot. He can't walk. He collapses and becomes unconscious, but the Yamadūtas have no compassion. They force him to rise again, whipping him on the back. He must walk. He's hungry and thirsty, but there's no shelter. There's nothing to drink. Nowhere to rest.

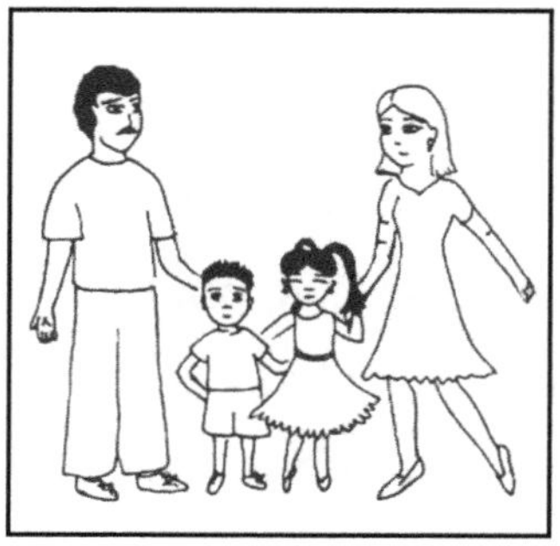

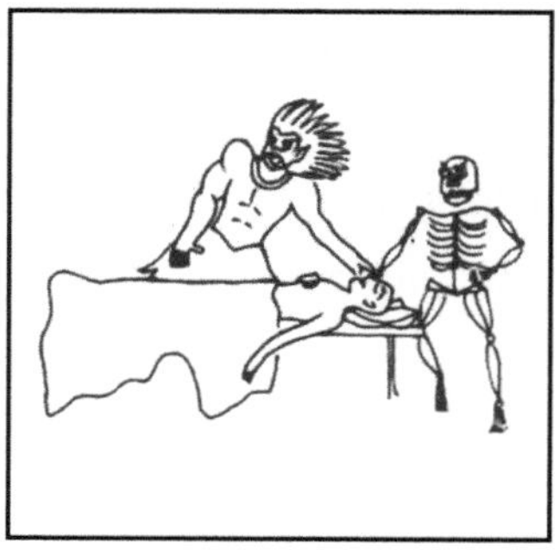

"However, he passes this long road only within a few moments, and he is brought to the presence of Yamarāja – the demigod of the underworld.

"And now the punishments begin based on what he is destined to suffer.

"The Yamadūtas place him in burning pieces of wood, setting his limbs on fire. He struggles frantically but it's no use. He can't die. He is already dead. He is then forced to eat his own flesh, and sometimes it's eaten by others."

"Eaten…by…others?" Devahūti was pale, her voice faint.

"Shall I continue?"

Devahūti swallowed. "Yes, my son. I asked about this. I need to know."

"Hounds and vultures pull out his insides, yet he is still alive to see it all and feel it all. He is tormented by serpents, scorpions, gnats, and other creatures that bite him; elephants chop and tear his limbs; he is hurled from hilltops and even held captive in water or caves. It just doesn't stop.

"My dear mother, even on Earth we can experience hell or heaven, for hellish punishments are visible here too.

"So as you can see, mother, the materialistic man who maintains himself and his family through sinful activities and black methods goes to the darkest regions of hell, to *Andha- tāmisra*, after quitting his body.

"After going through these hellish conditions, he passes through the lower animal life forms and eventually, as he is purged of his sins, he is reborn as a human being on this earth."

Themes and Key Messages

Please go through this table of themes and key messages, with corresponding verses, and discuss each topic further.

Theme	Reference	Key Messages
Time destroys everything, yet people in material consciousness do not realize the power of the time factor.	3.30.1–2	People waste time to improve material life, but they don't know that their life in a particular body is like a flash in their eternal journey. Whatever they produce with great pain and labor is taken away by time in the form of death.
The materialist thinks that everything in this material world is permanent although the world is temporary. He thus tries to enjoy in illusion.	3.30.3–6	A materialist thinks that he will enjoy his home, family, and money forever, but a Kṛṣṇa conscious person knows that all this is temporary and is taken away at death. A materialist enjoys his body even in abominable species of life and does not feel like casting off that body. He thinks his condition is perfect due to his attraction to the body, family, and friends.
Under the influence of illusion (*māyā*), a person attached to family performs all kinds of sinful activities to maintain his family. A Kṛṣṇa conscious person, however, lives with family to develop Kṛṣṇa consciousness.	3.30.7–18	A *gṛhamedhī*, a householder who is simply focused on maintaining his family, remains in family life controlled by his senses. He commits violence and secures money out of greed, and when he is unsuccessful in his endeavors, he remains at home to suffer old age, illness, and death. A *gṛhastha*, on the other hand, focuses on his relationship with Kṛṣṇa and works towards entering Kṛṣṇa's abode where his eternal family resides.
When a materialistic man dies, the Yamadūtas, the messengers of death, come to take him to the abode of Yamarāja where he suffers various punishments.	3.30.19–27	When a sinful man quits his body, the Yamadūtas takes the soul, accompanied by the subtle body that experiences pain and torment, to the abode of Yamarāja. He experiences various hellish conditions that remind him of his sinful activities. He thus laments and grieves while going through further punishment in various hellish planets.
One has to suffer if one acquires money through illegal means.	3.30.30–33	When a person earns money by unfair means he goes to hell alone even though the money was enjoyed by his family members. The money that he earned remains in this world while he takes only the reaction of his sinful activities. Therefore it is better to use one's money and possessions for the Lord's service, which will guarantee only good rewards and an auspicious destination after death.
After being cleansed of all his sins, the living entity enters the human form of life again.	3.30.34	Just as a prisoner who has finished his term of suffering in prison and is freed, a person who is engaged in impious activities is put in hellish conditions, and when he has finished suffering in the bodies of different species of life, he is born again as a human being. In the human form of life, one can advance on the spiritual path and avoid the hellish conditions. Kṛṣṇa consciousness protects all human beings from going to hell and taking birth in lower forms of life.

Higher-Thinking Questions

Now try to deepen your understanding of this chapter by delving into Śrīla Prabhupāda's purports and reflecting on the following questions:

1. By reading this chapter it is clear that the conditions of hell are fearful and horrific. Explain why the materialistic person goes through hellish conditions and why he tends to stay there, not wanting to cast off his body. See verse 5 purport.
2. In verses 3 to 7 Lord Kapila explains how everything in this material world is temporary. Can you think of an instance when you lamented over something temporary? How was it difficult? By now understanding the effects of the time factor, how could you view this differently?
3. If our bodies and work in this world are temporary, why work? Explain how we can work as described in text 2 and 3 purports. How can you perform your duty and serve Kṛṣṇa?
4. In verse 10 purport, Śrīla Prabhupāda explains that serving others can lead to *māyā*, or

illusion. Explain how this is so. How can you prevent this downfall?

5. Everyone who is born in this world has to go through the miseries of old age. According to Vedic scripture, what is the process for avoiding the misfortunes of old age and the road to hell soon after? See verses 13–15 purports.
6. Can you think of a time in the scriptures where there was hell on earth? What about in modern society? What about heaven on earth? Please describe the events and circumstances.
7. According to this chapter, a man is destined to hell because of his sinful activities. How can you prevent sinful activities in your life?
8. One might think that a man who supports his family, even through sinful means, is doing his duty. However, according to 31–34 verses and purports, why is this not true?
9. In verse 7 purport Śrīla Prabhupāda explains that family in the material world is the perverted reflection of our family in Kṛṣṇaloka. How is it a perverted reflection?
10. According to verse 8 purport, what is the difference between a *gṛhamedhī* and a *gṛhastha*?
11. According to verse 9, what is happiness for conditioned souls in the material world?
12. Verse 31 purport explains that a direct offender is more responsible for sinful activities than the indirect enjoyer. How should one see his possessions so that he can avoid becoming a direct offender? See verse 31 purport.

ACTIVITIES

In this section you will find many exciting things to do. These activities will get you thinking, moving, drawing, and having loads of fun.

Analogy Activity . . . to bring out the scholar in you!

THE TIME FACTOR

> "As a mass of clouds does not know the powerful influence of the wind, a person engaged in material consciousness does not know the powerful strength of the time factor, by which he is being carried." (*SB* 3.30.1)

This analogy illustrates the power of the time factor.

Answer the following questions to understand this better:

1. What effect does the wind have on the clouds? Why is this effect powerful?
2. In the same way, what effect does time have on a person with material consciousness? Why is this effect powerful?

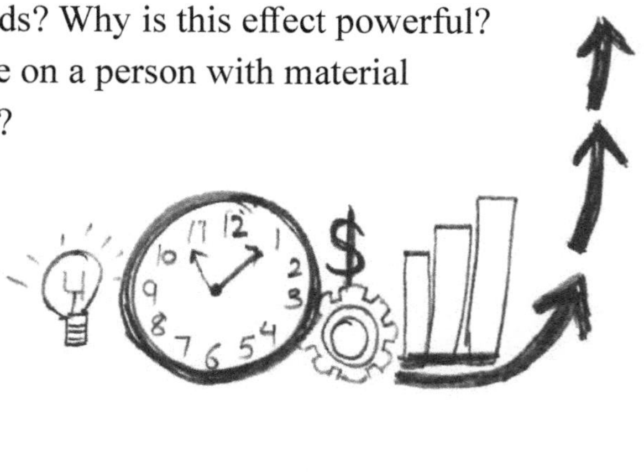

Artistic Activity

. . . to reveal your creativity!

THE CLOCK OF ILLUSION

Make a clock to show the effects of time on material existence.

What you will need: heavy cardboard (from recyclable boxes), thin card; paper; pens; color pens or crayons; either paper binder or office pin.

Steps:

1. Draw a large circle on heavy cardboard and cut it out. This will be your clock face.
2. On a separate sheet of paper draw items/objects that represent the effects of time, e.g., the sun; different stages of the body's development; or even a plant in different stages. Color the images and cut them out.
3. Paste your images on the rim of the clock (see illustration) where the hours are meant to be.
4. Now make an hour-hand marker from a thin piece of cardboard and cut it out. Pierce a small hole at the center of the clock and the end of the marker. Insert a paper binder with two prongs through the holes so that the marker is fastened onto the cardboard but can still move around (see illustration).
5. Now move your hour hand around to the different images, showing how time affects our life. The illusion is that we are not aware that time is passing by so quickly; we are under time's control.

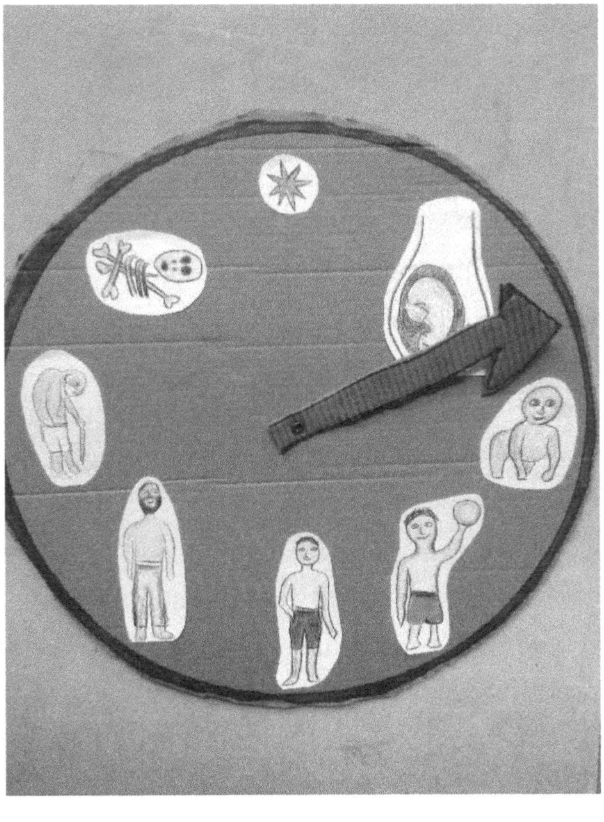

Critical-Thinking Activities
. . . to bring out the spiritual investigator in you!

THE LAW OF KARMA

This chapter describes the reactions a sinful materialist gets in this life and the next. This concept of action and reaction forms the law of *karma*. In today's world, people do not believe that the law of *karma* exists, nor that hell is a real place where sinful souls are sent.

In this activity we will logically demonstrate that the law of *karma* exists and fairly directs the journey of the living being in the material world.

A. The Logic Behind Karma

Look at the six cards below. Each of them states a fact, showing that the law of *karma* is real and logical in everyday life. For each statement, give examples from everyday experience and then draw a connection to the law of *karma*, the universal law of cause and effect, and write it out in the space below. The first one has been done as an example.

1
Laws of action and reaction are seen to control physical elements.

2
We are all controlled by systems and rules in our daily lives.

3
A good citizen tries to abide by the laws of the state.

4
A criminal cannot blame the law for being punished.

5
We have all experienced cause and effect.

6
None of us hope to achieve success without working hard for it.

1. Everything in nature has a cause and effect; if we plant a seed it will sprout and bear leaves, flowers, and fruit; if a male and female mate, they produce a child; if cells are in a healthy environment they grow; the planets move in certain orbits. Therefore we can conclude that if physical phenomena in the world comes with cause and effect and has a specific order, then there must be universal laws that govern living beings as well.

2. ……………………………………………………………………………..

……………………………………………………………………………..

……………………………………………………………………………..

3. ....

....

....

4. ....

....

....

5. ....

....

....

6. ....

....

....

B. Diminishing Karma

Since the soul is eternal and continues in different lifetimes, the law of *karma* continues for the conditioned soul throughout those lifetimes. Therefore, we may not understand why bad things happen to good people. They may be suffering a reaction for a sinful activity from a previous life; in other words, the law of *karma* is complex and difficult to analyze, although we can understand how it exists.

The best would be to understand how to end the influence of the law of *karma* forever. Even if we perform good activities, we have to be reborn in this world and reap the favorable rewards.

From your understanding of this chapter, what advice would you give someone to diminish the law of *karma* in their life, or the negative effects of their past sinful activities? How can we end the cycle of birth and death caused by the law of *karma*? Write your answer in the space below:

ILLUSION AND REALITY

In this chapter Lord Kapila describes the family man's life and illusions based on his lack of true knowledge. He always thinks he is happy by continuing his miserable life in sense gratification and fruitive activities.

In this activity you will be breaking the illusions of this family man by providing the reality. Counteract the statements below with the truth:

1. **Illusion:** Thinking he is the human body.
   Reality:

2. **Illusion:** Thinking his home belongs to him.
   Reality:

3. **Illusion:** Thinking his spouse and children are the most important people to serve.
   Reality:

4. **Illusion:** Thinking his friendships are critical to maintain in order to have a nice social life.
   Reality:

5. **Illusion:** Thinking his body is the safest place to be even in hellish conditions.
   Reality:

6. **Illusion:** Thinking his life is perfect as it is.
   Reality:

7. **Illusion:** Thinking happiness is derived from having deeper relationships with family members.
   Reality:

8. **Illusion:** Thinking that committing violence or sinful activities is excusable if it is for the purpose of maintaining his family.

Reality:
Illusion: Thinking the more he earns, the more he can enjoy.
Reality:

9. **Illusion:** Thinking that he still needs to remain at home and work hard till the end of his life without seeking spiritual knowledge.

10. **Reality:**

Introspective Activity

. . . to bring out the reflective devotee in you!

In the second verse of this chapter Lord Kapiladeva states that the time factor is a representative of the Supreme Lord and it destroys everything produced by the materialist. This is similar to what Lord Kṛṣṇa states in the *Bhagavad-gītā* (11.32): *"Time I am, the great destroyer of the worlds, and I have come here to destroy all people."*

- Examine all the things you have created that have been destroyed in the course of time. Make a list of as many things as you can think of.
- Is there anything in this world that will remain forever?

In the introduction to the *Bhagavad-gītā*, Śrīla Prabhupāda explains: *"In this material world we find that everything is temporary. It comes into being, stays for some time, produces some by-products, dwindles and then vanishes. That is the law of the material world, whether we use as an example this body, or a piece of fruit or anything."*

So everything in this world comes to an end. But then Śrīla Prabhupāda describes that the soul is eternal, Kṛṣṇa is eternal, His abode is eternal, and our relationship of love with Kṛṣṇa is eternal.

- Now make a list of the things you have done for Kṛṣṇa with love. These are eternal, and the effects will last forever.

Temporary in existence

Eternal loving service to Kṛṣṇa

Language Activities

. . . to make you understand better!

FILL IN THE BLANKS

1. A mass of ________________ does not know the powerful influence of the wind; similarly, a person engaged in material consciousness does not know the strength of the __________________.
2. A conditioned soul lives in a particular body for a _____________ amount of time.
3. The attraction to ___________, _____________, and wealth are in relationship to the body, which is temporary.

4. However, when one is situated in ________________________________, he can use land, home, and wealth for the service of the Lord.
5. The satisfaction of the living entity in a particular body, even if it is most abominable, is called ___________________.
6. *Māyā* has two phases of activities: one is called *āvaraṇātmikā* which means "__________________". And the second one is called *prakṣepātmikā* which means "___________________________"
7. The so-called perfection of human life is a _____________________.
8. It is said that is it easier to maintain an entire empire than to maintain a _________________________.
9. Here in this material world, _________________________means successful counteraction to the effects of distress.
10. Therefore, all our attempts to become happy in this material world are simply a delusion offered by ___________.

A SINFUL MAN'S JOURNEY TO HELL

Directions: Complete the sinful man's journey to hell.

1. Attaches himself to the____________ and home, thinking these material things are permanent.
2. Commits __________________ activities.
3. Accepts a ____________________and family enchanted by false love.
4. Lives a life of ___________________________.
5. Maintains family through ______________________ activities.
6. Fails at his job, accepts ____________________ from others, and in turn his family loses respect for him.

7. Even though they have no ____________________ for him, he still maintains his attachment for his family, falls sick, and dies with them grieving all around him.
8. _______________________ take him to Yamarāja.
9. He suffers the pains of hell, being bit by _______________ and tortured severely.
10. Those whose lives are built on sex enjoyment go to ___________________.
11. After purifying his existence, suffering in hell, and being born in the lowest forms of animal life, he is reborn as a ______________________ on this earth.

INFERRING QUESTIONS

Which questions do you agree with and disagree with, using the story summary and what you know? Back up your argument with reasons.

1. The description of the family man is noted in this chapter. Based on this description, you could infer that anyone partaking in sex life and earning money, as a "family man," will be going to the hellish realms after he leaves his present body.
2. When the Lord responds to His mother that "there really is no true happiness in this material world. The only real happiness is beyond time, in the spiritual world while serving the Lord," you could infer that as long as one is within this material world, there is no real happiness. One must go to the spiritual world to experience happiness.

ANSWERS

The Time Factor

1. Wind carries the clouds from one place to another; the clouds have no power to stop the wind or control the direction in which they are carried.
2. Time carries a person's life, giving him what he deserves and causing old age and death; man has no control over the activities of time although he can use his time wisely.

The Law of Karma (Potential Answers)

2. We all need to follow rules in schools, offices, at public places, etc., otherwise we will have consequences; similarly, the law of *karma* is a universal law governing our behavior in the world, and we need to follow it.
3. The government makes laws that all citizens of a country must follow otherwise they will be punished; similarly, there are universal rules to govern our behavior for which we will get punished in this life or the next.
4. Law breakers are responsible for their actions and can neither deny the existence of nor blame the government laws for their condition; similarly, even those who don't believe in the law of *karma* will be judged and will have to face the consequences of their actions.
5. If we eat unhealthily, we fall sick; if a person smokes, he may end up with lung cancer or respiratory disease; similarly, just as cause and effect is evident in the world, it is not difficult to understand the law of *karma* based on cause and effect.
6. We all experience how we cannot achieve something without hard work, so we can see that the law of *karma* exists: "as you sow, so shall you reap."

Illusion and Reality

1. He is an eternal spirit soul.
2. His home belongs to the Lord.
3. Lord Kṛṣṇa is the most important person to serve; however, if he engages his family in devotional service then they can be served as devotees of Kṛṣṇa.
4. Relationships and association with devotees are most critical to maintain and develop for the purpose of spiritual life, the permanent end of suffering.
5. His identification with and attachment to his body is the cause of his hellish condition.
6. His life is imperfect because of his suffering. He needs to seek spiritual guidance and perform devotional service to free himself from material bondage and achieve the perfection of life, love of God.
7. Real happiness is derived from deepening and strengthening our relationship with the Lord.

8. He needs to live a life of piety/non-sinful activities to be blessed with good fortune or ability to maintain his family.
9. Kapiladeva says there is a limit to how much one can enjoy; for example, the stomach is only big enough to hold a certain amount of food.
10. As a man gets old and becomes less able to provide, he should give up family attachment and take shelter of the Supreme Personality of Godhead, so He can take control of his life and future life.

Fill in the Blanks

1. clouds; time factor
2. fixed
3. home; land
4. Kṛṣṇa consciousness
5. illusion
6. "covering"; "pulling down"
7. concoction
8. small family
9. happiness
10. *māyā*

The Family Man's Journey to Hell

1. body
2. sinful
3. wife
4. sense gratification
5. criminal
6. money
7. respect
8. Yamadūtas
9. dogs
10. Andha-tāmisra
11. human being

Inferring Questions

1. **False:** The description of the family man is distinct from a family man practicing Kṛṣṇa consciousness (*gṛhastha*). Because the center of attention is Kṛṣṇa, the destiny of a family man changes. (3.30.34)
2. **False:** By practicing Kṛṣṇa consciousness and performing devotional service, which is the true duty of the eternal soul, one can experience true spiritual happiness even within the human body.

31
Lord Kapila's Instructions on the Movements of the Living Entities

STORY SUMMARY

Lord Kapila had described the process of death at his mother's request. Now he would talk about birth in this material world.

"Mother," he began, "when the soul is ready to take birth in a human body, under the supervision of the Lord the soul enters a particle of a man's semen. When the man unites with a woman, the semen enters her womb. On the first night, the semen and ovum mix, and by the fifth night, the mixture ferments into a bubble. Now, this bubble becomes denser and denser, and by the tenth night it turns into a lump of flesh.

"By the first month, the head is formed, and at the end of the second month the hands, feet, and other limbs take shape. By the third month, the nails, fingers, toes, hair, bones, skin, eyes, ears, nose, mouth, and anus are all formed, and by the fourth month, the seven essential ingredients of the body come into existence. By the fifth month, the fetus in the womb starts to feel hunger and thirst, and by the sixth month, enclosed by the amniotic fluid, it moves to the right side of the abdomen.

"The fetus continues to grow, getting nutrition from the food and drink of the mother, but the baby is not comfortable and suffers immense pain. Excruciating pain."

Devahūti was taken aback. The baby in the mother's womb is uncomfortable? He isn't cosy and protected in the womb? And even more…he is hurting? Why? How?

With a solemn face Lord Kapila continued to expose the hard truth of the process of birth in this material world.

"Because the mother eats bitter, pungent, salty, and sour food, the baby suffers incessant pain. As he grows, he is cramped with his head turned towards the belly and his neck and back arched like a bow. He is trapped like a bird in a cage and surrounded by the mother's intestines, stool, and urine. Worms breed in the abdomen and they bite the child's tender skin again and again. There is nothing he can do. The pain is so intolerable that he loses consciousness, then regains it, and again loses it moment after moment. How can he be peaceful in such a state?"

Devahūti shook her head in disbelief.

"But mother…" Kapila's voice brightened. "If the baby is fortunate, he may remember the troubles of his past one hundred births and then grieve deeply."

Devahūti was confused. "How is this fortunate?"

"You see, mother, by the seventh month, the consciousness of the baby has developed. He's suffering, but when he remembers the suffering of his past one hundred births, he laments and remembers the Lord. This now fortunate soul prays to the Lord with folded hands:

" 'My Lord, I take shelter of You,' he says. 'Only You can take away all my fears. I have the body I am meant to get. I deserve this from my past sinful actions. I know I'm a pure soul that is simply bound in the womb by the reactions of my past activities, but I also know that if my heart feels deep regret for my past activities, I can see You.

" 'Oh Lord, we struggle to survive in this material world because we have forgotten our relationship with You, so how can we engage in devotional service if we've forgotten You? It is only possible by Your mercy.

" 'I thank You for making me fully conscious of You even at the tender age of ten months. I know I am suffering, but I don't want to leave this womb if it means that I will forget You again by *māyā*'s influence.

" 'Thank You for this human body in which I can control my senses and understand the goal of life. Now I know what to do…I will keep Your lotus feet in my mind always and be saved from entering the wombs of many mothers in future lives. I'll never forget You, my Lord. I'll never forget You.'

"But then the fateful day comes.

"The wind in the abdomen gets stronger and pushes the baby, head downwards, through the birth canal.

" 'I'll never forget You, my Lord!' the baby continues to cry, as he endures the trauma of birth. 'I will keep my consciousness clear! I promise! I'll always remember Your lotus feet!'

"…and then he is out.

"Breathless. In a pool of blood and stool, and under the spell of *māyā*. He wonders, 'Who am I? Where am I? Where did I come from? What just happened?' He looks

around… but it's no use. He has forgotten everything. He knows nothing but to cry, and cry he does, oh so pitiably.

"He's then picked up and cared for by those who simply don't know what he wants. They place him on a bed of germs and sweat where the insects continue to bite his delicate skin, and he can't even scratch…so he cries even more.

"And as he grows, his suffering doesn't stop. When he becomes a child, he wants things that he can't have and so he becomes angry and sad. And as he gets older, his suffering worsens.

"He believes more and more that he is the material body and accepts the temporary people and objects in this world as his own. He harbors anger and lust and expects much adoration and respect from others. This causes him to clash with enemies who are similarly lusty.

"In this way he becomes bound to the actions and reactions of this world, which causes him repeated birth and death. By associating with people who live to enjoy their senses, the embodied soul loses all his good qualities, such as truthfulness, cleanliness, mercy, gravity, spiritual intelligence, austerity, forgiveness, and many other pious qualities. As a result, he goes to hell as before.

"Therefore, O mother, do not associate with a fool bereft of self-realization and who is like a dog in the hands of a woman.

"This is the tightest grip in this material world – the attachment to women or the attachment to a man who is fond of women just to enjoy his senses. Try to understand this *māyā* of mine in the form of a woman. She can control the greatest conquerors of this world simply by the movement of her eyebrows. Even Lord Brahma became bewildered by a woman's charms and shamelessly ran after her. Associating with such women is a sure gateway to hell;

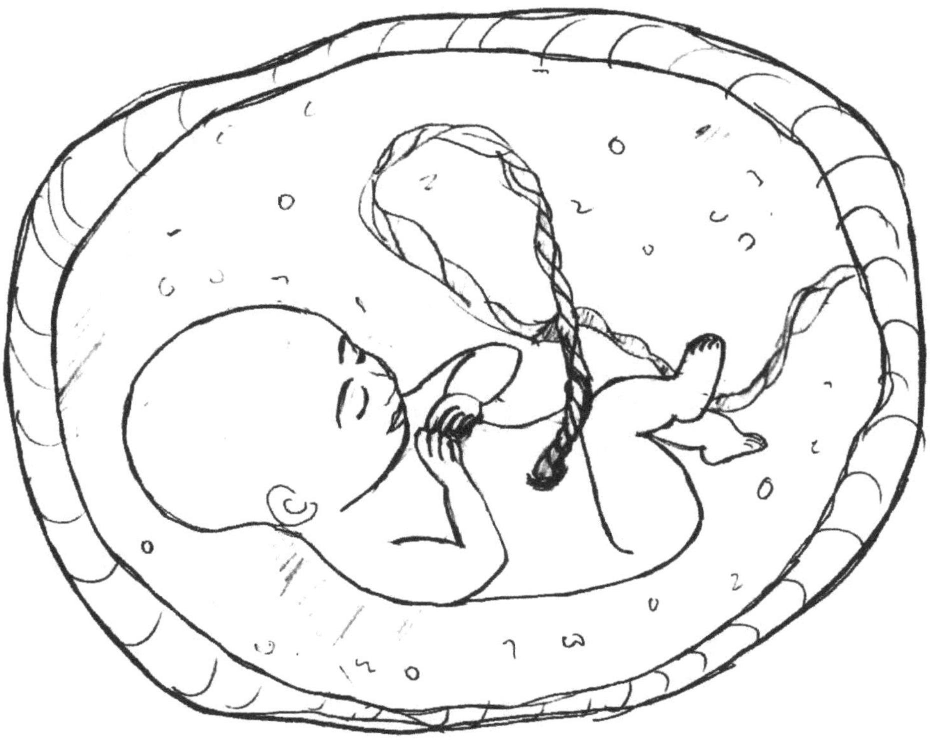

therefore, anyone who wants to advance in Kṛṣṇa consciousness must guard against this."

Māyā's allurement in the form of a woman didn't apply to Devahūti, but Kapila would now explain what is a woman's *māyā*.

"Those attached to women in their previous life take birth as a woman in the next life," Kapila said, "and their *māyā* becomes the man – the husband. He provides wealth, children, a home, and other material needs for her; all these things are her *māyā*, like the sweet singing of the hunter for the deer."

So that was that. Even women weren't exempt from *māyā*.

"So whatever body one has, one acts simply for enjoying the results. This is called fruitive activities. In this way, birth after birth, a person performs fruitive activities and enjoys the reactions over and over again. Such materialistic life involves a series of actions and reactions. When the results of one set of fruitive activities are finished and the body can no longer enjoy its senses, there is death. Then, when another set of reactions begin and one feels and thinks that he is the body, there is birth.

"Therefore, mother," Kapila concluded, "instead of seeing death with horror and that you are simply the body meant to enjoy, see the true nature of the soul. With this vision, stay detached in this world and determined in your purpose – loving service to the Lord. Strengthened by devotional service, you will be unconcerned with this material world."

Themes and Key Messages

Please go through this table of themes and key messages, with corresponding verses, and discuss each topic further.

Theme	Reference	Key Messages
It is not the semen of a man that creates life. The soul gives life to the baby in the womb.	3.31.1–3	When a living entity comes again to the human form of body after suffering hellish conditions, it enters the womb of a woman through the semen of a man. However, it is not the semen that gives life; because of the presence of the soul there is life. Then within days the fertilized egg turns into a lump of flesh (in the case of mammals) or an egg (in the case of birds).
The womb of the mother is a hellish place for the growing fetus.	3.31.5–10	As the fetus in the womb grows, it remains with stool and urine and bitten by worms. The child suffers pain from the mother's eating of bitter, pungent, salty, and sour food and lies in an uncomfortable position without freedom of movement.
Conditional life is due to our forgetfulness of our relationship with the Lord.	3.31.11, 13–14	The suffering soul in the womb awakens his consciousness and surrenders to the Lord, realizing that he is suffering because he has forgotten his relationship with Kṛṣṇa. He thus promises to never forget the Lord and never to commit sinful activities again. But soon after he is born, he forgets everything and commits the same sins again. Nevertheless, he can revive his relationship through devotional service to the Lord.
The human form of life is the highest, for it has the consciousness to get out of the cycle of birth and death.	3.31.18–19	Among the 8,400,000 species of life, there is a gradual and systematic evolution from lower species to higher forms of life. The baby in the womb is grateful to the Lord for blessing him with the human body because the human form has developed consciousness to realize the self and the Supreme Lord. Therefore we should properly utilize the human form of life for spiritual realization. If we cannot control the senses through *bhakti-yoga* and develop our relationship with God, we are no better than animals.
Simply by remembering the Lord, one can develop clear consciousness and be saved from entering the womb of many mothers for repeated births and deaths.	3.31.21	The child in the womb fears that when he enters the world he will forget the Lord and fall victim to *māyā*. He would rather stay in the dark suffering condition of the womb and remember the Lord than be in the material world and forget Him. By taking to the process of Kṛṣṇa consciousness, specifically chanting the holy names of the Lord, one can remember the Lord and the cycle of birth and death can be stopped for good.
We suffer because we accept the body as our self.	3.31.29–33	When the child is born, he accepts the material body as himself under the influence of *māyā*, and his suffering continues into childhood and youth due to lust. When he associates with people who are simply interested in gratifying their senses through sex life or eating and drinking, he can be influenced to commit sinful activities and again go to hell.
When one is attached to women for sex enjoyment or associates with someone who is attached to women, he is bound to the material world.	3.31.34–39	In Kali-yuga, association with and attraction to women is very strong and is the main reason for our conditional life in the material world. In Vedic culture only *gṛhasthas* (householders) are allowed to associate with women, but even then with restriction. The senses are very strong. It's best to control the senses by practicing *bhakti-yoga*. When we become attracted to Kṛṣṇa's beauty, we won't be attracted to the beauty of a man or woman.
A man should not be attached to a woman and vice versa – both should be attached to the service of the Lord.	3.31.41–42	To be a man or a woman is just a bodily dress. On the spiritual platform the living entity is feminine by nature, to be enjoyed by the Lord. If a man and woman are simply attracted to each other, in the next life they will be born as either a man or woman. But if they become Kṛṣṇa conscious, they both can go back to Godhead by serving the Lord. It's a question of attachment. If attachment is transferred to Kṛṣṇa, then they become Kṛṣṇa conscious and marriage is very favorable.
The living being gets a suitable body according to his fruitive activities and thus wanders from one planet to another.	3.31.43–47	One gets a material body according to one's past fruitive activities. Fruitive activities are activities that bear fruit, that give results. When the reactions of one's fruitive activities come to an end, it is called death, and when another series of reactions begins, it is called birth. Therefore, one should not fear death but should realize one's true nature and move in this world detached and fixed in purpose.

Understanding the Story

Now it's time for you to check how well you understood the story by answering these multiple-choice questions.

1. In how many ways does the body of a living entity develop?
   a) 5
   b) 4
   c) 3
2. In which month does the Lord awaken the baby's consciousness?
   a) 8 months
   b) 6 months
   c) 7 months
3. How many past births does a fortunate soul remember when in the womb?
   a) 100 births
   b) 1,000 births
   c) 50 births
4. What does the baby do when he remembers his past lives?
   a) He rejoices at another chance to enjoy life.
   b) He apologizes to Kṛṣṇa for all the wrong things he did and offers his obeisances to the Lord.
   c) He tries to forget as the information is overwhelming for him.
5. What is the soul's determination after he realizes he is purely spiritual in nature?
   a) He wants to retain his pure identity and protect himself from *māyā* by serving the Lord.
   b) He wants to enjoy things that he could not enjoy in previous births.
   c) He wants to reunite with his family from past birth.
6. What happens to the child's determination after he is born?
   a) He remembers everything and pursues his spiritual goals after birth.
   b) He surrenders to Kṛṣṇa as soon as he is born.
   c) The spell of *māyā* makes him forget his determination, and he falls into materialistic life.
7. What is the most dangerous thing about material life?
   a) Attraction to money
   b) Attraction between man and woman
   c) Attraction to fame

8. What makes it difficult for the living entity to come out of material life?
   a) Association with materialistic people who enjoy the senses
   b) Association with women for sense pleasure
   c) Both of the above

Higher-Thinking Questions

Now try to deepen your understanding of this chapter by delving into Śrīla Prabhupāda's purports and reflecting on the following questions:

1. Under the spell of *māyā*, the living entities become attracted to a so-called happiness in their conditioned bodies (see verse 6 purport). What is their idea of happiness? What do you think is true happiness?
2. Once the baby in the womb is born and captured by the spell of *māyā*, he forgets his promise to remember the Lord. How much in an average day do you think you remember the Lord? In what ways can you remember Him more?
3. In verse 15 purport Śrīla Prabhupāda explains that the Supreme Lord directs the forgetfulness of the conditioned soul (also in *BG*. 15.15). According to the purport, what is the initial cause of the soul's forgetfulness of the Lord? What is the solution to this forgetfulness? See the purport to verse 20 for more details.
4. Verse 16 purport states that the Lord gives knowledge to anyone who fully surrenders to Him. Can you think of examples in scripture of the Lord giving knowledge to a devotee within the heart or in person? How did they surrender to Him?
5. Verse16 purport says that hearing the spiritual master's instructions fructifies the seed of Kṛṣṇa consciousness. Can you think of other activities that fructify (or waters) the seed of Kṛṣṇa consciousness?
6. Why is the baby in the womb grateful for the human form of life? Can you think of other reasons why *you* are grateful to have a human body? See verse 19 purport.
7. According to verses 15–16 purport, without the Lord's mercy no one can engage in His devotional service. Why is this so? How does the Lord give His mercy?
8. What is the fundamental difference between the Lord and the living entity as described in the last paragraph in verse 19 purport?

9. Once a child is born, he is often misunderstood and given what he does not want and deprived of what he does want or need. Can you remember a time when you were not given what you wanted? How did you respond? How could you have responded better?
10. According to verses 32–33 purports, why is it that even a religious person or *yogī* can find himself entering a hellish situation?
11. Śrīla Prabhupāda explains in verse 42 purport that the main issue with the relationship between man and woman is their attachment for each other. How can they maintain their relationship with each other while learning how to dissolve their material attachments?
12. Verse 38 purport describes that even Kṛṣṇa has the propensity to be attracted to women. How is His attraction different from the conditioned souls'? What is the mundane attraction to women a reflection of?
13. Explain the difference between false renunciation and true renunciation as described in verse 48 purport? Why is it impossible to renounce everything material?

ACTIVITIES

In this section you will find many exciting things to do. These activities will get you thinking, moving, drawing, and having loads of fun.

Analogy Activity . . . to bring out the scholar in you!

PHOTO ALBUM OF THE JĪVA

> "Materialistic life involves a series of actions and reactions. It is a long film spool of actions and reactions, and one life-span is just a flash in such a reactionary show." (*SB* 3.31.44, purport)

A film spool is a reel of photographic film that captured photographs in older cameras. When we take pictures, we capture special moments of different stages of our lives on them. When we look through these old photos, we can easily remember our past experiences.

In this analogy Śrīla Prabhupāda compares the journey of a soul through different species to photographs of memories or stages of existence captured on a film spool. There are, however, differences between the two.

Let us first understand the analogy a little more. In the following table, match each item on the left to its corresponding item on the right:

Film spool	Species of life
Photograph	Conditioned soul
Person in the photograph	Record of action and reaction

1. How are the pictures we take of our lives different from the pictures Śrīla Prabhupāda is talking about?
2. Now summarize what you understand about the analogy.
3. Create a photo album to illustrate this analogy. Give your album an interesting name to depict the position of the *jīva* in it. Your album cover can depict the conditioned soul, and the different photographs in the album could be of different species of life that the *jīva* goes through. At the end of the photo album, add a small note about how action and reaction are responsible for this journey, and what can the *jīva* do to quickly recover his original identity. (You can draw pictures if you cannot take photos. You can also create a Powerpoint slideshow and play it on slideshow mode to see the film spool effect as the photos change every few seconds.)

Artistic Activity

. . . to reveal your creativity!

COLLAGE – PROCESSES OF DEVELOPMENT

Description:
Śrīla Prabhupāda points out in the purport to verse 2 that the living entity takes a body that develops in one of four different ways:

- Sprouting – like a tree
- Fermenting – like germs
- Hatching – like an egg
- Growing in an embryo – like a mammal (human/animal)

In this activity you will create a collage of the above processes.
What is a collage? It is a piece of art created by combining photos, clippings, or small objects onto a surface.

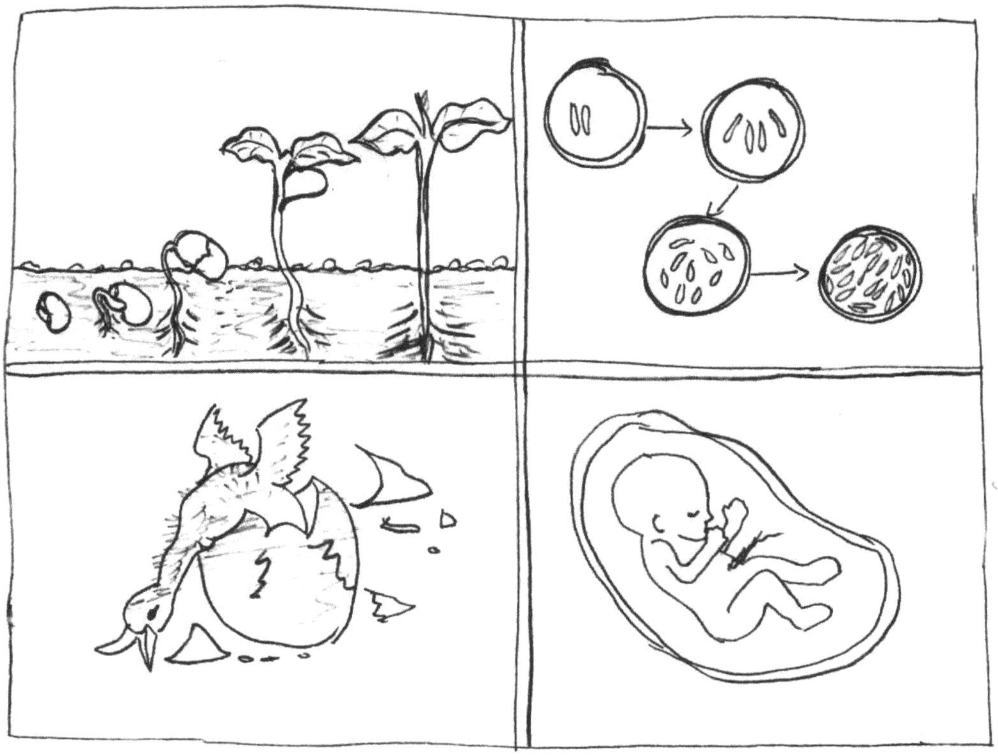

What you will need:
Access to the internet; printer or photocopier; paper; glue; scissors; chosen art media

Directions:

1. Find images on the internet of these four different processes; they look really interesting up close.
2. Choose four images that would complement each other, either by color, style, or even their contrasting nature.
3. Now you can make your collage in one of the following ways:
   a) Print the images and place them on a sheet of cardboard or paper in an interesting pattern to resemble a collage. Now glue the pictures on.
   b) You can use a software program like Powerpoint or Microsoft Word to assemble your images and design your collage. Seek help from someone who would know how to do this.

Introspective Activity

. . . to bring out the reflective devotee in you!

HOW TO BECOME FREE FROM SUFFERING

This chapter allows us to introspect about our position of suffering in this world. How did we come here and where will we go after? What is the purpose of life? What is the difference between me and my body, and how is my consciousness in the human body different from the consciousness in an animal body?

Whatever body we are in, our suffering is due to accepting our body as the self. As a result, we want to simply enjoy the senses out of lust; we perform activities to satisfy our material desires, becoming entangled in fruitive action and reactions. When one set of reactions are finished, we experience death; when another set of reactions begin, we experience birth. In this way, we continue suffering in the repeated cycle of birth and death.

An intelligent person will find out the root cause of his suffering, which is the attachment to the material body and everything related to the body.

- According to this chapter, how can you become free from material contamination and desire and end suffering forever?
- According to verse 15 purport, without the Lord's mercy no one can understand the Lord and be liberated from birth and death and all suffering. What is the Lord's mercy to make us understand His form, quality, and name?
- In the same purport Śrīla Prabhupāda explains that our memory is lost because we are now covered by the Lord's material nature. Why did the Lord put us under the influence of material energy if He wants us to go back to Him?
- Ultimately the Lord instructs us to surrender to Him if we want to become free of the material energy and repeated birth and death. What does "surrender" mean? List ways in which you can surrender to the Lord more.

Writing Activities . . . to bring out the writer in you!

ESSAY: REGRETS

The child in the womb regrets his past sinful activities that caused him to be in such an abominable condition, and he promises the Lord never to commit sinful activities again. He also vows that he will always remember the Lord, knowing that the Lord is his eternal shelter and well-wisher.

Directions: Write an essay about a time you felt regretful. What did you do? Why were you regretful? How did you feel? Describe your thoughts at the time. Did you pray to Kṛṣṇa? If you made any promises to Him or to yourself, did you keep them?

To conclude the essay, explain how will you react to a moment of regret in the future? What can you do now to prevent any regrets?

A LETTER OF SURRENDER

According to verses 11–12 and purports, consciousness develops from the seventh month for the child in the womb. The child then remembers the miseries of his past one hundred births. And now because of the miseries he experiences in the womb, he is ready to surrender to the Lord.

Directions: For this activity, ***study*** the above texts and purports and compose your own letter of surrender to the Lord based on your own life, as you know it. Start first by ***offering*** respects and ***glorifying*** the Lord. Next, try to express ***why*** you want to surrender and ***what*** you want instead, and based on your knowledge of this chapter, ***how*** you might accomplish this.

Language Activities

. . . to make you understand better!

THE DEVELOPMENT OF THE HUMAN BODY

Even before modern science discovered the development of the fetus in the mother's womb, *Śrīmad-Bhāgavatam* gave a vivid description of the development of the child in the womb and the process of birth. Thus, we can see that *Śrīmad-Bhāgavatam* is not merely a philosophy based on belief but presents scientific knowledge. It gives a complete analysis of birth, including the suffering a child experiences in the womb and the spiritual evolution of the soul after birth.

Directions: In the table below, describe the development of the baby for each month within the mother's womb. Use the chapter summary and verses 3–24 for details.

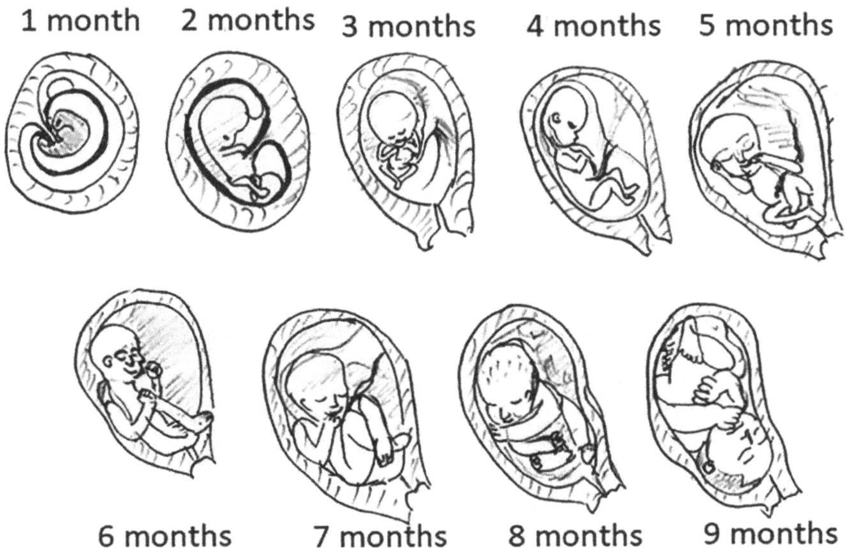

Month 1	
Month 2	

Month 3	
Month 4	
Month 5	
Month 6	
Month 7	
Month 8	
Month 9	
Month 10	

FOUR WAYS THE LIVING ENTITY CAN DEVELOP

Directions: Determine which group each of the living entities in the table is a part of.

Groups

1) Sprouting, like trees.
2) Perspiring or fermenting, like how germs multiply.
3) Hatching from eggs, like birds and fish.
4) Growing from an embryo, like the animals and humans.

Potato	
Octopus	
Dolphin	
Spider	
Rose	
Hummingbird	
Bat	
Bacteria	
Avocado tree	
Worm	
Tulip Flower	
Butterfly	
Koala Bear	

Turtle	
Mushroom	

FILL IN THE BLANKS

1. At the end of six months if it's a boy, he tries to move on the ____________ side of the abdomen, and if it's a girl, she tries to move on the ________________ side.
2. In the abdomen there are many ______________________ that bite the child.
3. Because the baby's ______________________ is not very developed, the child can tolerate the miseries.
4. We have a very efficient boat in this _______________ body, and there is a very expert captain, the spiritual master, who guides the boat; the scriptural injunctions are like favorable winds.
5. The worms born in the mother's womb, according to Śrīla Prabhupāda, are actually the baby's ______________, like all living entities are considered.
6. As the Supreme Lord can put a living entity into a condition of horrible existence, He can also ____________ him.
7. Material contamination is _____________________, and the living entity's actual position is that he is liberated.
8. One is liberated not by the knowledge of the Lord, but by the ______________ of the Lord.
9. The human baby in the womb can realize his ___________________ position as human and is thereby distinguished from other bodies.

10. Real consciousness means to develop the consciousness of "I am not ____________________ . I am a ____________________, an eternal part and parcel of the Supreme Lord."
11. By material energy, one forgets everything just after ____________________ due to contact with ____________________.
12. The Supreme Lord gives knowledge internally as ________________________ and externally as ______________________________.

WHAT DO YOU THINK?

Set 1 – Tick those statements that you think are correct. If false, write the true sentence by providing the correct information.

1. The living entity again obtains a particular human body depending on the results of his present activities.
2. At three months in the mother's womb, the baby's head is formed and at the end of five months his hands, feet, and other limbs take shape.
3. In the fourth month, the seven essential ingredients of the body – the digestive fluids, blood, flesh, fat, bone marrow, and semen – are produced.
4. Many gross things such as stool, urine, and gas surround him while in the womb – even gnats surround him and bite him!
5. *Māyā* is so strong with the so-called pleasures of this life!
6. Like a cat in a cage, he has no freedom to move at all.
7. With his pure love given by the Lord, the baby is able to see what he did wrong in past lives and why it was wrong.
8. The soul realizes that he is purely spiritual in nature, but because he is within a material body, his senses are being disturbed.
9. The baby says: "You have given me this body for which I can control myself and understand my destination."
10. The beauty and attraction the conditioned soul experiences in this material world are just imitations of the real attraction and beauty in the spiritual world.

Set 2 – INFERRING QUESTIONS

Which questions do you agree with and disagree with, using the story summary and your knowledge? Back up your argument with reasons.

1. When Lord Kapila says that just as a man's attraction to a woman is dangerously strong, a woman's attraction for a man is also strong. We can infer that regardless of gender a person in either male or female body has weakness for the opposite gender and there is no real advantage in being in either a male or female body.
2. The child within the womb awakens with pure consciousness given by the Lord and prays: "O Lord, I wish to stay here in this womb to protect myself from the materialistic life outside!" We can infer here that since the pure consciousness has been given by the Lord, the child's prayer is sensible, and although the womb is uncomfortable, it is safer than the outside world.

ANSWERS

Understanding the Story: 1) b, 2) c, 3) a, 4) b, 5) a, 6) c, 7) b, 8) c

Photo Album of the Jīva

film spool – record of action and reaction; photograph – species of life; person in the photograph – conditioned soul.

1. Differences: we choose to take pictures for memories, but nature does not give us choice of species – it depends on our actions and reactions; we take pictures only of nice experiences, but nature gives us bodies based on our proper and improper behavior; we remember these experiences in our lives, but a soul cannot remember past lives.
2. Sample summary: One lifetime of the conditioned soul is just a tiny part of its long journey through different experiences, much like we go through many experiences within one life. These experiences are determined by a series of actions and reactions.

Development of the Human Body

Month 1: A head is formed.

Month 2: Hands, feet, and other limbs take shape.

Month 3: Nails, fingers, toes, body hair, bones, and skin appear and the whole body grows with eyes, nostrils, ears, a mouth and anus.

Month 4: The seven essential ingredients of the body – the digestive fluids (chyle), blood, flesh, fat, bone marrow, and semen – are produced.

Month 5: Hunger and thirst are produced.

Month 6: The body begins to move.

Month 7: The Lord awakens the baby's consciousness within the womb.

Month 8: The baby counts the months until he is released; He is surrounded by blood, stool, urine, and gastric fire.

Month 9: He is unable to move and lies in an uncomfortable position with head downward to be born.

Month 10: Child is born; he is pushed downward through the birth canal by the wind of the mother's abdomen; he comes out with great trouble, head downward, breathless, and deprived of memory due to agony.

Four Ways the Living Entity Can Develop

- **Sprouting:** potato; rose; avocado tree; tulip flower
- **Perspiring or fermenting:** bacteria; mushroom
- **Hatching from eggs:** octopus; spider; hummingbird; worm; butterfly (originally a caterpillar); turtle
- **Growing from an embryo:** dolphin; bat; koala bear

Fill in the Blanks

1. right; left;
2. worms;
3. consciousness;
4. human;
5. brothers;
6. deliver/liberate;
7. temporary;
8. mercy;
9. superior/fortunate;
10. this body; spirit soul;
11. birth; *māyā*;
12. Supersoul; spiritual master

What do you think?

1. **False:** The living entity again obtains a particular human body depending on the results of his **previous** activities.
2. **False:** At **one month** in the mother's womb, a head is formed and at the end of **two months** his hands, feet, and other limbs take shape.
3. **True.**
4. **False:** Many gross things such as stool, urine, and gas surround him while in the womb – even **worms** surround him and bite him!
5. **True.**
6. **False:** Like a **bird** in a cage, he has no freedom to move at all!
7. **False:** Because with his pure **consciousness** given by the Lord, the baby is able to see what he did wrong in past lives and why it was wrong.
8. **False:** The soul realizes that he is purely spiritual in nature, but because he is within a material body, his senses are being **misused**!
9. **False:** The baby says: "You have given me this body for which I can control my **senses** and understand my destination."
10. **True.**

Inferring Questions

1. **True and False:** Śrīla Prabhupāda states in verse 41 purport: "In the body of a man there is a greater opportunity to get out of the material clutches; there is less opportunity in the body of a woman." However, Prabhupāda also mentions that if the two individuals are Kṛṣṇa conscious, the body can be seen as simply a dress, and the process of Kṛṣṇa consciousness can make them equally eligible to get out of material entanglement.
2. **False.** Neither inside nor outside of the womb is safer. The forces of material nature, or *māyā*, work within and outside of the womb; if a person is Kṛṣṇa conscious, such conditions cannot act unfavorably upon him. (See verse 21 and purport)

32
Entanglement in Fruitive Activities

STORY SUMMARY

Birth and death are painful and miserable. Only serving Lord Kṛṣṇa with love can get us out of this nightmare. This is what the scriptures tell us.

Wait a moment…there are other ways to get out of the cycle of birth and death that are recommended in the scriptures – ones that don't involve devotion to Lord Kṛṣṇa. Surely following any of these ways can also free us from birth and death – what does Lord Kapila say?

He's about to tell His mother what happens to those who follow different paths in the scriptures.

"Mother, there are some people who follow the scriptures so they can prosper and enjoy their lives. They're not interested in Lord Kṛṣṇa. They're only attached to enjoying themselves. Indeed, they worship the demigods to fulfill their material desires, and they may even go to the heavenly moon planet at the end of their lives. They enjoy there for thousands of years and drink the most heavenly *soma rasa*, but when they use up their pious credits, they must come back down to Earth. Even if they remain on the moon, at the time of annihilation when Lord Viṣṇu sleeps on Ananta Śeṣa, all the material planets – including the moon – are destroyed.

"Birth and death continue for these materialists. They can't escape it.

"Then there are those who follow the scriptures, are detached, and perform their duties to please the Lord. They don't consider whether they get prosperity, praise, criticism, or good or bad results from their actions. Oh no. They simply do their duty as the scriptures have recommended. These are intelligent people. Pure. Free from the modes of material nature. They directly approach Lord Kṛṣṇa and can therefore easily enter the spiritual world.

"Then there are some who worship

Hiraṇyagarbha, a plenary expansion of Garbhodakaśāyī Viṣṇu. They do not approach the Supreme Lord in Vaikuṇṭha. They therefore stay in this world until the end of Brahmā's life, and then they go back to Godhead.

"There are also expert *yogīs* who have controlled their minds and their breathing. When they leave their body, they go to Lord Brahmā's planet. When they leave their heavenly bodies, they enter Lord Brahmā's body, and only when Lord Brahmā leaves his body, the *yogīs* go to the spiritual kingdom of God with Lord Brahmā.

"But mother, I am here as your son. You can directly engage in My devotional service.

"You see, if anyone worships the Lord with self-interest, wanting to be equal to the Lord in any way, they may reach Mahā-Viṣṇu, but they must return to the material world. Even great demigods like Lord Brahmā, and great sages like Sanat-kumāra and Marīci come back to the material world at the time of creation.

"Then there are people who perform their duties nicely but are attached to the results. They are driven by passion. They are anxious and really want to enjoy this material world, so they worship their forefathers to improve their quality of life. Only interested in making money and enjoying this world, they are pious people but have no interest in Lord Kṛṣṇa or hearing of His pastimes. They may go to the planet of the forefathers, but they must take birth again in their family and continue.

"Birth and death continue for them.

"Lord Kṛṣṇa is certainly not impressed by this. They are like hogs eating stool who don't want to hear about Kṛṣṇa but would rather

hear of the activities of materialists.

"Therefore, mother, please take shelter of the Supreme Personality of Godhead with love and devotion. That's all you need to do.

"Knowledge will come.

"Detachment will come.

"Self-realization will come.

"Your mind will be calm. You will no longer be affected by good and bad situations as you will only want what Lord Kṛṣṇa wants.

"Engage in *bhakti* to Lord Kṛṣṇa, dear mother, for you can see Him in complete knowledge. Other spiritual paths reveal Him differently: as an impersonal energy (the impersonal Brahman) or as the Supersoul (the Paramātmā) in everything. Only through *bhakti-yoga* can you see Lord Kṛṣṇa face to face. The highest spiritual understanding is the Personality of Godhead."

Lord Kapila looked up at the sun, which was setting in the west. This would be His last day with His mother. The next morning He would leave.

"Mother, let me now conclude. All *yogīs* have a common understanding: we must become detached from matter. But some don't believe in Me and so decide that everything in this world is false; nothing is real. They use this understanding to detach themselves from the material world. But this is simply not true, mother. This whole universe comes from Me. This material world is my energy. And, in fact, if one were to engage in devotional service, they would be able to see this.

"Now, the *jñānī* through mental speculation will ultimately see Me as impersonal Brahman. It's like seeing milk and only appreciating that it is white.

"The *aṣṭāṅga-yogī* through practicing the eightfold *yoga* system will ultimately see me as the Supersoul in everyone's heart. This is like seeing the whiteness of milk and also smelling its aroma.

"Now if they later associate with devotees and engage in *bhakti-yoga,* devotion to the Lord, they will be able to progress further and be able to see Me. This is like seeing the milk, smelling the milk, and tasting the milk.

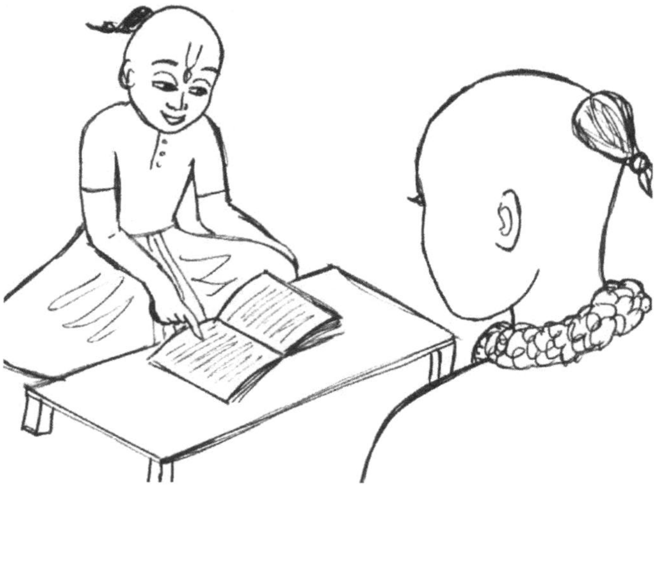

"Now the *bhakti-yogī* can either engage in philosophical research of the scriptures until he is free from the modes and then engage in devotional service, or he can simply engage directly in devotional service.

"As a young boy, one must study the various scriptures under the guidance of the spiritual master. As a householder, one must perform sacrifices, distribute charity, and act according to one's social order. As a retired man, one must be austere, study the Vedic literatures, and conduct philosophical research. And as a renounced man, one must control one's mind and senses and absorb oneself in Kṛṣṇa consciousness. More importantly, whatever activity a person may perform in any stage of life, it should be done in *bhakti-yoga*: devotional service to the Lord, otherwise his activities would bear no fruit. Also, through *bhakti-yoga* one automatically becomes more attached to Lord Kṛṣṇa and more detached from this material world.

"Mother, I've talked about devotional service in the mode of goodness, passion, ignorance and pure goodness. I've also explained how time chases the living entities and what happens to a living entity who chooses to work outside of devotional service. In his forgetfulness, he could go anywhere in this material existence; he won't know where he'll end up.

"This philosophy should not be heard by envious people, atheists or agnostics, or people who behave badly. Neither should it be heard by hypocrites, proud or greedy people, or those too attached to their family.

"The listener must be faithful, my dear mother. He must be respectful to his spiritual master, nonenvious, friendly to all, eager to serve, clean, and detached from anything not Kṛṣṇa conscious. The Supreme Personality of Godhead must be more dear to him than anything else.

"Anyone who once meditates upon Me with faith and affection, who hears and chants about Me, surely goes back home, back to Godhead."

Themes and Key Messages

The following table summarizes some of the key messages and themes of this chapter. Use it as a quick reference guide to the verses listed and discuss each theme and message further with your teacher or friends.

Theme	Reference	Key Messages
Worship of the demigods cannot award liberation from birth and death.	3.32.1–4	The materialistic householders, or *gṛhamedhīs*, worship the demigods to get material benefits and fruitive results. They may reach the heavenly planets or the moon planet in the next life, but because they cannot control their senses and still have material desires, they have to return to Earth to continue in the cycle of birth and death.
The Lord's devotees do not act for their sense gratification but for the pleasure of the Lord.	3.32.6–7	Arjuna didn't want to kill his enemies in the battle of Kurukṣetra, but he fought following the order of the Lord just to please the Lord. In the same way, the devotee only works for the satisfaction of the Lord and at the end of life goes back home, back to Godhead.
It is better to directly take shelter of the Supreme Personality of Godhead than take shelter of the demigods or follow any other process of spiritual realization.	3.32.8–12 16–21	Demigod worshipers cannot achieve liberation from birth and death because the demigods themselves are not liberated and hence cannot award liberation. Even the *yogīs* who indirectly worship the Lord by meditating on the plenary expansion of Viṣṇu go to Brahmaloka at the end of their life where they merge into Brahmā's body, and only at the end of Brahmā's life they go to the spiritual world or return to the material world. The *bhakti-yogīs*, however, who worship the Supreme Personality of Godhead directly, go to the spiritual world.
When the results of fruitive activity is exhausted, one has to come back to Earth.	3.32.20–21	Materialistic persons only do work to enjoy the results, and they don't like to hear the glories of the Lord. They may go to Pitṛloka, the planet of their forefathers, or the heavenly planets, but as soon as the results of their pious activities are finished, they return to Earth to continue in fruitive activity.
When one is Kṛṣṇa conscious and engages in devotional service, he automatically becomes most knowledgeable, detached, and self-realized.	3.32.22–28, 30	One does not need to practice detachment or gain knowledge separately like the *jñānīs*. By devotional service one automatically develops all good qualities and becomes detached and self-realized. Devotees have perfect knowledge of the Supreme Lord in His different features (Brahman, Paramātmā, and Bhagavān), and because they focus on the Bhagavān feature of the Lord, they have complete understanding of the Lord and eventually see Him face to face.
For any activity to be successful one must execute it in *bhakti-yog*a, and when *bhakti-yoga* is prominent in every activity then one reaches the ultimate goal of life.	3.32.31–36	People belonging to different social orders (*brahmacārīs*, *gṛhasthas*, *vānaprasthas*, and *sannyāsīs*) are recommended to perform certain activities according to their position in society; however, if devotional service to the Lord is missing, then their activities are meaningless and unsuccessful. But if they add *bhakti-yoga* to all their activities, then they understand their constitutional positions as servants of Kṛṣṇa and reach the Lord's abode.

Understanding the Story

Now it's time for you to check how well you understood the story by answering these multiple-choice questions.

1. Who do persons with material desires worship?
   a) Lord Viṣṇu
   b) Demigods
   c) Themselves
2. Where do demigod worshipers go to after death?
   a) Moon planet
   b) Spiritual sky
   c) Pitṛloka
3. What is the best way to reach Kṛṣṇa?
   a) By performing all our activities with the goal to reach Kṛṣṇa
   b) By praying to the demigods to help us reach Kṛṣṇa
   c) By performing *aṣṭāṅga-yoga* and meditation
4. What is the difference between a *yogī* and a devotee?
   a) A yogī stops work and detaches from all activities, and a devotee engages in activities to become Kṛṣṇa conscious and to please Kṛṣṇa.
   b) A *yogī* serves the Supreme Lord, and a devotee performs meditation and *yoga*.
   c) A *yogī* serves the Supreme Lord, and a devotee likes to read philosophical books.
5. What is the destination of a man who is very attached to his family?
   a) The moon planet
   b) Brahmaloka, Lord Brahmā's planet
   c) Pitṛloka, the planet of his forefathers
6. What is Kṛṣṇa's advice to people taking different paths to get to Him?
   a) They should directly serve Him, always keep Him as their goal, and not get distracted.
   b) They should focus on demigods of their choice, who will then guide them to Him.
   c) They should perform their activities with knowledge and detachment.
7. What is the key factor in devotional service?
   a) It should be performed strictly according to the instructions in the Vedas.
   b) It should be performed with love for Kṛṣṇa.
   c) It should be performed however one likes.

8. What feature of the Lord do *bhakti-yogīs* focus on?
   a) Paramātmā
   b) Bhagavān
   c) Brahman

Higher-Thinking Questions

Now try to deepen your understanding of this chapter by delving into Śrīla Prabhupāda's purports and reflecting on the following questions:

1. In verses 1, 2, and 4, Śrīla Prabhupāda describes the difference between the *gṛhastha* and the *gṛhamedhī*. Explain the difference, and give an example of each from world history, scripture, or your personal life. The *gṛhastha* and *gṛhamedhī* also perform different religious activities as described in verse 6 purport. What are they and what is the purpose of each?
2. Verse 5 describes how devotees who are completely satisfied are called *praśāntāḥ*. How does a devotee reach this stage of satisfaction? What is the opposite of *praśāntāḥ*? Describe.
3. What is the difference between the oneness the Māyāvādīs desire to achieve and the oneness the Vaiṣṇavas achieve? (see verse 11 purport) How do Māyāvādīs see diversity in this world as opposed to how the Vaiṣṇavas see diversity? (see verse 28 purport)
4. Lord Brahmā and some of the great sages go to the spiritual world at the dissolution of the universe, and yet they sometimes return to the material world. Please explain why as noted in verse 15 purport. Therefore, what is the great mistake of the impersonalists also noted in the purport?
5. Can a person worshiping a demigod be liberated from the clutches of *māyā*? Why or why not? (see verse 16 purport)
6. According to verse 22–23 purport, why is devotional service to Kṛṣṇa the highest perfection of life for the human being?
7. In verse 29 purport, Śrīla Prabhupāda describes how it is because of mental speculation that the conditioned soul remains in ignorance under the spell of the illusory energy. How then can one attain liberation?
8. In verses 32–33 why does Lord Kapila tell His mother that devotional service is better than the path of philosophical research? What chapter in the *Bhagavad-gītā* also explains this? Are the *jñānī*'s and devotee's destinations the same? If not, explain how and why they are different.

9. As described in verse 36, what is the result for people who perform the duties prescribed in the scriptures while worshiping the demigods?
10. *Karma* (fruitive action) and *jñāna* (philosophical research) are considered inferior to *bhakti* (devotional service) in this chapter. Why is this so?
11. Verse 33 purport describes that *jñāna-yoga* and *bhakti-yoga* are meant to reach the same destination – the Personality of Godhead. But to understand the Lord in full, one must perform *bhakti-yoga*. Śrīla Prabhupāda uses the analogy of milk to explain the differences in perceiving the Supreme Lord. Explain this analogy, relating it to different processes of understanding the Lord.
12. Verse 16 explains that persons who are in the mode of passion and work simply to gratify their senses worship the forefathers. And verse 17 explains that these people are called *trai-vargika* because they are interested in the three elevating processes. What are these three processes, and how are they detrimental to understanding God?
13. One of the five chief devotional activities noted in verse 42 purport is to accept the shelter of a spiritual master. Why do you think this is important?
14. What is the real humanitarian work Śrīla Prabhupāda describes in verse 42 purport? How can you actively preach in your community? Try and give three different ways.

ACTIVITIES

In this section you will find many exciting things to do. These activities will get you thinking, moving, drawing, and having loads of fun.

Analogy Activity . . . to bring out the scholar in you!

A HUNGRY MAN'S SATISFACTION

"A hungry man feels strength and satisfaction from eating, and at the same time he gradually becomes detached from eating any more. Similarly, with the execution of devotional service, real knowledge develops, and one becomes detached from all material activities." (*SB* 3.32.34–36, purport)

This analogy compares doing devotional service to eating – just as food keeps the body nourished, devotional service keeps the soul nourished. Just as we feel strength and satisfaction from eating and as our hunger lessens we don't desire to eat any more, we get real knowledge and satisfaction when we execute devotional service; then naturally we become detached from material activities.

The following two diagrams illustrate the positive effects of eating and devotional service on the right side, and the final result on the left side. In your notebook, explain how each activity in the analogy, eating and devotional service, achieves the effect or result mentioned in the bubbles on the right and left. For example: How does eating give strength? How does eating result in detachment from eating?

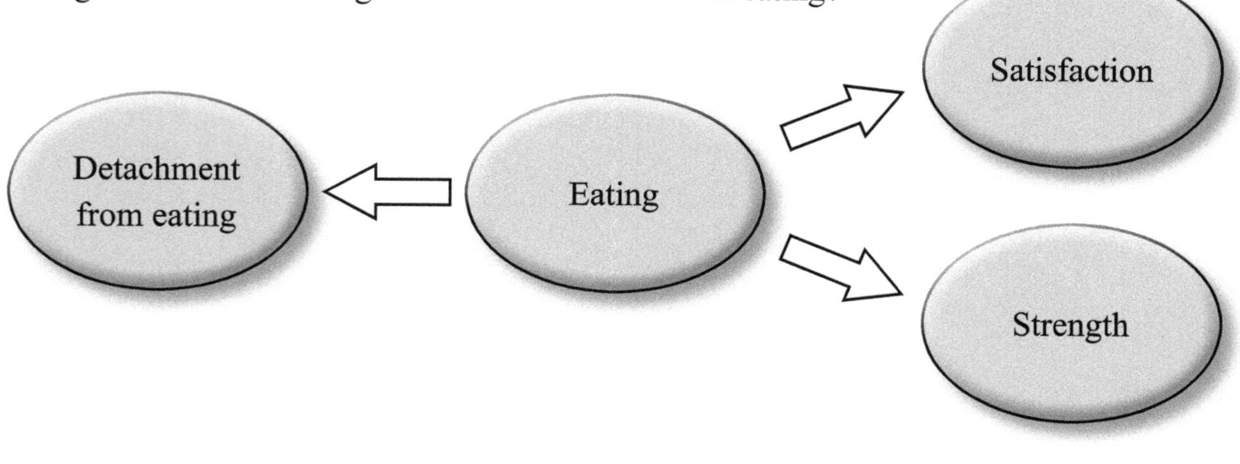

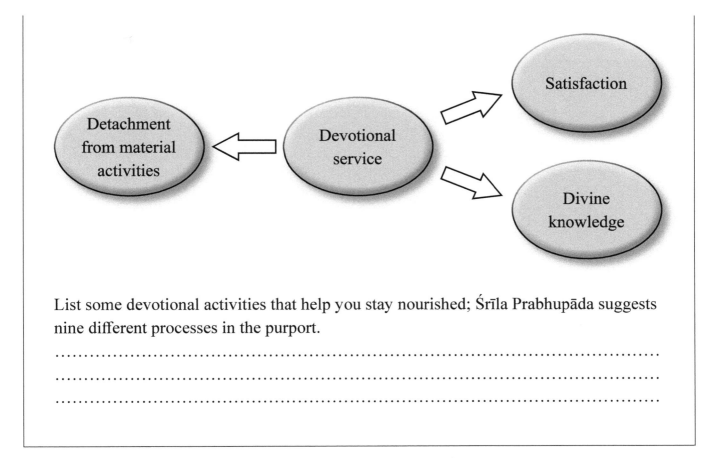

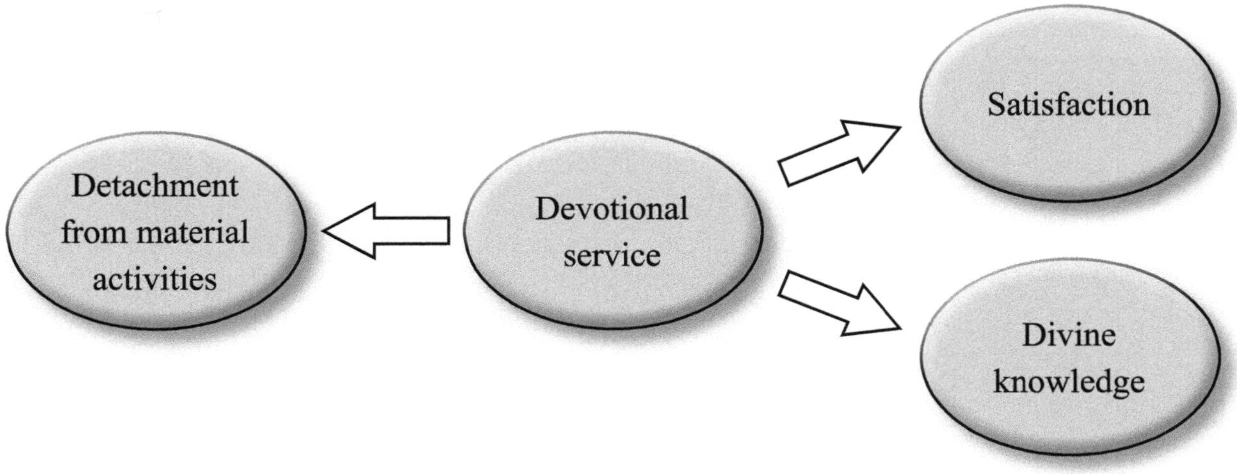

List some devotional activities that help you stay nourished; Śrīla Prabhupāda suggests nine different processes in the purport.

....

....

....

Artistic Activity

. . . to reveal your creativity!

PLANET ART

In this chapter we learn about the different destinations of *yogīs* who follow their own religious path. Some go to the moon planet, some attain the heavenly planets, some go to Lord Brahmā's planet, some to the Vaikuṇṭha planets, and many fall back to the earth planet.

In this fun activity, you will be creating any planet you like!

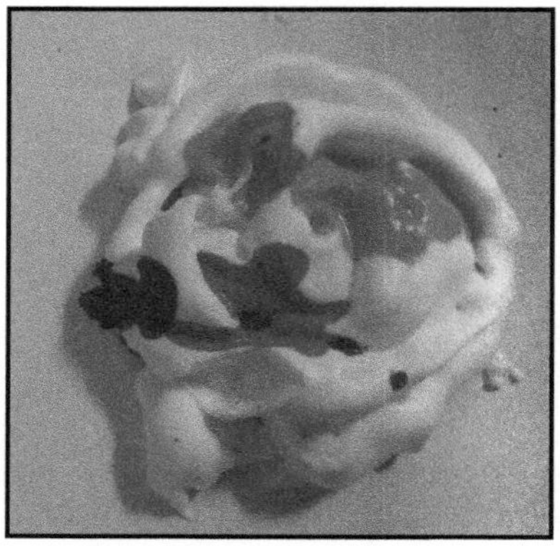
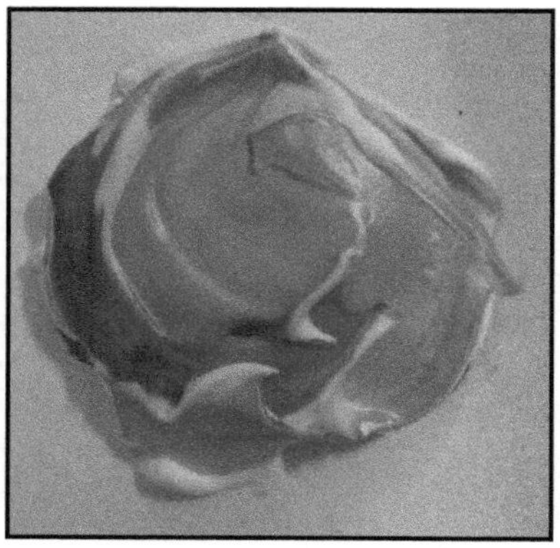
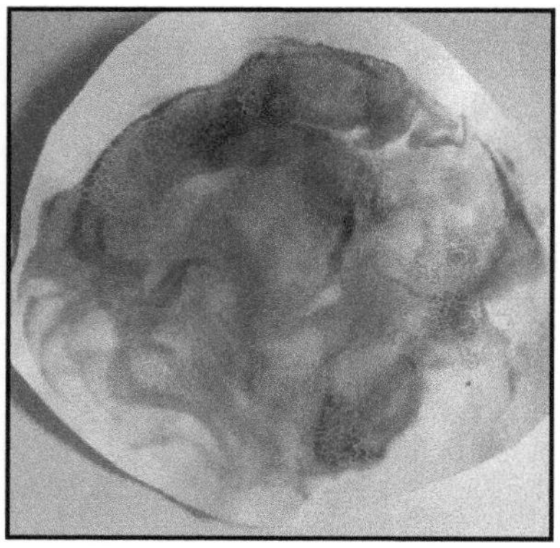

What you will need: Shaving foam; baking paper; food coloring or acrylic paints; stick or straw; cardboard

Directions:

1. Cut out your cardboard in different size circles to represent different planets and leave them aside.
2. Squirt some white shaving foam onto a sheet of baking paper. Spread it smoothly and evenly with a spoon, stick, or straw.
3. Now add drops of different colored food coloring or paint all over the shaving foam and swirl with the straw.
4. Gently place one of your card circles on top of the colored shaving foam and leave it there for a few seconds.
5. Peel the card off gently and leave it to dry. A beautiful multi-colored pattern should appear on your card.
6. Now repeat with different size cards on different colors of shaving foam.
7. You may hang your planets up with string as a mobile.

Introspective Activity
. . . to bring out the reflective devotee in you!

CHANTING CONNECTS US TO KṚṢṆA

This chapter describes many different paths of elevation which can be followed, and Lord Kapila recommends to His mother that she should follow the direct path of devotional service.

Lord Caitanya Mahāprabhu recommends that of all processes of devotional service, the most essential in this age is the chanting of the holy names of God, specifically the *mahā-mantra, Hare Kṛṣṇa Hare Kṛṣṇa Kṛṣṇa Kṛṣṇa Hare Hare, Hare Rāma Hare Rāma Rāma Rāma Hare Hare.*

- If you don't already practice chanting, then try sitting for 10 or 15 minutes every day and chant this *mantra* attentively on japa beads. See if it makes you feel different.
- If you already practice chanting, then see how you can improve, either by increasing the time you chant or the number of rounds on your beads. To see if you are pronouncing every word correctly and clearly, record yourself chanting and then hear the recording.

It also helps to have a sacred space where you chant every day, where you will not be distracted. To help you focus, chant in front of your altar or Deities or in a quiet, serene atmosphere. When your mind wanders, bring it back to hearing the holy names, knowing that the name is nondifferent from Kṛṣṇa.

Saying prayers before chanting also helps you to remain focused on the holy name. Learn and recite the *Pañca-tattva mantra*, or any other prayer related to the holy name, before chanting.

- Now write down your experience when you tried to improve your chanting in this way. Did you feel different? Describe.

Critical-Thinking Activity

. . . to bring out the spiritual investigator in you!

DIFFERENT DESTINATIONS FOR DIFFERENT YOGĪS

This chapter explains how different *yogīs* understand the Supreme Personality of Godhead in different ways.

Directions: In your notebook give at least three examples of *yogīs* who understand Kṛṣṇa. What is their destination? What does their destination look like and how do they understand Kṛṣṇa? How do they get to their destination? (Refer to verse 27 purport)

If you like, draw a picture or find a picture of their destination.

Now explain why the *bhakti-yogī*'s destination is considered the supreme destination.

Language Activities

. . . to make you understand better!

INSTRUCTIONS FOR WHOM?

Exercise 1:

At the end of the chapter Lord Kapiladeva describes for whom His instructions are meant and for whom they are not meant. Describe them in the table below.

These instructions are meant for…	These instructions are not meant for…

Exercise 2:

In verses 32–36 the Lord also instructs the social classes (*brahmacārīs*, *gṛhasthas*, *vānaprasthas*, and *sannyāsīs*) to engage in specific activities. For the following activities, give the social order that is meant to perform the activity, and give at least two examples of each activity.

- **Performing Sacrifice:**

- **Charity:**

- **Austerity:**

- **Studying the Vedas:**

- **Controlling the mind:**

- **Becoming renounced:**

- **Performing one's normal duties:**

FILL IN THE BLANKS

Fill in the blanks by choosing the appropriate answer from the box below:

independent	faith		sense gratification
life	religiosity	*nirguṇa*	uncontaminated
hellish	face to face		economic development
elevated	day		anxieties

1. People who think that each demigod is a separate God cannot be __________________ to the spiritual world.
2. There are two universal dissolutions: One at the end of Brahmā's _____________ and another at the end of Brahmā's _______________________.
3. Lord Brahmā comes back to the material world after being liberated because he still thinks he is ____ of Lord Kṛṣṇa.
4. Persons who are too addicted to this material world execute their prescribed duties very nicely and with great____.
5. People in the mode of passion and aspiring for sense gratification are full of _____________________.
6. According to Vedic thought, there are three elevating processes, namely ___________________________, ______________________________, and ______ ______________________________.
7. Materialistic persons are considered condemned because they are interested in _______________________ activities and not transcendental activities.
8. *Bhakti* is _________________________, free from all tinges of material qualities.
9. If Brahman is impersonal, then there is no question of *darśanam*, which means seeing the Lord ___________________________.
10. The pure devotee is equipoised in his vision and sees himself to be ________________________________ by matter.

ANSWERS

Understanding the Story: 1) b, 2) a, 3) a, 4) a, 5) c, 6) a, 7) c, 8) b

A Hungry Man's Satisfaction *(Potential Answers)*

Eating:
Strength – the food nourishes us and gives us energy; satisfaction – a good meal can make us feel nice because of its delicious taste; detachment – we do not desire to eat more because we are full, and by avoiding eating too much, we avoid disease.

Devotional service:
Divine knowledge – being food for the soul, devotional service gives knowledge of the soul's *sat-cit-ānanda* nature, giving it strength to sustain in the harsh material atmosphere; satisfaction – satisfying the Supreme Lord by serving Him is like watering the root of a tree; the soul automatically feels happy when the Lord is happy; detachment – through devotional service the conditioned soul gets a distaste for material activities and a higher taste for spiritual activities; therefore, he becomes automatically detached from sense gratification.

Different Destinations for Different Yogīs

1. The *jñāna-yogī*: He uses mental reasoning and logic to understand that material sense enjoyment is false. His destination is to become one with the Brahman effulgence. He sees Kṛṣṇa as light.
2. The *aṣṭāṅga-yogī/mystic yogī*: He tries to control the senses by practicing the eight-fold mystic *yoga* system: *yama*, *niyama*, *āsana*, *prāṇāyāma*, *pratyāhāra*, *dhāraṇā*, *dhyāna* and *samādhi*. He wants to realize Paramātmā, or the Supersoul, in his heart. His destination is the heavenly planets.
3. The *bhakti-yogī*: He engages his senses in the service of the Lord and practices transcendental loving service to the personal form of the Lord. His destination is Goloka Vṛndāvana or the Vaikuṇṭha planets where he interacts with the Lord in a loving relationship.

Bhakti-yoga is the easiest and direct process of *yoga* because you are not repressing the mind and senses but engaging them in the Lord's service. The mind and senses alone are very difficult to control. In *bhakti-yoga* the practitioner directly connects with Kṛṣṇa, and he reaches the supreme destination, Goloka Vṛndāvana, where he can engage in a loving and personal relationship with God. By practicing *bhakti-yoga*, knowledge, detachment, and liberation are automatically attained.

Instructions for Whom?

Exercise 1:

These instructions are meant for...	These instructions are not meant for...
• The faithful devotees who are respectful to the spiritual master • The nonenvious • Those friendly to all • Those eager to render service with faith and sincerity • Those who have taken the Supreme Lord to be dearer than anything else • Those who have developed detachment for everything outside the purview of Kṛṣṇa consciousness	• Those envious of devotees • The hypocritical • The prideful • The unclean • The greedy • Those attached to family life • The nondevotees

Exercise 2: *(Potential Answers)*

- **Performing Sacrifice:** (*gṛhasthas*) Preparing *prasādam*; bearing children.
- **Charity:** (*gṛhasthas*) Sponsoring a temple feast; sponsoring a cow.
- **Austerity:** (*brahmacārīs*, *vānaprasthas*, *sannyāsīs*) Getting up early and chanting; fasting on Ekādaśī.
- **Studying the Vedas:** (*brahmacārīs*) Reading *Śrīmad-Bhāgavatam*; studying *Bhakti-Śāstrī.*
- **Controlling the mind:** (*sannyāsīs*) Not associating with women; clean and regulated in habits.
- **Becoming renounced:** (*vānaprasthas*; *sannyāsīs*) Traveling to propagate the Lord's teachings; not endeavoring for worldly things.
- **Performing one's normal duties:** (*gṛhasthas*) Working for the sake of the family's well-being; working in an occupation according to one's nature.

Fill in the Blanks

1. elevated; 2. day; life; 3. independent; 4. faith; 5. anxieties; 6. religiosity; economic development; sense gratification; 7. hellish; 8. *nirguṇa*; 9. face to face; 10. uncontaminated

33
Activities of Kapila

STORY SUMMARY

Devahūti felt different. The dark cloud of ignorance was gone. The beauty of devotional service lit up her heart. She was immersed in knowledge, transcendental knowledge.

Kapila rose. His work was done. With her heart overflowing with gratitude, Devahūti fell to the Lord's feet, offering Him her obeisances. Kapila slowly lifted her up as her tear-filled eyes met the warm, loving comfort of His.

Bringing her palms together, she said in a quivering voice, "My son, I realize now."

"What's that?" he asked, smiling.

"I realize that even though Lord Brahmā was born from You, he must still meditate on You to reach You. I realize that even though You are personally not doing anything to manage this material world, You do everything. The energy that creates this world, maintains it, and eventually destroys it comes from You.

"I realize now that it's not extraordinary that You once lay in my womb, because You have laid in more extraordinary places."

"Have I?" Kapila laughed.

"When this material world is destroyed, You lie as a baby on a banyan leaf that floats on the waters of devastation, and while doing so, you suck Your toe."

Kapila bit His lip and looked down.

"O my Lord, You have come to take away the sins of Your dependents. You incarnate in different forms just to enrich people with knowledge and devotion so they can go back to the spiritual world. And now I know how they can do this! By chanting Your name, hearing about You, offering obeisances to You, or remembering You."

Devahūti's heart leapt with joy speaking about this process.

"Even if they belong to a family of dog-eaters, they are qualified to perform Vedic sacrifices if even once…just once…they chant Your holy name, hear Your glories, or remember You. In fact, these persons are worshipable. Their tongues are glorious! Even though they may be from a lowly family, what must be the weight of their past pious activities to be chanting Your holy name? They must've done all kinds of austerities and fire sacrifices and achieved the good behavior of the Aryans; they must've bathed at holy places of pilgrimage and studied the Vedas.

"My son, I realize that You are the Supreme Personality of Godhead under the name of Kapila. By Your mercy, saints and sages are released from the shackles of this material world simply by meditating on You."

Devahūti said no more. Tears trickled down her face. The inevitable moment had come for her son to leave. The Lord spoke gravely, His lotus eyes full of affection for His mother.

"Mother, this path of self-realization is very easy. Please follow My instructions and soon you will be liberated even in this present body."

Devahūti nodded. "I will, my son."

"If you follow this process properly, you'll be free from fear and ultimately come to Me. Anyone who doesn't know about devotional service cannot escape birth and death."

"I'll follow this process; I will," promised Devahūti.

Kapila smiled and asked, "Mother, may I have your permission to leave home now?"

Devahūti whimpered. She knew the time had come. Trembling, she lifted her right hand to offer blessings and said faintly, "Yes…my son."

Devahūti watched with tear-soaked eyes as Kapila set out towards the northeast. His mission of distributing the transcendental knowledge of Sāṅkhya philosophy was complete. Now He would set the example of retiring from family life and dedicating Himself to spiritual realization although He had no need of it.

Devahūti followed her son's instructions and lived a life of devotional service in the *āśrama* of Kardama Muni, which was beautifully decorated with flowers. She lived in *samādhi*, bathing three times a day and engaging in austerity. In time, her curly black hair turned gray, her body became thin, and her garments worn out.

The home of Kardama Muni was opulent

as a result of his mystic powers. The residents of heaven who flew by in their majestic airplanes sometimes envied the gorgeous furnishings and gardens."

"Who lives there?" asked a heavenly lady to her husband one day as she gazed down at Devahūti's palace. "It's a beautiful place…maybe more exquisite than ours in the heavenly planets."

They glided further down, desiring to see more.

"Look, my dear husband," said the heavenly damsel, pointing to the house, "look how white those mattresses and bedsheets are! They look like the white foam of milk. And…" she gasped, "the couches are gold and the cushions look ever-so soft! Look at those ivory chairs and benches covered with lace cloth and golden filigree, and the marble walls decorated with such valuable jewels!"

They came closer.

"Oh my! This place doesn't even need any light. These jewels are so bright they're lighting up the rooms themselves. And look at the damsel maids; even they are decorated with jewelry."

"This place is known as the flower crown of the Sarasvatī," replied the husband.

"I can understand why," replied the heavenly lady in amazement. "The gardens

are gorgeous. I have never heard birds chirping so sweetly, or smelled such fragrant flowers, or seen such beautiful tall trees with this much fresh fruit. I love this atmosphere! Oh…here's the lady of the house right now!"

They were shocked to see Devahūti, expecting to see a lady of royalty.

Devahūti walked towards the lotus pond to bathe. They saw her frail and withered body dressed with old garments. At that moment, the sky filled with the Gandharvas' melodious song about Kardama's household life.

However, Devahūti wasn't concerned in the least about this or the comforts that surrounded her. Her husband had left and now her son was gone.

Although she knew the truths of life and death and her heart was cleansed, she still lamented for her son – the Supreme Lord – like a cow cries for her lost calf. She meditated upon Him and remembered His words. She also constantly meditated on Lord Viṣṇu in devotion and lived simply, accepting only what her body needed.

Very soon her mind was completely absorbed in the Lord, and she realized His impersonal Brahman feature, seeing everything as Kṛṣṇa's spiritual energy. This gave her divine bliss. She became so detached from this material world and situated in spiritual trance that she forgot to take care of her body. But the spiritual damsels created by Kardama Muni cared for her.

Very soon, she also realized Kṛṣṇa as the Supersoul within everyone and everything. She had reached the perfection of life. She left her body in perfect Kṛṣṇa consciousness, and it melted into water, which became a flowing river, the most sacred of all rivers. She returned to Vaikuṇṭha and reunited with her son. The place where she left is a sacred spot called Siddhapada. If you bathe in that river, you too will achieve perfection.

In the meantime, Kapila had traveled northeast. During his travels, celestial beings, like the Cāraṇas and Gandharvas, offered their prayers and respects to the Lord. The ocean offered Him oblations and a place to stay within its waters. Even to this day, Kapila continues to live in the ocean's depths where the Ganges meets the sea to deliver the conditioned souls. Sāṅkhya teachers continue to worship him there.

Vidura had listened attentively to the wonderful narration of Lord Kapiladeva's pastimes. Maitreya Ṛṣi told him that the conversation between Lord Kapila and His mother is very confidential and the purest of discourses. Whoever hears or reads their conversation will become a devotee of the Supreme Personality of Godhead and enter His abode to engage in loving service to the Lord.

Themes and Key Messages

Please go through this table of themes and key messages, with corresponding verses, and discuss each topic further.

Theme	Reference	Key Messages
Although the Lord is aloof from the material world, he incarnates in this world to give divine knowledge.	3.33.3, 5	The Lord has nothing to do with the material world, but His energies create, maintain, and dissolve the world – nothing is independent of Him. He creates the material world to fulfill the desires of the living beings to enjoy separately from Him. At the same time, He incarnates in different forms in different millenniums out of His mercy to deliver the fallen souls. As Kapila, He gave divine knowledge of how to develop our love for Him and return to the spiritual world.
The Lord's holy name is so powerful that even if degraded people utter it once without offense, they become eligible to perform Vedic sacrifices.	3.33.6–7	Usually only *brāhmaṇas* are qualified to perform Vedic sacrifices and have to go through many purificatory processes beforehand, but those who chant the holy names purely and hear about and remember the Lord, even from a degraded family, are automatically purified of all sinful reactions and can thus perform Vedic sacrifices. In fact, they are so glorious that in their past lives they already passed all lower stages, such as performing Vedic ritualistic sacrifices, studying the Vedas, and practicing good behavior.
If we aim to serve the Supreme Personality of Godhead under the direction of the spiritual master, we are already liberated even within the material body.	3.33.10	Liberation means being situated in our natural positions as eternal servants of Kṛṣṇa. Since the body is material, we have material necessities; nevertheless, if we fully engage in devotional service, following the instructions of the spiritual master as Devahūti did, we are already liberated.
We can give up all attachments only when we are attached to the Supreme Lord. Such attachment elevates us to the spiritual world.	3.33.20–22	Devahūti had all material comforts that were even envied by the demigods, but she was detached and gave them up. This is because she was fully attached to her son Kapila, who was the Supreme Personality of Godhead. She also meditated on the Lord within the heart and became so attached to Him that she went to Vaikuṇṭha at the end of her life.
If one realizes the Supreme Person (Bhagavān), he automatically realizes the Supersoul (Paramātmā) and impersonal Brahman feature of the Lord.	3.33.26	Devahūti followed Kapila's instructions to meditate on Lord Viṣṇu, and thus she automatically realized the impersonal Brahman feature of the Lord, His presence as the all-pervading spiritual energy, and His Paramātmā feature, the Supersoul in everyone's heart. When one meditates on and realizes the personal feature of the Supreme Personality of Godhead in His *sat-cid-ānanda* form, he automatically realizes the Lord's Paramātmā and Brahman features as well.
When one is absorbed in the Lord's service, he forgets his bodily existence but is still taken care of by the Lord.	3.33.27–29	In the conditioned state the senses are absorbed in the body, family, society, or country. But when one realizes one's position as an eternal servant of Kṛṣṇa, one is no longer interested in these things for sense gratification. Devahūti was not interested in her bodily necessities, but she was still taken care of by the Supreme Lord.

Understanding the Story

Now it's time for you to check how well you understood the story by answering these multiple-choice questions.

1. What is the specific name of the philosophy taught by Lord Kapila?
   a) *Sāṅkhya*
   b) *Bhakti*
   c) *Aṣṭāṅga*
2. What is the benefit of hearing Lord Kapila's philosophy?
   a) One is freed from material ignorance.
   b) One reawakens his love for the Lord and returns to the spiritual world.
   c) One merges into the impersonal Brahman.
3. What was bewildering for Devahūti?
   a) The Supreme Lord who had appeared as her son was leaving her.
   b) She was able to understand all of Lord Kapila's complicated instructions.
   c) The Supreme Lord chose to take birth as her son even though she appeared to be an ordinary person.
4. Why did Lord Kapila take birth as a human being?
   a) To only help Devahūti become liberated
   b) To save the whole world by teaching devotion to God
   c) To spread impersonal philosophy in the world
5. What was Devahūti's realization after hearing Lord Kapila's instructions?
   a) She could be liberated by becoming austere.
   b) She could practice breathing exercises to achieve liberation.
   c) She could purify herself by chanting the holy names of the Lord.
6. What kind of people easily take up chanting of the holy name?
   a) People who have lived piously in their past lives
   b) People who have no qualification
   c) People who are always seeking enjoyment in this material world
7. What is Lord Kapila's promise to Devahūti and to humanity in general if His instructions are followed?
   a) They will attain liberation and reach Him.
   b) They will live happily in this world.
   c) They will get mystic powers.

8. What will be the situation of those who do not follow the instructions of Lord Kapila?
   a) They will remain in the repeated cycle of birth and death.
   b) They will enjoy in the material world.
   c) They will attain the heavenly planets.
9. What did Devahūti do after Lord Kapila left home?
   a) She continued to live and enjoy her life in the aerial mansion.
   b) She continued practicing devotional service and eventually gave up her body and went back to Godhead.
   c) She became morose because she missed her son and then eventually gave up her body.
10. What is the name of the place where Devahūti attained liberation?
   a) Bindu-sarovara
   b) Ganges
   c) Siddhapada

Higher-Thinking Questions

Now try to deepen your understanding of this chapter by delving into Śrīla Prabhupāda's purports and reflecting on the following questions:

1. In verse 4 Devahūti is amazed that the unlimited Lord took birth from her womb, yet she remarks that it is not so astonishing. Why is this so? In the scriptures there are many instances when the Lord acts in an ordinary manner for the benefit of humanity and when He performs extraordinary activities. Give a few examples of each. Which is your favorite and why?
2. Why does the Lord suck His toe as described in verse 4 purport. Explain how Lord Caitanya also came to this world to taste the sweetness in Himself.
3. Verse 6 describes how any man, even a person born in a family of dog-eaters, can become as qualified as a *brāhmaṇa* by chanting the holy name of the Lord even once. What does this tell you about the holy name? What are the other benefits of the holy name as described in the purport?
4. In verse 7 purport Śrīla Prabhupāda describes that the holy name should be chanted only for the purpose of pleasing the Lord, then it will give the full benefits. When one chants in this pure mentality, what is the result? Give an example of a Vaiṣṇava from the purport who chanted like this even though born in a lower family. How was he better than the *smarta-brāhmaṇas*?
5. How is a person liberated in the present material body according to verse 10 purport? What is the true meaning of liberation?
6. According to verse 8 purport, why did Lord Kapila leave home to seek spiritual realization if He is the Supreme Lord?
7. Regardless of what *yoga* one pursues, one should voluntarily accept some penance and difficulty as mentioned in verse 14 purport. Can you think of any benefits of voluntarily accepting difficulties? Have you performed any austerity and derived some benefit from it? Explain.
8. In Vedic times why did *gṛhasthas* keep valuable items, such as silk cloth or gold ornaments and furniture? See verse 17 purport. How is this different from today's view of wealth?
9. Devahūti easily became detached from her opulent possessions. According to verses 21–22 and purports, why was she able to become detached? We can see that you can become easily detached or disinterested in mundane things when you replace that attachment with a

spiritual activity that makes you happier. What spiritual activity or practice you enjoy that makes you disinterested in other activities?

10. At the end of verse 26 purport, Śrīla Prabhupāda explains that the purpose of all *yoga* systems is to come to the point of devotional service. Explain why devotional service is considered the highest *yoga* system and the most effective way to understand the Lord fully.
11. Verse 28 describes that Devahūti appeared "like a fire surrounded by smoke." Explain this analogy and how it relates to her detachment from material luxuries.
12. Verses 27 to 29 describe how Devahūti completely forgot about her body because of her absorption in the Lord. Compare her situation with today's ordinary women in society who are beautifully dressed and groomed. Have you been so completely absorbed in something that you forgot about your outward appearance? Describe.

ACTIVITIES

In this section you will find many exciting things to do. These activities will get you thinking, moving, drawing, and having loads of fun.

Analogy Activity . . . to bring out the scholar in you!

FROM BELL METAL TO GOLD

"As a base metal like bell metal can be changed into gold by a chemical process, any person can similarly be changed into a *brāhmaṇa* by *dīkṣā-vidhāna*, the initiation process." (*SB* 3.33.6)

Let us first understand the analogy clearly by identifying the comparison properly. In the following question, fill out the blanks to understand what is being compared to what:

Bell Metal	⇨	
Chemical Process	⇨	
Gold	⇨	

Now, let us understand why each element is compared in this way. In the following table are statements about the elements on the left side of the table above. Understand them and fill in the blanks in the table below based on the analogy.

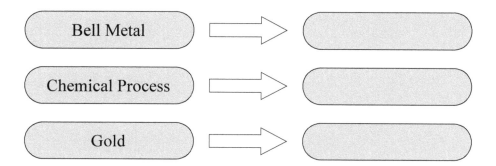

Bell metal is not considered very pure or precious, and therefore is not considered to have great value.	A person not practicing _____________ is not considered very pure because __________________________________ __________________________________
The chemical process changes this impure bell metal into a valuable, pure and precious metal – gold.	__________________________________ is the method of changing a person from ______________________________ to _________________________________. Śrīla Prabhupāda instructed that the process involves __________________ __________________________________ __________________________________
Gold is very valuable and precious because it is pure and lustrous.	__________________________________ is considered pure because __________________________________

Introspective Activities
. . . to bring out the reflective devotee in you!

In verse 7 of this chapter, the glories of chanting the Lord's holy names are described. In the purport Śrīla Prabhupāda states that "a person who has once offenselessly chanted the holy name of God becomes immediately eligible to perform Vedic sacrifices." So we should try to chant the holy names without offenses.

- In the Nectar of Devotion, Śrīla Prabhupāda describes the ten offenses to be avoided:

1. To blaspheme the devotees who have dedicated their lives for propagating the holy name of the Lord.
2. To consider the names of demigods like Lord Śiva or Lord Brahmā to be equal to, or independent of, the name of Lord Viṣṇu.
3. To disobey the orders of the spiritual master.
4. To blaspheme the Vedic literature or literature in pursuance of the Vedic version.
5. To consider the glories of chanting Hare Kṛṣṇa to be imagination.
6. To give some interpretation on the holy name of the Lord.
7. To commit sinful activities on the strength of the holy name of the Lord.
8. To consider the chanting of Hare Kṛṣṇa one of the auspicious ritualistic activities offered in the Vedas as fruitive activities (*karma-kāṇḍa*).
9. To instruct a faithless person about the glories of the holy name.
10. To not have complete faith in the chanting of the holy names and to maintain material attachments, even after understanding so many instructions on this matter.

- Discuss the ten offenses with your teacher and devotee friends and listen to their understanding of each offense. Now memorize the ten offenses so that you are aware of them when you chant.

Prabhupada further states: *"The holy name has to be chanted to please the Supreme Lord, and not for any sense gratification or professional purpose."*

So if we chant the holy name without offenses with the goal of pleasing Lord Kṛṣṇa, we will please Him and make our life successful.

PRACTICING TRANSFORMATIVE THOUGHT

"Even a person born in a family of dog-eaters immediately becomes eligible to perform Vedic sacrifices if he once utters the holy name of the Lord or chants about Him, hears about His pastimes, offers Him obeisances or even remembers Him." (*SB*. 3.33.6)

In the conditioned state, we have the tendency to make judgments in our minds about others. But who is to say when the seemingly "lowest of people" may be attracted to the holy names and be freed from their sinful reactions? Anyone from any family or background can be eligible to chant the holy names and go back to Godhead. Although discernment is necessary in life, most of our judgments are not useful to others and ourselves.

How do we turn this tendency around to benefit others and ourselves?
One option is to recognize and transform our thoughts as soon as they come to our minds. Recognize that *everyone* is a spirit soul and *everyone* has the Supersoul in his or her heart. Try to imagine the best scenario for this person. Imagine them taking to the process of Kṛṣṇa consciousness or performing some devotional service.

Let's put this into practice.

Below are descriptions of different kinds of people you might see around town, in the temple, or at school. Give two positive thoughts about that person and one specific prayer to Kṛṣṇa that may illustrate their spiritual success in this life.

For example:

You see...

A homeless person walking down the street with a big backpack. He is dirty and has a cane. He is walking into a homeless shelter.

Two positive thoughts:

1. He has already attained a human body!
2. He may be a holy man in disguise, or maybe something devastating happened to him and he is ready to hear about Kṛṣṇa.

Prayer to illustrate his success:

Please, Kṛṣṇa, send one of your devotees (in whatever way or form) to influence this person's heart and enthuse him to make steps towards You. Maybe he will have a great moment of realization and gain a higher taste.

Now try to transform your thoughts! Choose four of the following scenarios. Be free to write your additional thoughts, as you need, using the headings above.

1. You see a young woman in her twenties wearing a mini skirt. She is walking on the side of the road with two young men.
2. You see your school teacher downtown eating at a restaurant. He or she is enjoying a non-vegetarian dinner with a glass of wine.
3. You see a serious religious missionary at your school campus yelling and condemning all non-Christians. He argues with everyone who approaches him.
4. You see two dogs fighting and eventually the dog owners start to fight with each other.
5. You see a politician win an election based on his platform to save the world by implementing eco-friendly regulations for citizens and encouraging an eco-friendly lifestyle.
6. You see a disabled woman reading a religious book. Another young woman who looks like her daughter is by her side smoking a cigarette.
7. You see a devotee chastising another devotee in a loud, harsh tone. The other devotee looks hurt but tolerant.

Critical-Thinking Activity

. . . to bring out the spiritual investigator in you!

A HIGHER TASTE

In this chapter we saw how Devahūti became disinterested in material things – even her body – because she developed a higher taste for devotional service. This shows that material desires and attachments can only be given up when they are replaced by a higher taste for spiritual activities.

In essence, the best way to gain a higher taste is to chant the holy name, which will remove all impurities from the heart; one will then naturally give up lower tendencies for the greater taste of loving and serving Kṛṣṇa.

Below are different activities and/or addictions of this material world that distract people and keep them from advancing in spiritual life. For each activity/addiction, give a solution or a higher taste that will break the attachment. The first one has been done for you.

1. Sleeping too much: Sleep in a regulated fashion, enough for the body's health and maintenance. Commit to a fun, enlivening Kṛṣṇa conscious activity that will motivate you to get up and become active. Think of waking up early as a sacrifice you are performing out of love for Kṛṣṇa.
2. Reading love stories
3. Watching movies
4. Gossiping or talking about mundane subjects
5. Eating too many sweets and opulent food
6. Drinking alcohol
7. Buying a big house
8. Attending recreational parties
9. Enjoying a relationship with the opposite sex
10. Making/spending money for fun
11. Fighting with others
12. Trying to control others

Writing and Language Activities

. . . to make you understand better!

REPORT: GAṄGĀ-SĀGARA-TĪRTHA

Directions:

Write a report on Gaṅgā-sāgara-tīrtha, where Lord Kapiladeva resided and where he is still worshiped. Find information on the internet, in books, or from devotees.

1. Create an attractive **cover page with a picture** and title. Then create a **table of contents** with headings related to the topics below.
2. Write a **small summary** on the significance of Gaṅgā-sāgara-tīrtha according to this chapter of the *Bhāgavatam* and your research.

3. After the summary, write on the following topics (you may use these headings or make your own based on the topics):

3.1 LOCATION OF GAṄGĀ-SĀGARA-TĪRTHA

Where is Gaṅgā-sāgara-tīrtha located?

- What is the terrain like?
- What are the people like?
- What language is commonly spoken there?
- Anything else?

3.2 REASONS FOR TRAVEL

Why do people travel to Gaṅgā-sāgara-tīrtha?

- For religious/pilgrimage purposes
- Tourism
- Other

3.3 SEASON AND REASON FOR VISITING

Is there a particular time of year people go to Gaṅgā-sāgara-tīrtha?

- What is the occasion?
- What do they do there?
- Are there particular rituals they follow?
- Whom do they worship?
- Whose teachings do they follow?
- How is Lord Kapila in the *Bhāgavatam* different from the Kapila sometimes followed at Gaṅgā-sāgara-tīrtha? (see verse 34 purport)

3.4 FROM THE EYES OF A PILGRIM

Have you ever been to this holy place? Do you know anyone who has visited? Find out their experience or describe your own experience. Now that you know more about Gaṅgā-sāgara-tīrtha, what will you do if you go there or the next time you go there? Share your report with your peers, family, and friends

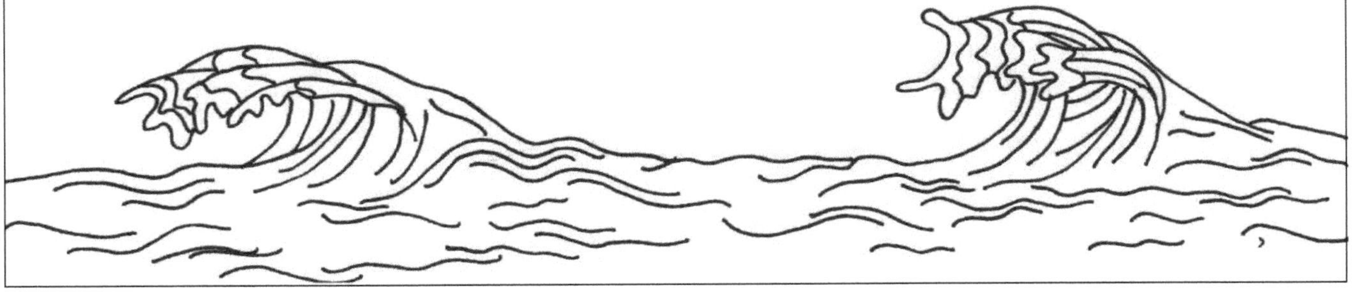

REFLECTION: THE IMPORTANCE OF THE HOLY NAME

Devahūti glorifies the holy name and persons chanting the holy name in this chapter. Such persons are worshipable. Why does she say this? (Refer to verse 7 and purport)

Now, reflect upon your own life and think about the following:
- The people who have influenced you to keep chanting and performing devotional service.
- Your own struggles in Kṛṣṇa consciousness.
- What kept you motivated and kept giving you a higher taste.
- Your greatest motivation to continue chanting and performing devotional service.

Now, write a letter to a new devotee who has just begun chanting and explain these personal reflections to him or her. Try to encourage them to continue and increase their chanting and devotional practices. Explain how fortunate they are to be chanting and how advanced a *yoga* they are performing. Describe your own story, your struggles (to the extent you want), and what keeps you performing devotional service every day. Express what makes you happy in devotional service, so the person can feel inclined to follow in your footsteps. See the importance of setting a good example for others in whatever capacity you can!

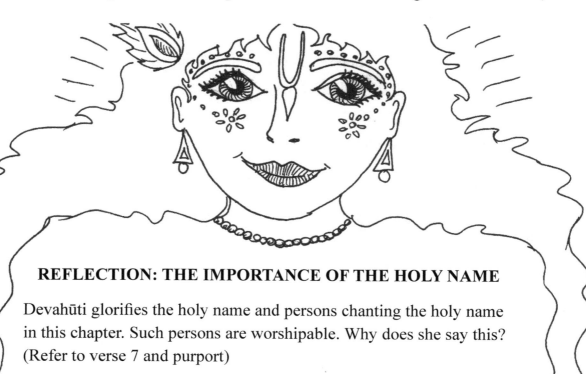

IMAGINING THE POSSIBILITIES

Devahūti describes in her prayers to Lord Kapiladeva that He can do *anything* amazing. He lies as a baby on a banyan leaf at the time of dissolution and sucks his toe for His pleasure, and He chooses to enter her womb of a common woman to become her son. What then is not possible for the Lord?

Keeping this in mind, contemplate your future. Do you desire anything you think is impossible? List three of your impossibilities or big dreams for life below. Write about your dreams in detail and plan to execute them with goals in mind and the means to get there. Challenge any reasons that the dreams are impossible.

Describe:

- What is your dream?
- Is this a spiritual or material dream? "Material" is for your own satisfaction and pleasure, and "spiritual" is for Kṛṣṇa's satisfaction and pleasure. See how you can dovetail your dream to make it spiritual.
- What skills do you need? Describe.
- Will it take practice or study?
- Do you need to find a teacher or mentor?
- What can you do today to start executing this dream?

Now think of a dream to have Kṛṣṇa as your master, child, friend, or lover as Śrīla Prabhupāda describes in this chapter and as Devahūti attained. Is this dream better than your "material" dreams? How so? Think of ways to connect your dreams to Kṛṣṇa. For example, if you want to be a doctor, think of ways you can help Kṛṣṇa's devotees or give your hard-earned money for Kṛṣṇa's service. If you dream to have a family, think of how you can have a loving family serving Kṛṣṇa together or helping each other to become Kṛṣṇa conscious. Ultimately, connecting with Kṛṣṇa in any way gives lasting results and fulfills the best dream of being with Him in the spiritual sky.

ANSWERS

Understanding the Story: 1) a, 2) b, 3) c, 4) b, 5) c, 6) a, 7) a, 8) a, 9) b, 10) c

From Bell Metal to Gold

Table 1: bell metal – an ordinary person; chemical process – devotional service; gold – a purified devotee.

Table 2: A person not practicing **devotional service** is not considered very pure because **he does not know that real happiness comes from serving Lord Kṛṣṇa because we are all His eternal servants.**

Devotional service is the method of changing **an ordinary conditioned soul** to **a devotee of the Lord**.

Śrīla Prabhupāda instructed that the process involves **accepting *dīkṣā* (initiation) from a bona fide guru and following his instructions – chanting the holy name and following the regulative principles of devotional service.**

A devotee of the Lord is considered pure because **he understands that he is a servant of Kṛṣṇa and always engages in His service, thus remaining happy and peaceful.**

A Higher Taste *(Potential Answers)*

2. Reading love stories: Read or hear the pastimes of Lord Kṛṣṇa with His pure devotees.
3. Watching movies: Read instead, or watch movies about Lord Kṛṣṇa's pastimes; watch videos of lectures or plays related to glorifying Kṛṣṇa.
4. Gossiping or talking too much: Talk about Kṛṣṇa and/or philosophical and other Kṛṣṇa conscious topics, which are beneficial to self-realization.
5. Eating sweets and opulent foods: Make nice homemade sweets and other preparations and offer them to Kṛṣṇa. Then distribute the *prasāda* to others.
6. Drinking alcohol: Drink sweet drinks offered to Kṛṣṇa first, including soda, juices, sweet milk drinks, etc.
7. Buying a big house and expensive cars: Buy a house and car that meets the family's needs without being extravagant, therefore facilitating simple living and high thinking.
8. Attending recreational parties: Host or attend *satsangas*, house programs, or temple festivals with a lot of *prasādam* and *kīrtana*.
9. Enjoying a relationship with the opposite sex: Get married to a suitable devotee of the opposite sex and have a family according to the regulations of *śāstra*; have harmonious family relationships with Kṛṣṇa in the center.
10. Making/spending money for fun: Spend money for basic necessities and for service to Kṛṣṇa and His devotees.

11. Fighting with others: If a person is angry in nature, they should consult a bona fide spiritual master and find an occupation they can execute in order to fulfill these inclinations, while chanting Kṛṣṇa's name.
12. Controlling others: Under guidance from a bona fide spiritual master, become involved in temple administration and find opportunities to execute this propensity, such as coordinating a major festival.

APPENDIXES

APPENDIX 1

RELATED VERSES

Let's memorize these beautiful verses related to each chapter. As you learn the verses, engage your hands and body in movements that help you express each word in the verse. Another fun way to memorize *ślokas* is to draw simple images or symbols of the translations. Remember to recite these *ślokas* from your heart!

CHAPTER 17

Bhagavad-gītā 16.21

tri-vidhaṁ narakasyedaṁ
dvāraṁ nāśanam ātmanaḥ
kāmaḥ krodhas tathā lobhas
tasmād etat trayaṁ tyajet

There are three gates leading to this hell – lust, anger and greed. Every sane man should give these up, for they lead to the degradation of the soul.

Bhagavad-gītā 16.23

yaḥ śāstra-vidhim utsṛjya
vartate kāma-kārataḥ
na sa siddhim avāpnoti
na sukhaṁ na parāṁ gatim

He who discards scriptural injunctions and acts according to his own whims attains neither perfection, nor happiness, nor the supreme destination.

CHAPTER 18

Śrī Brahma-saṁhitā 1

īśvaraḥ paramaḥ kṛṣṇaḥ
sac-cid-ānanda-vigrahaḥ
anādir ādir govindaḥ
sarva-kāraṇa-kāraṇam

Kṛṣṇa who is known as Govinda is the Supreme Godhead. He has an eternal blissful spiritual body. He is the origin of all. He has no other origin and He is the prime cause of all causes.

Bhagavad-gītā 18.66

sarva-dharmān parityajya
mām ekaṁ śaraṇaṁ vraja
ahaṁ tvāṁ sarva-pāpebhyo
mokṣayiṣyāmi mā śucaḥ

Abandon all varieties of religion and just surrender unto Me. I shall deliver you from all sinful reactions. Do not fear.

CHAPTER 19

Śrīmad-Bhāgavatam 1.2.17

śṛṇvatāṁ sva-kathāḥ kṛṣṇaḥ
puṇya-śravaṇa-kīrtanaḥ
hṛdy antaḥ stho hy abhadrāṇi
vidhunoti suhṛt satām

Śrī Kṛṣṇa, the Personality of Godhead, who is the Paramātmā [Supersoul] in everyone's heart and the benefactor of the truthful devotee, cleanses desire for material enjoyment from the heart of the devotee who has developed the urge to hear His messages, which are in themselves virtuous when properly heard and chanted.

Śrīmad-Bhāgavatam 1.2.19

tadā rajas-tamo-bhāvāḥ
kāma-lobhādayaś ca ye
ceta etair anāviddhaṁ
sthitaṁ sattve prasīdati

As soon as irrevocable loving service is established in the heart, the effects of nature's modes of passion and ignorance, such as lust, desire and hankering, disappear from the heart. Then the devotee is established in goodness, and he becomes completely happy.

CHAPTER 20

Bhagavad-gītā 10.10

teṣāṁ satata-yuktānāṁ
bhajatāṁ prīti-pūrvakam
dadāmi buddhi-yogaṁ taṁ
yena mām upayānti te

To those who are constantly devoted to serving Me with love, I give the understanding by which they can come to Me.

Bhagavad-gītā 10.11

teṣām evānukampārtham
aham ajñāna-jaṁ tamaḥ
nāśayāmy ātma-bhāva-stho
jñāna-dīpena bhāsvatā

To show them special mercy, I, dwelling in their hearts, destroy with the shining lamp of knowledge the darkness born of ignorance.

CHAPTER 21

Śrīmad-Bhāgavatam 1.2.8

dharmaḥ svanuṣṭhitaḥ puṁsāṁ
viṣvaksena-kathāsu yaḥ
notpādayed yadi ratiṁ
śrama eva hi kevalam

The occupational activities a man performs according to his own position are only so much useless labor if they do not provoke attraction for the message of the Personality of Godhead.

Śrī Caitanya-caritāmṛta Madhya-līlā 19.170

sarvopādhi-vinirmuktaṁ
tat-paratvena nirmalam
hṛṣīkeṇa hṛṣīkeśa-
sevanaṁ bhaktir ucyate

Bhakti, or devotional service, means engaging all our senses in the service of the Lord, the Supreme Personality of Godhead, the master of all the senses. When the spirit soul renders service unto the Supreme, there are two side effects. One is freed from all material designations, and one's senses are purified simply by being employed in the service of the Lord.

CHAPTER 22

Śrī Caitanya-caritāmṛta Madhya-līlā 22.54

'sādhu-saṅga', 'sādhu-saṅga'— sarva-śāstre kaya
lava-mātra sādhu-saṅge sarva-siddhi haya

The verdict of all revealed scriptures is that by even a moment's association with a pure devotee, one can attain all success.

Śrīmad-Bhāgavatam 1.2.13

ataḥ pumbhir dvija-śreṣṭhā
varṇāśrama-vibhāgaśaḥ
svanuṣṭhitasya dharmasya
saṁsiddhir hari-toṣaṇam

O best among the twice-born, it is therefore concluded that the highest perfection one can achieve by discharging the duties prescribed for one's own occupation according to caste divisions and orders of life is to please the Personality of Godhead.

CHAPTER 23

Bhagavad-gītā 9.31

kṣipraṁ bhavati dharmātmā
śaśvac-chāntiṁ nigacchati
kaunteya pratijānīhi
na me bhaktaḥ praṇaśyati

He quickly becomes righteous and attains lasting peace. O son of Kuntī, declare it boldly that My devotee never perishes.

CHAPTER 24

Śrīmad-Bhāgavatam 1.2.21

bhidyate hṛdaya-granthiś
chidyante sarva-saṁśayāḥ
kṣīyante cāsya karmāṇi
dṛṣṭa evātmanīśvare

Thus the knot in the heart is pierced, and all misgivings are cut to pieces. The chain of fruitive actions is terminated when one sees the self as master.

Bhagavad-gītā 9.11

avajānanti māṁ mūḍhā
mānuṣīṁ tanum āśritam
paraṁ bhāvam ajānanto
mama bhūta-maheśvaram

Fools deride Me when I descend in the human form. They do not know My transcendental nature as the Supreme Lord of all that be.

CHAPTER 25

Bhagavad-gītā Introduction

oṁ ajñāna-timirāndhasya
jñānāñjana-śalākayā
cakṣur unmīlitaṁ yena
tasmai śrī-gurave namaḥ

I was born in the darkest ignorance, and my spiritual master opened my eyes with the torch of knowledge. I offer my respectful obeisances unto him.

Bhagavad-gītā 2.14

mātrā-sparśās tu kaunteya
śītoṣṇa-sukha-duḥkha-dāḥ
āgamāpāyino 'nityās
tāṁs titikṣasva bhārata

O son of Kuntī, the nonpermanent appearance of happiness and distress, and their disappearance in due course, are like the appearance and disappearance of winter and summer seasons. They arise from sense perception, O scion of Bharata, and one must learn to tolerate them without being disturbed.

CHAPTER 26

Bhagavad-gītā 18.55

bhaktyā mām abhijānāti
yāvān yaś cāsmi tattvataḥ
tato māṁ tattvato jñātvā
viśate tad-anantaram

One can understand Me as I am, as the Supreme Personality of Godhead, only by devotional service. And when one is in full consciousness of Me by such devotion, he can enter into the kingdom of God.

Bhagavad-gītā 11.32

śrī-bhagavān uvāca
kālo 'smi loka-kṣaya-kṛt pravṛddho
lokān samāhartum iha pravṛttaḥ
ṛte 'pi tvāṁ na bhaviṣyanti sarve
ye 'vasthitāḥ praty-anīkeṣu yodhāḥ

The Supreme Personality of Godhead said: Time I am, the great destroyer of the worlds, and I have come here to destroy all people. With the exception of you [the Pāṇḍavas], all the soldiers here on both sides will be slain.

CHAPTER 27

Bhagavad-gītā 5.29

bhoktāraṁ yajña-tapasāṁ
sarva-loka-maheśvaram
suhṛdaṁ sarva-bhūtānāṁ
jñātvā māṁ śāntim ṛcchati

A person in full consciousness of Me, knowing Me to be the ultimate beneficiary of all sacrifices and austerities, the Supreme Lord of all planets and demigods, and the benefactor and well-wisher of all living entities, attains peace from the pangs of material miseries.

Bhagavad-gītā 6.1

śrī-bhagavān uvāca
anāśritaḥ karma-phalaṁ
kāryaṁ karma karoti yaḥ
sa sannyāsī ca yogī ca
na niragnir na cākriyaḥ

The Supreme Personality of Godhead said: One who is unattached to the fruits of his work and who works as he is obligated is in the renounced order of life, and he is the true mystic, not he who lights no fire and performs no duty.

CHAPTER 28

Śrīmad-Bhāgavatam 1.8.36

śṛṇvanti gāyanti gṛṇanty abhīkṣṇaśaḥ
smaranti nandanti tavehitaṁ janāḥ
ta eva paśyanty acireṇa tāvakaṁ
bhava-pravāhoparamaṁ padāmbujam

O Kṛṣṇa, those who continuously hear, chant and repeat Your transcendental activities, or take pleasure in others' doing so, certainly see Your lotus feet, which alone can stop the repetition of birth and death.

CHAPTER 29

Bhagavad-gītā 6.47

yogināṁ api sarveṣāṁ
mad-gatenāntar-ātmanā
śraddhāvān bhajate yo māṁ
sa me yukta-tamo mataḥ

And of all *yogīs*, the one with great faith who always abides in Me, thinks of Me within himself and renders transcendental loving service to Me – he is the most intimately united with Me in *yoga* and is the highest of all. That is My opinion.

Bhagavad-gītā 7.19

bahūnāṁ janmanām ante
jñānavān māṁ prapadyate
vāsudevaḥ sarvam iti
sa mahātmā su-durlabhaḥ

After many births and deaths, he who is actually in knowledge surrenders unto Me, knowing Me to be the cause of all causes and all that is. Such a great soul is very rare.

CHAPTER 30

Bhagavad-gītā 16.10

kāmam āśritya duṣpūraṁ
dambha-māna-madānvitāḥ
mohād gṛhītvāsad-grāhān
pravartante 'śuci-vratāḥ

Taking shelter of insatiable lust and absorbed in the conceit of pride and false prestige, the demoniac, thus illusioned, are always sworn to unclean work, attracted by the impermanent.

CHAPTER 31

Bhagavad-gītā 14.4

sarva-yoniṣu kaunteya
mūrtayaḥ sambhavanti yāḥ
tāsāṁ brahma mahad yonir
ahaṁ bīja-pradaḥ pitā

It should be understood that all species of life, O son of Kuntī, are made possible by birth in this material nature, and that I am the seed-giving father.

CHAPTER 32

Bhagavad-gītā 7.23

antavat tu phalaṁ teṣāṁ
tad bhavaty alpa-medhasām
devān deva-yajo yānti
mad-bhaktā yānti mām api

Men of small intelligence worship the demigods, and their fruits are limited and temporary. Those who worship the demigods go to the planets of the demigods, but My devotees ultimately reach My supreme planet.

Bhagavad-gītā 9.23

ye 'py anya-devatā-bhaktā
yajante śraddhayānvitāḥ
te 'pi mām eva kaunteya
yajanty avidhi-pūrvakam

Those who are devotees of other gods and who worship them with faith actually worship only Me, O son of Kuntī, but they do so in a wrong way.

CHAPTER 33

Śrīmad-Bhāgavatam 6.3.31

tasmāt saṅkīrtanaṁ viṣṇor
jagan-maṅgalam aṁhasām
mahatām api kauravya
viddhy aikāntika-niṣkṛtam

Śukadeva Gosvāmī continued: My dear King, the chanting of the holy name of the Lord is able to uproot even the reactions of the greatest sins. Therefore the chanting of the *saṅkīrtana* movement is the most auspicious activity in the entire universe. Please try to understand this so that others will take it seriously.

APPENDIX 2

PLAY OR PUPPET SHOW: LORD KAPILA INSTRUCTS DEVAHŪTI

Perform a play with different actors, props, and costumes with the following script. Alternatively, you may perform a skit in class or a puppet show.

SCENE 1

(Kardama sitting in meditation)

Narrator: Many, many years ago on the bank of the sacred river Sarasvatī, the great sage Kardama Muni, who had been instructed by Lord Brahmā to beget children, sat in meditation for ten thousand years. Pleased by His devotee, the Lord appeared before Kardama Muni.

(Enter Lord Viṣṇu)

Kardama Muni: (offering obeisances): Oh my Lord, Your lotus feet can award all spiritual desires. Only foolish people would worship You for things of this world, but You are so kind that You are even merciful to them. So my Lord, I ask for your help; I am looking for a nice wife.

Lord Viṣṇu: Dearest sage, I have already read your mind and have arranged to fulfill your desire. The day after tomorrow, Emperor Svāyambhuva Manu will come with his queen to see you. His beautiful daughter is ready for marriage and is searching for a husband. She is just the type you have been looking for and will serve you to your heart's content. She will give you nine daughters, and through your daughters, the sages will beget children. O sage, I shall then manifest Myself through your wife, and I shall instruct her in Sāṅkhya philosophy.

(Exit Lord Viṣṇu)

SCENE 2

(Enter Svāyambhuva Manu and his wife on chariot)

Kardama Muni: (offering obeisances to Manu) O King, please accept my humble obeisances!

Manu: O great sage, it is my fortune to see you. Please listen, for my mind is troubled by my love for my daughter. She is seeking a suitable husband, and the moment she heard from the great sage Nārada Muni of you, she fixed her mind upon you. Therefore, please accept her, for I offer her to you with faith, dear sage.

Kardama Muni: Why, yes! I do want to marry, and your daughter is very qualified and beautiful. Yes, I shall accept your daughter as my wife, on the condition that I may accept a life of devotional service to Lord Viṣṇu after we give birth to our children.

(Śatarūpā, Devahūti's mother, steps forward with Devahūti. Devahūti offers obeisances. Śatarūpā gives Kardama Muni gifts.)

Manu and Śatarūpā: (Embracing Devahūti and crying) O, we will miss you. O, we will miss you, dear one!

(They exit on chariot)

Narrator: After her parents left, Devahūti served her husband constantly with great love. Over time she grew weak due to all her service. Kardama Muni noticed her selfless service and her frail conditon.

Kardama Muni: O daughter of Svāyambhuva Manu, I am very pleased with your devotion and service. I have achieved Kṛṣṇa's blessings, and I will offer them all to you for your unconditional service.

Devahūti: O husband, you once made a promise to me that you would give me children. Please grant me this and a house for us; this is my desire.

Narrator: To please his wife, Kardama produced an aerial mansion by his *yogic* powers that could travel anywhere. (Kardama gestures to the sky)

Devahūti: O my lord! This is wonderful! But look at me; I'm a mess!

Kardama Muni: Do not worry. Bathe in the sacred waters of the Bindu-sarovara, and you will regain your former beauty.

(Devahūti dives into the lake, and maidens attend to her; then she emerges beautiful. Kardama Muni and Devahūti mount the mansion and fly around.)

Narrator: Many, many years later (Kardama and Devahūti still flying around)

Devahūti: This has been fun seeing all the universes, my lord, but I still have no children.

Kardama Muni: Oh yes; here are nine daughters for you.

Devahūti: Oh, that was quick!

Kardama Muni: Now I must prepare to leave home.

Devahūti: My dear husband, you have fulfilled all your promises, but I am feeling sad. You are a great devotee, and I have had your association, but I traveled the universe simply enjoying my senses. Now I need to ask something for my spiritual life. Please give me fearlessness so I can be freed from this material position.

Kardama Muni: Don't be sad, my dear Devahūti. The Lord will shortly enter your womb as your son.

Devahūti: (face brightens) Thank you, dear husband!

SCENE 3

Narrator: Lord Brahmā could understand that the Lord had appeared in Devahūti's womb to speak knowledge of *Sāṅkhya-yoga*, so he came to Kardama Muni's *āśrama*.

Lord Brahmā: Thank you for following my instructions of begetting children. Now you have nine wonderful daughters; please give them to great sages to increase the population more. O Kardama! I know that the Supreme Personality of Godhead has now appeared in your wife's womb as Kapila Muni. He will travel all over the world to enlighten souls! Jaya!

(Exit Lord Brahmā)

SCENE 4

(Lord Kapiladeva sitting alone. Kardama Muni enters)

Kardama Muni: My Lord, I offer my respectful obeisances unto you. My Lord, I have something to ask. Now that I have been freed from my debts to my forefathers, I wish to accept the order of a mendicant *sannyāsī* and think always of You in my heart. Is this possible?

Lord Kapila: Please, dear Muni, go as you desire, surrendering all your activities to Me and worshiping Me for eternal life. I will also describe this process of surrender to My mother, Devahūti, so she will also attain perfection, self-realization, and freedom from all material fear.

(Kardama Muni circumambulates Lord Kapila and then leaves, chanting. Devahūti enters.)

Narrator: When Kardama left for the forest to live a renounced life, Lord Kapila stayed with His mother at Bindu-sarovara. As the Lord sat before her, Devahūti remembered Lord Brahmā telling her that Lord Kapila would show her the goal of life. Thus she began to inquire from Him.

Devahūti: O dear Lord, I am so disturbed. Please dispel my ignorance and describe to me the difference between spirit and matter. I take shelter at Your lotus feet.

Lord Kapila: Dear mother, I will now explain the *yoga* system that relates to the Lord and the individual soul and that gives detachment from all happiness and distress. This is the highest *yoga* system!

Attachment for material life is the greatest entanglement, but attachment to the *sādhus* opens the door to liberation. If the mind is absorbed in sense gratification, you become bound to the false ego. But if the mind is engaged in the Lord's service, it is better than liberation because the false ego is dissolved by devotional service just as fire digests what we eat. By glorifying My devotees, you will become free from material activities and attain the perfection of life. Become attached to such holy men and hear, chant, and perform devotional service with them. Then you will lose the taste for sense gratification.

Devahūti: O Supreme Personality of Godhead, please explain to me the relationship between You and Your energies.

Lord Kapila: Yes, dear mother. It is very complicated, but for now, let me give you a simple example by showing you this picture of the universal egg.

This universal egg, or the universe in the shape of an egg, is called the manifestation of material energy. Its layers of water, air, fire, sky, ego, and *mahat-tattva* increase in thickness one after another. Each layer is ten times bigger than the previous one, and the final outside layer is covered by *pradhāna*. Within this egg is the universal form of Lord Hari, of whose body the fourteen planetary systems are parts. Dearest mother, after injecting Himself as time, the Lord places Himself within all souls and in every atom as the Supersoul.

Devahūti: This is amazing!

Lord Kapila: O mother, when the soul realizes that the Lord is the proprietor of everything, he begins to serve the Lord. If he doesn't do this, he will never be freed from the cycle of birth and death.

Devahūti: No way! I don't want to remain in this material world for even one more lifetime...O son, help free me from this painful cycle of birth and death.

Lord Kapila: The soul suffers so much because he is trying to be the boss. But if he engages his mind in devotional service to Me and offers everything to Me, without desiring to enjoy, he will see that he is actually spiritual and becomes free from this suffering.

Devahūti: What a relief! But how can the spirit become free from the material world?

Lord Kapila: By always hearing about Me and serving Me with love. Always work your best in life and try not to do other people's work. Try to be satisfied with what the Lord has given you and thank Him for His gifts!

Lord Kapila: O mother, the path of a true *yogī* is to fix the mind on the Lord Himself and His pastimes. Try to eat only what is necessary and live in a secluded and peaceful place. Practice nonviolence, truthfulness, austerity, and cleanliness; study the Vedas; and worship the Lord. Observe silence, steadiness, controlled breathing, and sense control by concentrating the mind on the beautiful form of the Supersoul. By gradually devoting your mind to this meditation, you will develop pure love for the Lord.

Devahūti: O my son, please tell me more!

Lord Kapila: The pure devotee offers his respects to every living entity because he knows I am inside everyone's heart as the Supersoul, in every form of life. I am even in stonelike matter; then there are the trees, better than the trees are the fish because fish have developed the sense of taste. Better than the fish are the bees, who have developed the sense of smell, and better than them are the serpents because serpents have developed the sense of hearing.

Living entities that have many legs, like the wasp, are better than those that have no legs. Four-legged animals are better than many-legged living entities, and better than the animals is the human being, who has only two legs. Among the humans, the *brāhmaṇas* are the best and one who knows the actual purport of the Vedas is the best. And better than him is a pure devotee, who executes devotional service without expecting a reward.

(Devahūti looks with wide eyes.)

Lord Kapila: Do you notice that everything created is destroyed by time? That everything material is only temporary!

A man works very hard in this life to maintain his family, and sometimes he maintains his family by doing terrible activities that will cause him to suffer in the future. And then after spending his life maintaining his family, in his old age when he can't provide for them anymore, they don't even take care of him!

Devahūti: O, how sad!

Lord Kapila: When such a man dies, the messengers of Yamarāja, the Yamadūtas, come to him and he is terrified! They take him to suffer in hellish conditions for many lifetimes, and after taking birth in all the lower species of life on earth, he again gets a particular human body, depending on the results of his previous activities.

Devahūti: I have noticed different species are produced in different ways.

Lord Kapila: Yes, sprouting, like a tree does, fermenting such as a germ, hatching from an egg like a bird or fish, and then developing as an embryo in the womb like a human. The human in the womb goes through a very complex growth, and it's very uncomfortable for the baby. The baby is squished in there, and if the mum eats too much spicy food the baby feels terrible pain. He has no freedom to move…

Devahūti: Oh, how miserable!

Lord Kapila: Yes, he is like a bird in a cage, trapped! However, the good part is, at around seven months, the soul is fortunate enough to remember the troubles of his past one hundred births and he grieves.

Devahūti: How is he fortunate to grieve?

Lord Kapila: With his pure consciousness given by the Lord, he is able to see what he did wrong in the past life and why it was wrong. In this state of realization, he deeply regrets and calls to Kṛṣṇa: "O Kṛṣṇa, I'm so sorry! Please help me keep Your lotus feet within my mind."

But once the baby is born, the child forgets his determination.

Devahūti: I was hoping you would not say this. O Lord, how bewildering!

Lord Kapila: Māyā is so, so strong. If a person does not watch himself, he will continually suffer and travel through various planets and universes in the cycle of birth and death.

Devahūti: Oh no! Will this cycle ever end?

Lord Kapila: Yes, only when he has the fortune to meet a bona fide spiritual master who instructs and guides him on the path of devotional service. In this way he can gradually come to Me. This universe is very difficult to get out of, and if one forgets Me, he will be unable to understand where he is going next. But one who meditates on Me with faith and affection, hearing and chanting about Me, will surely go back home, back to Godhead!

(Devahūti bowing to Lord Kapila)

Lord Kapila: My dear mother, please follow My instructions and you will definitely attain liberation. Now with your permission I shall go on pilgrimage to perform devotional service to set an example for everyone!

Devahūti: Yes, my Lord.

(Devahūti returns to her aerial mansion chanting "Hare Kṛṣṇa Hare Kṛṣṇa ....")

Narrator: Because of Devahūti's devotional service, her whole mansion became so beautiful that it was considered to be the flower crown of the river Sarasvatī! Because she had performed many austerities in her life, it was easy for Devahūti to give up all her opulence. The only person she truly missed was Lord Kapila. She had sincere love for Him. And because her son was the Lord Himself and her attachment to Him was so strong, she simply meditated upon Him and was able to give up all possessions very quickly and attain perfection.

(Lord Kapila slowly walks off stage towards the Himālayas)

Narrator: Lord Kapila left His mother and His home; He went to the Himālayas and followed the Ganges all the way to where it meets the ocean at Gaṅgā-sāgara-tīrtha. To this day people travel there and offer their respects to Lord Kapila. He is said to still be in trance, ready to save any fallen soul!

Kṛṣṇa who is known as Govinda is the Supreme Godhead. He has an eternal blissful spiritual body. He is the origin of all. He has no other origin and He is the prime cause of all causes.

CPSIA information can be obtained
at www.ICGtesting.com
Printed in the USA
BVHW051022211221
624600BV00008B/908

9 781733 927246